Gender and Biopolitics

Studies in Critical Social Sciences Book Series

Haymarket Books is proud to be working with Brill Academic Publishers (www.brill.nl) to republish the *Studies in Critical Social Sciences* book series in paperback editions. This peer-reviewed book series offers insights into our current reality by exploring the content and consequences of power relationships under capitalism, and by considering the spaces of opposition and resistance to these changes that have been defining our new age. Our full catalog of *SCSS* volumes can be viewed at https://www.haymarketbooks.org/series_collections/4-studies-in-critical-social-sciences.

Series Editor
David Fasenfest (Wayne State University)

New Scholarship in Political Economy Book Series

Series Editors
David Fasenfest (Wayne State University)
Alfredo Saad-Filho (King's College London)

Editorial Board
Kevin B. Anderson (University of California, Santa Barbara)
Tom Brass (formerly of SPS, University of Cambridge)
Raju Das (York University)
Ben Fine ((emeritus) SOAS University of London)
Jayati Ghosh (Jawaharlal Nehru University)
Elizabeth Hill (University of Sydney)
Dan Krier (Iowa State University)
Lauren Langman (Loyola University Chicago)
Valentine Moghadam (Northeastern University)
David N. Smith (University of Kansas)
Susanne Soederberg (Queen's University)
Aylin Topal (Middle East Technical University)
Fiona Tregenna (University of Johannesburg)
Matt Vidal (Loughborough University London)
Michelle Williams (University of the Witwatersrand)

Gender and Biopolitics

The Changing Patterns of Womanhood
in Post-2002 Turkey

Pınar Sarıgöl

Haymarket Books
Chicago, IL

First published in 2021 by Brill Academic Publishers, The Netherlands
© 2021 Koninklijke Brill NV, Leiden, The Netherlands

Published in paperback in 2022 by
Haymarket Books
P.O. Box 180165
Chicago, IL 60618
773-583-7884
www.haymarketbooks.org

ISBN: 978-1-64259-798-1

Distributed to the trade in the US through Consortium Book Sales and Distribution (www.cbsd.com) and internationally through Ingram Publisher Services International (www.ingramcontent.com).

This book was published with the generous support of Lannan Foundation and Wallace Action Fund.

Special discounts are available for bulk purchases by organizations and institutions. Please call 773-583-7884 or email info@haymarketbooks.org for more information.

Cover design by Jamie Kerry and Ragina Johnson.

Printed in the United States.

10 9 8 7 6 5 4 3 2 1

Library of Congress Cataloging-in-Publication data is available.

Contents

Acknowledgements VII
Abbreviations IX

1 **Introduction**
   The Conceptualisation of Ideal Womanhood in Post-2002 Turkey 1
   1. The Conceptualisation of Problematic Womanhood and Governmentality 4
   2. Changing Patterns of Womanhood in Post-2002 Turkey 7
   3. Insights from Foucault's Method 10
   4. Selection of the Research Sources 16
   5. Structure of the Book 20
   6. Concluding Remarks 22

2 **The Closed Circuits of the Woman's Sexuality and *Temperate Seductiveness*** 24
   1. Islamic Virtues on Woman's Sexuality 27
   2. The Imagined Population in the New Gender Regime 35
      2.1 *Islamic Heteronormativity and Its Performances* 35
      2.2 *Contouring Gender Justice* 39
   3. Intimacy in Public or the Intimacy of the Public? 42
      3.1 *To Veil or Not to Veil* 44
      3.2 *On the Political Representations of Women* 54
      3.3 *Policing Public Morality* 58
   4. Concluding Remarks 64

3 **The Sacred Family Portrait**
   Balance, Uniformity, Patience and Piety 67
   1. Understanding the Family in Its Cooperative Manner 70
   2. True Womanhood and Unmanageable Fields of Government 86
      2.1 *The New Definition of Womanhood* 88
      2.2 *Awakening the Sense of Motherhood* 96
      2.3 *Some Facts: Adultery, Homosexuality, Prostitution, Brothels and the Like* 100
   3. The Last Sight on Family 103
      3.1 *Consulting Services for the Betterisation of Family* 103
      3.2 *Divorce as an Impossible Practice* 106
   4. Concluding Remarks 108

4　Reconsidering Violence as a Disciplinary and Regulatory
   Apparatus　111
   1　Statistical Facts and the Hard Truth　116
   2　Rape as a Justified Reaction against the Impropriety　119
   3　From Crimes of Honour to Crimes of Passion　128
   4　Political Reality and the Depoliticisation of Violence　136
      4.1　*Protective Mechanisms and Legal Applications*　139
      4.2　*Manhood and Violence*　143
      4.3　*Gendered Mediation*　148
   5　Concluding Remarks　152

5　Islamic Neoliberal Female Subjectivity in Post-2002 Turkey　155
   1　Reading Political Islamism in Its Own Governmental Nature in Turkey　160
   2　Islamic Neoliberal Governmentality: Challenging the Unity of Sovereign Power, Disciplinary Power and Biopower　166
   3　Rethinking Gender Justice in the Context of Islamism and Neoliberalism　178
   4　The Exclusion and Inclusion of Women at the Intersection of Differences　190
   5　Concluding Remarks　203

6　Conclusions
   Resistance for the Better　205

   References　215
   Index　243

Acknowledgements

This book is based on my PhD dissertation, which I completed in 2020. The adaptation from dissertation to book would not have been possible without the trust and generous support of people who believed in me and in my study more than I did.

In 2003, when I graduated from high school, the AKP had already acceded as the ruling party in Turkey. It was still in power when I completed my doctoral programme, and it may also be in power as of the publication of this book. In Turkey, those of my age group have become witnesses to the epoch-defining transformations that have been underway since 2002. Since the AKP came to power, the Islamic neoliberal turn that had begun to shape my generation during early youth has been dramatically sharpened. We have also observed the changing face of a political culture, and the consequences of it. Most of these consequences affected and are still affecting the lives of women and youth. The period since 2002 has been marked by both the most murders of women within the familial context and the most public protest against such violence and the political shifts that enabled them. As a female researcher of such an intense structuring and transformation process, I feel that this research is one piece of a collective effort among the friends and colleagues I came to know during my time with the Department of Political Science and Public Administration at Middle East Technical University. I credit METU with cultivating my critical thinking skills during my undergrad years, as well as with providing a stimulating academe that holds an irreplaceable position in my memories. For this reason, I will always owe my professors a debt of gratitude for not just helping me get a bachelor's degree, but in many respects raising me.

I thank Jemima Repo and Kyle Grayson, who invited me to Newcastle upon Tyne. The time I spent there was probably the most fertile period of this study's preparation process. I also specifically thank Jemima Repo not only for her criticism of my study through her sharp intelligence and candour, but also for her friendship. The most important criterion for this study's efficacy was being welcomed into rigorous academic environments in Bielefeld, Frankfurt, Berlin, Göttingen, Newcastle upon Tyne and Helsinki. I'm grateful to everyone who read my study at various stages of its development with great curiosity and amity, who made time in their busy schedules to discuss my project with me, and with whom we shared our grief and laughed from time to time.

Fatih Çağatay Cengiz expressed harsh criticisms about this work at its early stages; this was made possible by our long and robust friendship. He has been with me as a classmate since the beginning of this process and had his hand on my shoulder even during the toughest times. I thank him for his encouragement and his patience. Likewise, I thank Emre Gömeç for his presence, friendship and comradeship, which became valuable in time. I thank Emmanuel Yenkyi, Serdar Çakmak, Fehmi Odabaş for their friendships, and Elsia Papageorgiou for her enchanting honesty, as well as for being special by standing her ground. Nesrin Orun pointed out things I had not seen or thought of, not only during the preparation of my master's thesis, but also during my doctoral study, and I thank her for her frank criticism; it perplexed me, but in the way that always leads to a better final result. I thank my family and especially my mother Menekşe Çalış for supporting me unquestioningly in all my decisions. I'm really grateful to my mother – who transferred to me not only the sharp edges of her personality but also her vulnerability– for everything she taught me, and for her infinite strength and love. As another highlight, I thank Ceyhun Gürkan for his love, patience and understanding. He was with me during each phase of my study, and I might not have been able to complete this work without him. Whenever I felt discouraged or indeed hopeless, and when the issues and their solutions became meaningless, Ceyhun stood by me in all candour and honesty. He was right to tell me not to leave this study incomplete despite all its difficulties. Perseverance for me has meant saying no and holding onto the modest belief in being able to make a change. Ceyhun never allowed me to forget this; I'm as grateful for that as I am for the melodies coming from his guitar that accompanied my silent work.

I thank my editors David Fasenfest and Alfredo Saad-Filho, who relieved my burden with their unique guidance and understanding as I turned my dissertation into a book. I also thank Janine Su for her edits, which helped to make my book readable, and to get my point across.

We are passing through a dreary period that affects everyone. This book is dedicated to 'the ones who live with great seriousness' despite everything (as characterized by Nazım Hikmet in his poem *On Living* (*Yaşamaya Dair*), and to the 'undaunteds of life', who try to stand despite increasing soreness of the world.

Abbreviations

ANAP	*Anavatan Partisi* –The Motherland Party
AKP / official AK Party	*Adalet ve Kalkınma Partisi* –Justice and Development Party
AIRB	*Aile İrşat ve Rehberlik Büroları* –Family (Spiritual) Guidance and Counseling Offices
ASPB	*Aile ve Sosyal Politikalar Bakanlığı* –Ministry of Family and Social Policies
CHP	*Cumhuriyet Halk Partisi* –The Republican's People Party
Diyanet	*Diyanet İşleri Başkanlığı* –Directorate of Religious Affairs / Presidency of Religious Affairs
DP	*Demokrat Parti* –The Democratic Party
FP	*Fazilet Partisi* –The Virtue Party
MEB	*Milli Eğitim Bakanlığı* –Ministry of Education
MHP	*Milliyetçi Hareket Partisi* –The National Movement Party
MNP	*Milli Nizam Partisi* –The National Order Party
MSP	*Milli Selamet Partisi* –The National Salvation Party
MÜSIAD	*Müstakil Sanayici ve İşadamları Derneği* –The Independent Industrialists' and Businessmen's Association
RP	*Refah Partisi* –The Welfare Party
SB	*Sağlık Bakanlığı* –Ministry of Health
SP	*Saadet Partisi* –The Felicity Party
TBMM	*Türkiye Büyük Millet Meclisi* –Great National Assembly of Turkey
T.C.	*Türkiye Cumhuriyeti* –Republic of Turkey
TÜSIAD	*Türk Sanayicileri ve İşadamları Derneği* –Turkish Industry and Business Association

CHAPTER 1

Introduction

The Conceptualisation of Ideal Womanhood in Post-2002 Turkey

This book is an attempt to explore the changing patterns of womanhood in politics and the consequences of this change in the *life* of the woman in post-2002 Turkey in connection with the governmental rationality of the ruling party; namely, the AKP (Justice and Development Party). To face *life* and especially *the life of the woman* is to study the transformative relations of power from macro to micro by problematising womanhood in the scope of sexuality, family, violence, and neoliberal subjectivity, respectively. In this book, I argue that although the government in post-2002 Turkey aspires to construct a neoliberal society and Islamic subjectivities, it does not succeed in preventing violence against the woman despite multiple protective mechanisms. Between 2000 and 2014, 10,793 women were murdered, mostly by relatives, husbands, and boyfriends (Özbudun, 2016: 252). Without even including the rate of rape and sexual harassment, this number is devastating, and warrants a multifold analytical investigation that looks at the government's political and economic aims because influential political figures often talk about such cases and even womanhood in general using accusatory and upbraiding terms.

The AKP has taken decisive steps towards building neoliberalism through religio-cultural values since it came to power in 2002, which has had significant impacts on the lives of women. This book interrogates the changing nature of political *language* about womanhood, and the increasing interference in the lifestyle of the woman in social and population policies, in line with the merits of religious conservatism. It examines the transformation of power relations by questioning how a blend of Islamism and neoliberalism has become a certain discursive language and regulatory mechanism for the constitution of womanhood. The transformation of politics and society has produced positive and negative consequences for the woman; however, the negative outcomes have in a way outweighed the positive ones. This is the major challenge for and the paradox of the society and politics that this book attempts to explore. The overall argument is that in the post-2002 period the woman has become a central reference point in politics with respect to the idealisation of their gender status and social roles. This idealisation is observed in various forms, through which the woman has been described, ranging from member of society, to sexual object, to maternal actor, and to a body requiring certain behaviours and clothing. Yet at the same time, it is in this very period that the woman has become exposed to increasing violence, which has also resulted in an unprecedented visibility in gender-based criminality.

In this context, freedom and security are employed to regulate gender categories through constitutive norms of neoliberalism built in connection with religio-cultural values. As these norms and values spread throughout state apparatuses and civil society, regulative mechanisms seek to reconstruct power relations – which are always gendered – through womanhood. In other words, when the female body becomes one of the central points of politics, the woman's sexuality and her life are turned into objects of politics (Lemke, 2011). As the scope of discursive practices – such as institutional policies, political actors, and social authorities – is widened with an eye to creating more security for the woman, a new dimension based on gender roles is added to neoliberalism in order to manage womanhood in accordance with the conservative priorities of the day. However, gender categories and particularly idealised womanhood should be called into question because, I argue, there is an interplay at work between security and freedom in accordance with neoliberalism and conservatism. That is, strategies of security always seek to ensure the economy of power in that the interests of free individuals ultimately meet the collective interest (Foucault, 2008: 65).

This interplay between security and freedom becomes significant when disciplinary power and biopower join forces in order to regulate and reconstruct idealised womanhood by insistently pointing out failed women or "bad subjects" (Nadesan, 2008). That is to say, these combined powers of discipline and security are intended to normalise and optimise the advantages of gender categories in everyday neoliberalism. Emphasising biopolitical problems from the perspective of a problem-solution neoliberal rationality points to personal responsibility and self-entrepreneurship, which depoliticises governmental interventions and the fact of violence (Nadesan, 2008; Oksala, 2010, 2011). Therefore, this book suggests analysing womanhood through life spheres as a governmental field because government is able to produce transformative and regulative discursive practices oscillating between security and freedom. In other words, womanhood as a field of biopolitics provides a milieu within which one can study the rationality of the multifold transformation in post-2002 Turkey by considering not only normalised woman-subjects but also 'unregulated' and 'undisciplined' woman-subjects as purported social problems of (national) development.

Taking disciplinary power and biopower as two conceptions of power, I aim to question the linkage between the heightened political interest in the sexuality of the woman and the dramatic upsurge in gender-based violence. In this way, I examine discursive and subject formations by looking at "procedural practices employed by religion, medicine, which make individuals bind to his own truth" (Foucault, 2014: 24). Therefore, the governance of womanhood presents itself as a new truth regime that generates constitutive norms and rules of conduct between individuals and their relations with others. When speaking of power relations concerned with the new truth, I do not make a strict distinction between state power and micro power. Thus, I see a gender regime based on truth and *true* womanhood at the intersection of macro and micro power relations. In line with this, Islamist traditions and actors are able to compose the "counter-frames of civility and subject formation" (Ismail, 2011: 859). Namely, Islamist practices firstly target seizing the state as an important power apparatus and then target local settings to gain access to the micro. To do so, disciplinary power moves towards youth and women in order to reshape problematic social relations through the legitimised hierarchies of the order (Ismail, 2011: 859).

To put the matter another way, the state, government, and other macro-political and social structures, as well as institutions, come to be seen as political entities that affect womanhood. Therefore, the state and political actors are rated here as an 'effect'. *The state as an effect* means that the state is the result of wide-ranging governmental practices (Lemke, 2012: 31–34). This perspective is decisive for my method of research into power and power relations because it provides me with different vantage points from within the scope of the micro-power relations where the state is located. In a way, the state as an effect allows me to discern the linkage between the micro and macro realms by combining disciplinary power and biopower, in that this linkage enables me to look at the individual and society in the context of subject formation and discourse formation through the lens of governmentality. This being so, the imposed norms revolving around religious and traditional values, social honour, and self-esteem intrinsically constitute the truth regime in post-2002 Turkey by defining different states of womanhood in the public and private spheres. Accordingly, themes like "fundamental needs" and "true nature" are employed to *problematise* womanhood in the context of population, national development, social values, life quality, public health, and personal happiness (Foucault, 2014: 268; Rose and Miller, 1992: 174–175; Özbay et al., 2016: 17).

1   The Conceptualisation of Problematic Womanhood and Governmentality

Governmentality provides an analytical perspective on power techniques and political rationalities by marking their interwoven relations in the constitution of the state. That is, governmentality points to the art of government, in which the tactics and activities of power have to proceed on specific rationality in order that the government can produce and augment action plans. For this, the government discerns and defines problems, then solutions and interventions are deployed through power techniques, including agencies, institutions, procedures, and legal forms. Relying on the power techniques produced by political rationality, governmentality promises an array of strategies and interventions to identify and tackle problems of society and subject (Lemke, 2001: 191;2007: 43–45; Foucault, 1997a: 114).

Governmentality is therefore about power relations and processes of subjectivation because it not only refers to the management and control of the state within the political agenda but it also pokes at the self-government and "conduct of conduct" between subjects in line with religious, medical, cultural, traditional, or philosophical values and virtues (Foucault, 2001a: 341; Lemke, 2001:191; 2007: 43–45; Rose and Miller, 1992: 175). Thereby, the analytics of government "conceives of the state as an instrument and effect of political strategies that define the external borders between the public and the private, the state and civil society, and also define the internal structure of political institutions and state apparatuses" (Lemke, 2007: 44).

The notion of government in Foucault's setup has further meaning and function beyond state sovereignty. Through the conceptual promise of governmentality in terms of "governing the self" and "governing others", forms of government gain functionality and practicality under a specific statehood, by which the state as an effect opens up the ways by which the objects and subjects of problems and other constructive elements can be governed at a distance (Lemke, 2001: 191, 2007: 45–47; Rose and Miller, 1992: 175–176). In other words, political rationalities of government lead state agencies to knowledge of their own reality in terms of their history, geography, human capital, statistical facts and risks, scientific reports, bureaucratic rules, and popular and individual guidelines. The state's knowledge about its reality keeps political actions ready for entities and events. This accumulation of knowledge brings together technologies of government and power techniques in order to reconstruct subjectivities in line with the current truth regime (Lemke, 2007: 48; Rose and Miller, 1992: 183; see also Foucault, 1997b, 2001b).

Foucault's conception of the state and the relation between micro-power and macro-power relations raises essential questions to be answered from a critical gender perspective (Foucault, 1980a: 188–189). Lemke points out two of them: "What gender regime is coupled to concrete forms of statehood? What apparatus of sexuality, what forms of family and reproduction are promoted, marginalized, or even repressed?" (Lemke, 2012: 34; see also Lemke, 2007: 52–53). I evaluate state power in both macro-political and also daily relation to human life. From the perspective of biopolitics, everyday life and that of the political are interwoven. Therefore, the macro and micro realms relate to each other. In other words, as I shall argue, womanhood is constituted at this threshold. Norms, legal structures, administrative rules, and so on, can make sense in terms of womanhood from this comprehensive perspective.

In this context, the state is a domain wherein the discursive tools and practices of governmental rationality may be used to permeate the non-political and non-state spheres (Rose and Miller, 1992: 177). According to Rose and Miller's analysis (1992: 181), "government is a problematizing activity". Thus, the linkage between state strategising and government problematising is of utmost significance. With respect to the governmentalisation of the state, the state itself is an established term through which strategies are devised to prevent or solve problems; in other words, the state needs problems to solve. Therefore, tracing the problems faced by states and decoding their strategies help us understand the governmental rationalities of a given place and time, as well as the changing technologies and techniques of power then and now (Rose and Miller, 1992: 175; Rose, 1999: 5).

In a broader sense, Foucault develops his analysis of government through a "history of problematizations", which amounts to "the history of the way things pose a problem" (Foucault, 2014: 244). He uses the examples of madness and sexuality, which were both initially seen as problems. Looking at why and how societal problems tend to revolve around sexuality, madness, or criminality – which are the major technologies of biopolitics – gives us clues as to the solutions and interventions used to deal with them in a given time and place. In the context of sexuality, the population, subject, prostitution, and reproduction can all be problematised differently with reference to specific technologies (Foucault,1986, 1998, 2014). Therefore, sexuality itself is not a problem because it is regulated and managed according to family relations and gender roles. In line with this, sexual behaviours and relations are then subjected to norms and moral codes (Foucault, 1990, 1998, 2014). Namely, the political rationalities that form the art of government aim towards a reality represented by idealised images, which in turn inform the mechanisms used to solve problems (Rose and Miller, 1992: 178). We therefore need to think about the hidden facets of problematisation by carefully observing perceptions and practices because "they are acting blindly and that, as a result, a new light is necessary. A new light is necessary, a new lighting, and new rules of behavior. And here a new object appears: An object that appears as a problem" (Foucault, 2014: 245). As Majia Holmer Nadesan (2008: 6) sums up well, biopolitical problematics and the opportunities of problem-solving mechanisms simultaneously reveal governmental aims and approaches in accordance with their own governmental rationality. Biopolitical problematics intrinsically target utilitarian and beneficiary results in light of amendatory remedies with reference to the necessities of population, market or the actors of power (Nadesan, 2008: 6).

Leaning on the merits of biopolitical necessity, the development of problem-solving mechanisms brings with it knowledge of how to improve competency in identifying population problems (Nadesan, 2008: 8). Experts on such problems represent this competency as the biopolitical authority of knowledge (Nadesan, 2008: 94), through which the values and practices of individuals and institutions are deprivatised. Problem-solving mechanisms, in turn, publicly actualise the security and control apparatuses acting on everyday life (Nadesan, 2008: 10, 94). Additionally, the discursive practices around these necessities make individuals feel worthy of and motivated to take part in actualising governmental solutions to such problems. Therefore, as I shall argue, the weakness in the perspective of governmentality appears at the intersection of realisation of problems and the consent of individuals towards the fact that these problems must be solved in order to have a safer and healthier society. It can be understood that the political mechanisms to obtain consent from individuals are especially crucial for the state to realise itself. The consent of individuals also provides the representational field and acts as the tools through which power could permeate the private and public spheres. In this context, the strength of the state is also the success of governmental influence and permeation into spheres and souls (Nadesan, 2008: 25). Regarding biopolitical authorities, Rose and Miller (1992: 180) point out that a domain outside politics is ensured by the "proliferation of independent agencies including philanthropists, doctors, hygienists, managers, planners, parents, and social workers". This is because "political strategies" and "the activities of these authorities" need to know the everyday habits of individuals in order to merge them with orchestrated political, economic, and social decisions and actions (Rose and Miller, 1992: 180; Rose, 1999: 9).

Additionally, biopolitical authorities, or experts, are expected to produce free subjects who are conscious of self-monitoring and self-governing mechanisms in line with governmental reason (Nadesan, 2008: 29). Therefore, what government calls a situational case or personal problematic brings about very blunt questions of normalisation. To illustrate, the moral degeneration of subjects, local resistance, the demise of the family, and market rules are all indicators of abnormality in society, so the desire to normalise and stabilise the social order brings a string of diagnoses and risk analyses regarding the 'how' of the matter during the problem-solving process instead of the 'why' (Nadesan, 2008: 39; Lemke, 2007: 49; Foucault, 2008). Thereby, the normalisation of neoliberal exploitation is persuasive "in their promises to maximize personal liberty and happiness"; however, the promises of neoliberal rationality "offer limited vocabularies and technologies of government for addressing people, events, and phenomena rupturing liberal fantasies" (Nadesan, 2008: 215).

To sum up, thinking about the state as an effect of government problematisation denotes omnipresent power relations that also embrace it. The answer to "who governs whom" is the response to power that can gain its influence by stirring up "problems" in order to coordinate its strategies and solutions with the systems of thought and systems of action (Rose and Miller, 1992: 177). Therefore, by examining the multifold transformation of the state it should be possible to uncover the power relations between force and resistance. The desire for and belief in the power to solve problems for the good of all is actually the analytics of government. When looked at from this vantage point, the analytics of government leads me to develop a conceptual and theoretical framework through which I can re-problematise womanhood. This is how I propose to trace the problems of the AKP, and to question its strategies and problem-solving mechanisms regarding 'the why and how of problematic womanhood' in post-2002 Turkey. And, following Lemke, I keep in mind that:

> Practices instead of object, strategies instead of function, and technologies instead of institution – this is certainly not a light snack, but it might be the recipe for a state theory that opens up new directions and research areas for political analysis and critique and provides a better understanding of current political and social transformations.
> LEMKE, 2007: 58

2   Changing Patterns of Womanhood in Post-2002 Turkey

I aim to explore changing patterns of womanhood in post-2002 Turkey, and to point out the power/ power relations enacted upon the woman and her body. This power has rationality and a way of thinking in order to conduct bodies, as well as producing self-governable subjects in accordance with values in light of knowledge especially on religion, science, and culture. In this book, I examine the definition of idealised womanhood, which has been re-built in line with the governmental problems of the state under AKP rule.

Furthermore, the changing patterns make me think of idealised womanhood by exploring knowledge veins, which leads me to the question of how womanhood is regulated, and how the woman governs her own life. In doing so, I simultaneously unfold the neoliberal rationality of the state by tracing especially its problematisations revolving around womanhood. I develop a critical perspective on open-wound questions and restrictions on the woman, specifically their problem-solving mechanisms. Thus, this book approaches womanhood within the scope of gender and biopolitics in order to explore the woman's instrumental and transformative position in politics, economics, and culture.

Exploring the relation between biopolitics and gender, the reconstructive elements of womanhood in Turkey need to be looked at more closely, especially since the AKP came to power in 2002. Along with far-reaching changes in the economic, social, and political structure, Turkey under the AKP has evolved into a new phase of neoliberalism, and this has had a great impact on the female body, woman-subjects, and the definition of womanhood itself. Womanhood has always been regarded as a constitutive element in the making of state politics and social fabrication, even in the early periods of the Republic of Turkey, yet the woman has been constantly excluded from the realm of politics (Kandiyoti, 1987, 1991; Sirman, 1988/89).

This fact prompts me, first and foremost, to observe the basic interrelated and also paradoxical life spheres of womanhood. Closer examination of these life spheres shows that the instrumentalisation of womanhood and female subjectivity are disputed in accordance with neoliberalism and Islamic norms in the field of politics. I see some central concepts and themes in these discussions, such as competition, interest, benefit, risk, utility, happiness, peace, trust, and violence, which intrinsically regain their own neoliberal function through the bodily performances and choices of the woman. In other words, the political use of womanhood helps Islamic moral principles permeate micro-spheres by focusing on the intimacy of the female body and Islamic subjectivity. Therefore, as freedom and security become the central themes and targets of social and population policies in post-2002 Turkey, violence and discrimination against the woman in the name of social honour are increasing, and the disciplinary control mechanisms over the female body are deepening.

In this book, I treat neoliberalism as "a way of doing things" (Foucault, 2008: 318). Neoliberal rationality based on regulating and limiting governmental activity supports the freedom of individuals because "the contrived forms of the free, entrepreneurial and competitive conduct of economic–rational individuals" carve out "a form of the rational self-conduct of the governed themselves, but a form that is not so much a given of human nature as a consciously contrived style of conduct" (Burchell, 1996: 23–24). Therefore, contemporary neoliberalism is more than an economy or state. It must produce subjects, normative behaviours, or anything related to the individual, its body, its soul, its choices (Brown, 2003: 1). The rationality of neoliberal activity, thus, should be accepted beyond any institutional goals. Neoliberalism in the nexus of political rationality and the self requires the use of individual freedom, which is a technical condition of government (Rose and Miller, 1992: 201; Burchell, 1996: 24). Therefore, governmentality denotes the reasoning and practice of government. Governmentality has tools, apparatuses, strategies, techniques, and discourses (in short, *dispositifs*) to allow it to function. First of all, neoliberal governmentality targets freedom. Freedom for neoliberal governmentality is as much a target as a tool, strategy, technique, and discourse. As Foucault argues, neoliberal governmentality functions through the state apparatus and civil society in accordance with certain principles (Foucault, 2007, 2008). These principles, and the premises on which they are based, are the constitutive norms of social policies, which in turn shape social policies and discursive practices by highlighting ideal cases, including ideal womanhood. Therefore, governing through freedom means governing through these neoliberal norms.

Thinking womanhood in Turkish politics in the context of biopolitics and the analytics of governmentality provides me with a framework through which to view the relation of "the population-biological processes-regulatory mechanisms-State" and "the body-organism-discipline-institution series" (Foucault, 2003a: 250;Lemke, 2011: 37). This perspective would help to apprehend womanhood in Turkey in the context of both neoliberal state policies and neoliberal "self-technologies", both of which are essential for the neoliberal constitution of womanhood based on Islamism and subjectivity (Foucault, 1997b: 225; 2001b: 404).

This means that I should consider the connections of neoliberal social and population policies with the mechanisms of self-entrepreneurship, self-controlling mechanisms, self-interest, and self-regulation, as well as a new mode of mass-consumption society. This is the point at which gender and politics intersect. That is to say, the role of the woman is a specific and critical element of societal government. It is therefore essential to consider the intimate connection between gender and neoliberal governmentality in order to achieve an overall understanding of womanhood in Turkish politics and social and population policies through problems of government analytics. This fact

will be examined in the book by re-problematising womanhood through the following set of questions:
- What are the complex dynamics and motivations regarding the urge for disciplinary and regulatory efforts?
- What are the tensions and interwoven relations between neoliberalism and Islamism?
- How and why do these new disciplinary and regulatory attempts focus particularly on the lives of women?
- What is the relation between exacerbated manhood and authoritarian state practices?
- How did the female body become the target of politicised sexual practices?
- In which context can the female body be criminalised on the grounds of moral collapse?
- Why is the woman as a subject responsible for moral degeneration and moral hazards?
- Why have gender-based violence and crimes in Turkey become more visible since 2002, despite existing and remaining unresolved prior?
- What is the relation between the conservative governmental project of the gendered population and the increase in violence against women?
- What did the neoliberal transition *creatively* destruct in Turkey? And how?
- Under which circumstances does protective manhood need to be sharpened?
- Which kind of political-social reality left the woman defenceless, helpless, and vulnerable?
- Why do state actors see the core of the problems as the result of deficient religious values? If so, why cannot religion protect women then?
- Are there partial solutions for real problems? Are these real problems covered up by problematisations of government by locating them far away from their social context?

The crucial questions may be further generated. In answering these questions, my method is to trace the knowledge-power embedded in problems and solutions of governmentality regarding womanhood and socio-political life.

3 Insights from Foucault's Method

A research method according to biopolitics and the analytics of governmentality should focus on governmental practices. Foucault, in his piece *Question of Method*, explains this point in relation to his research into prisons:

> In this piece of research on the prisons, as in my other earlier work, the target of analysis was not 'institutions,' 'theories,' or 'ideology' but practices – with the aim of grasping the conditions that make these acceptable at a given moment; the hypothesis being that these types of practice are not just governed by institutions, prescribed by ideologies, guided by pragmatic circumstances – whatever role these elements may actually play – but, up to a point, possess their own specific regularities, logic, strategy, self-evidence, and 'reason.' It is a question of analyzing a 'regime of practices' – practices being understood here as places where what is said and what is done, rules imposed and reasons given, the planned and the taken-for-granted meet and interconnect. To analyze "regimes of practices" means to analyze programs of conduct that have both prescriptive effects regarding what is to be done (effects of 'jurisdiction') and codifying effects regarding what is to be known (effects of 'veridiction').
>
> FOUCAULT, 2001C: 225

This book has been based largely on qualitative analysis in the pursuit of a better understanding of ingrained womanhood and its social, political, and economic mechanisms, with the goal of answering the above-mentioned and further questions. Each answer paves new and different paths towards understanding the life spheres of womanhood. In answering these questions, new Islamic reference points lead me to religious mannerisms because political actors and state institutions lean heavily on religious knowledge in order to rationalise their regulations and interventions. Nevertheless, it is noteworthy that knowledge does not point to ideas and systematic thoughts as is the case with ideologies; on the contrary, it is a "central component of government", developing together with actors, theories, projects, experiments, and the like (Rose and Miller, 1992: 177). The *language* within the discursive practices makes knowledge plausibly transferable by using *apparatuses of truth*, that are composed of specific signs and special concepts, rules, procedures, and methods locating new ways to the truth (Rose and Miller, 1992: 177,179; Rose, 1999: 4). From great technologies to simple governmental techniques and tactics, anything ensuring governmental thoughts such as interviews, case records, brochures, and even diaries contribute to discerning governmental rationality by disclosing the *language* of knowledge and the *order* of things (Rose, O'Malley, and Valverde, 2006: 89). Therefore, knowledge-power itself gains a new political and economic ability in examining governmental rationality.

The vital shift in biopolitics comes from risk analysis, calculation, prediction of events, statistics, categorisations, and procreation within the population because the continuum of life makes up of the core of security mechanisms rationalised and regulated by knowledge-power. The conceptualisation of knowledge-power could find its way into Foucault's method oriented in terms of "archaeology" and "genealogy". While archaeology refers to "inscrib[ing] knowledges in the hierarchical order of power associated with science", genealogy is "a kind of attempt to emancipate historical knowledges from that subjection, to render them, that is, capable of opposition and of struggle against the coercion of a theoretical, unitary, formal and scientific discourse" (Foucault, 1980b: 85). Therefore, these two Foucauldian terms are employed to reveal local knowledges including tactics and description ignored by the scientific hierarchisation of knowledge and its effects on power; that is, knowledge-power (Foucault, 1980b: 85). Knowledge-*effects* on power can be explored at the level of pure methodological discussions. However, I do not aim to explain where knowledge-power comes in, but rather focus on questions of how knowledge-power governs us, conducts our behaviours, and how it thereby controls the population. In other words,

> There is not a real distinction between some and others. But within the system of knowledge-power, within the economic technology and management, there is this break between the pertinent level of the population and the level that is not pertinent, or that is simply instrumental. The final objective is the population. The population is pertinent as the objective, and individuals, the series of individuals, are no longer pertinent as the objective, but simply as the instrument, relay, or condition for obtaining something at the level of the population.
> FOUCAULT, 2007: 42

Therefore, it needs to be underlined that knowledge, which is obtained through surveillance, examination, tests, and confession, turns into power through the truth regime. That is to say, Foucault means that the analysis of mechanisms of power conjoins the history of economic transformation, which should be analysed as the politics of truth with regard to the individual and the population. In this context, political truth harbours the knowledge-effects produced by struggles, personal biographies, battles, and confessions, all of which have an important role to play in the practice of the tactics of power (Foucault, 2007). Thus, what is important here is that knowledge-power creates ruled-ruler relations and subjectivations, making it possible to grasp the norms of order and manage the self.

It should be noted here that sexuality, which is at the heart of these transitions, addresses the analytical framework for mobile and multiple discourses in the production process of truth in order to establish the basis for knowledge-power subjectivity and ethics (Foucault, 1998). This means that "if sexuality was constituted as an area of investigation, this was only because relations of power had established it as a possible object; and conversely if power was able to take it as a target, this was because techniques of knowledge and procedures of discourse were capable of investing it ... Techniques of knowledge and strategies of power are linked together on the basis of their difference" (Foucault, 1998: 98). Within these interwoven knowledge-heaps, based upon my understanding, any method that would fit the analytics of biopolitics and governmentality should take different sources and materials into account.

In a broader sense, there is a morality composed of normative values and determined actions. These values and relevant performances are taught and recommended to individuals through mediators of basic agencies such as families, religious institutions, schools, and state actors (Foucault, 1990: 25). Therefore, there must be a "systematic continuity" of tactical discursive practices in order to direct individuals on the way of knowledge-power(Foucault, 1998: 103, 2001d: 5). In this sense, power is composed of mobile and changeable relations based on tactical and strategic aims. That is why the examination of power is a method, technique, and perspective to disclose governmental rationality, and to uphold dominations, submissions, and confessions through the free subject by looking at all materials and documents left by the subject itself (Foucault, 2003a: 34, 1984a: 199, 1980c, 1980d). Within power relations, it is not who states the rules and actions but who listens to and obeys them that is important, which actually becomes the governmental domain of power (Foucault, 1998: 93–95). Thus, *examination* is crucial to disclose the governmental rationality of power through cases, actions, events, words, and expressions.

Therefore, strict, logical, positivist, and empiricist methods do not fit the analytics of biopolitics and governmentality. Instead, historical, sociological, and political concrete materials should be handled in a comprehensive way. What is essential for Foucault is to see knowledge and power, and their relation from below, not from a high vantage point. Accordingly, statistics, for instance, mean state-science, and are incorporated into the established power network. Foucault's aim is to display the genealogy of power and knowledge, and to inspire "the insurrection of the subjugated knowledges" (Foucault, 2003a: 7). As a method, genealogy in particular means putting up a fight against power, too. In his words, "Genealogy has to fight the power-effects characteristic of any discourse that is regarded as scientific" (Foucault, 2003a: 9). Foucault expresses this as follows:

> When I say 'subjugated knowledges', I mean two things. On the one hand, I am referring to historical contents that have been buried or masked in functional coherences or formal systematizations ... Second, I think subjugated knowledges should be understood as meaning something else and, in a sense, something quite different. When I say 'subjugated knowledges', I am also referring to a whole series of knowledges that have been disqualified as nonconceptual knowledges, as insufficiently elaborated knowledges: naive knowledges, hierarchically inferior knowledges, knowledges that are below the required level of erudition or scientificity.
>
> FOUCAULT, 2003a: 7

Foucault here explains knowledge-power relations and shows how they are closely related and interwoven into a complex power structure. The "subjugated knowledge" he refers to is knowledge that has been colonised by great narratives, state policies and discourses, systematic formulations, and strict logical theories. In his view, this results in producing and strengthening the established power relations and structures. From a genealogical perspective, it is essential that a critique of established power relations and structures aims to surmount colonised knowledges, as it were, through logical narratives and logical explanations, thereby inspiring "the insurrection of subjugated knowledges".

Interrelatedly, neoliberal governmentality has always sought to find cracks caused by political and economic crises so as to maintain its own subsistence, because *life itself has to continue* (Foucault,2003a). That is to say, contemporary neoliberal rationality with the rise of new-right discourses after the 1980s needed new discursive practices to stimulate individuals through new legitimate and regulative norms. Thus, in parallel with the increasing new-right conservative atmosphere, religion and traditional sensitivities became helpful for people to internalise this rationality, and thus permeated into every societal layer. In other words, the selfish, competitive, and pure rational subjects of neoliberal rationality were expected to learn how to practice self-sacrifice, patience, endurance, and frugality, all motivated and moralised by religion (Brown, 2006).

Deniz Ali Gür's book *The Religionisation of Knowledge* (*Bilginin Dinselleştirilmesi,* 2016) draws critical attention to the link between the neoliberalisation of Turkey and the rising application of religious knowledge based on the synthesis of modern knowledge and Islamic cultural accumulation. Religious knowledge seeks to bridge Islam with modern knowledge. Thus, the religionisation of knowledge aspires to develop a scientific approach loaded with values and virtues. In this respect, it is not a coincidence that neoliberalism and new-right policies met in 1980 in the global context. Likewise, this meeting of neoliberalism and the new right forced the development of new concepts such as neoconservatism, which embraced neoliberal values by leaning on religion, tradition, and culture. Under this global transformation, Turkey witnessed the rise of Islamic values and the establishment of neoliberalism with military intervention in 1980 (2016: 64–84). In this sense, it is worth mentioning that religious knowledge seems like a new form of knowledge targeted at convincing individuals through obscurity and spirituality. This new form of knowledge is based on undiscussable religious principles. It has an encompassing power on collective behaviour and thoughts for believers and non-believers alike. This is why religious knowledge under state-control affairs such as *the Directorate of Religious Affairs* (Diyanet)[1] would like to primarily target the public spheres and regulate public order through principles and rules based on morality and peace. Indeed, religious principles for morality and peace surely want to correct woman's behaviours and visibility. This kind of corrective and disciplinary power permeates into private spheres, as it filters problem-solving mechanisms for the betterisation of public order through the female body and womanhood.

Following these critical insights from research methodology discussion, Foucault's analytical perspective also helps guide how to handle knowledge as I analyse the conditions of womanhood. My *knowledge-power* sources enable me to *examine* gender and biopolitics in relation to Islamic neoliberal governmentality in post-2002 Turkey. This is because further elaboration is needed to clarify how and which sources are apt for *examination*, taking into account the links between micro and macro power relations, and between the different modes of power, *i.e.*, disciplinary power and biopower. This has an effect on society and intensifies patriarchal power relations, as I can see from the state of affairs in Turkey. Therefore, it should be clear that this book does not

---

1 *Diyanet* has worked as a state institution under the prime minister since 1924. Since 1965, *Diyanet* has continued its services under Law No. 633. The first code of this law informs us about its main duty: the "Presidency (*or Directorate*) of Religious Affairs is established under the Prime Ministry in order to carry out work related to the beliefs of Islamic Religion, worship and morality; to enlighten and manage the places of worship". *Diyanet* has served as a public service in order to meet the religious needs of the people. It is a state institution to teach and treat people according to moral and religious realities. Due to its public status, it has a lot more reliable sources in order to provide state-control Islamism (Mutluer, 2014). Therefore, "the Directorate of Religious Affairs was authorized to oversee the knowledge and practices of Islam, which included the supervision of all mosques and the public sermons given there, the appointment of imams, the production and dissemination of Islamic knowledge" (Çınar, 2006: 88–89; see also Çınar, 2005: 17).

essentially aspire to persuade anyone of the recent reality of Turkey by using, for example, statistical materials, which are basic data about the number of femicides, as well as other social and population statistics. I am arguing that there is a reality accepted by an array of citizens of Turkey, which says that gender-based crimes have increased and become more visible in comparison to pre-2002 Turkey.

In addition, several cases are being prosecuted in the courts over murders, rapes, and violence against women, and new regulations and reports continue to be prepared. People who have a sensibility for violence against women keep their eyes on these cases with the help of the media. The media, in turn, subtly rationalises gender-based crimes through family values. These, as laid out above, are the knowledge-power sources, materials, and data that govern the life spheres of womanhood in post-2002 Turkey, and my aim is to put these in perspective. Thus, statistics and other data based on the speech of political actors, Islamic principles, and guidance from state institutions are critical to my portrayal of the mechanisms of knowledge-power surrounding the woman and womanhood.

4   Selection of the Research Sources

My qualitative research relies first and foremost on the (monthly) publications and Friday Khutbahs[2] of Diyanet. The reason for this is that 77% of society believes that Diyanet is an institution operating according to the beliefs, rituals, and moral principles of Islam (Konda, 2014). Additionally, 72% of society finds these fatwas[3] and Friday Khutbahs reliable (Konda, 2014). In parallel with this, in 2006, 63% of society found the religious orientation of party leaders to be important; this increased to 72% by 2012 (Yılmaz, 2012). I state these rates here because this basic information shall be later crucial to grasp the increasing influence of Diyanet through protocols that have joined it with other state institutions to disseminate common values into each sphere of life. This is why it is necessary to open a special spot for Diyanet in the book.

According to Diyanet, *religion gains community and group consciousness by organising thoughts and values together for collective rituals* (Okumuş,

---

2   The Khutbah is a prayer and sermon that is said on Fridays and also Eid Salaahs. (http://www.tdk.gov.tr).

3   A fatwa is a religious document that can only be declared by sheyks-ul Islam or muftis, which offers solutions to the problems related to the Islamic Law, in compliance with the principles of religious law. (http://www.tdk.gov.tr).

2006: 18). Likewise, the production of religious knowledge ought to aim at avant-garde solutions for particular problems. For Diyanet, *religion is a need so religious knowledge may provide a remedy for the problem-solving process. Religious knowledge, by learning its values and principles, should be accessed through thought and conscience. Religious knowledge brings freedom to the individual upon arriving at the correct knowledge, namely, the truth of God* (Aydın, 2008: 20–23). In light of this, what we need to understand is that Diyanet serves as a mediator between *true religious knowledge* and the *individual at the level of society*, so it has responsibilities (Görgülü, 2015: 26–27).[4] This means that the influence of religion extends beyond the spiritual to earthly functions through the values and moral structure of society. Indeed, according to Diyanet,

> Religion as a potential social control protects the social structure. Religion with this functionality of social control related to conservatism and legitimisation draws a line and boundaries for the members of society; and actors in order to make them move within the limits of social and political order and regulations.
> OKUMUŞ, 2006: 19

In line with this, Diyanet emphasises that

> Religion helps social actors to learn and internalise their appropriate roles for the social structure and for their own socialisation by highlighting and promoting certain types of characters that adhere to religion, socio-economic, religious, and similar systems. With socialisation, the child

---

4 Leaning on its social responsibilities, in 1924, Diyanet began its broadcasting life with "courses in morals". Additionally, it produced 30 printed publications until 1950; since 1950 it has produced over 1200 printed publications. In 2012 Diyanet's video channel and in 2015 Diyanet's radio channel expanded their services. In 1979 Diyanet Children, 1968 Diyanet News and in 1991 the Diyanet monthly journal, in 1999 the Diyanet European journal began their publications with different responsibilities and insights on different issues; namely, divorce, the truth of woman, family, violence, the youth, mosque, suicide and so on. Among them, family, spiritual values, urbanization, migration, changes and continuities are always a matter and repeated thema (Görgülü, 2015: 26). For example, only in 2014, 118,703 sermons and 212 Khutbahs were given for the importance and problems of family structure. Additionally, 17,069 sermons and 55 Khutbahs were read at Friday meetings and other religious meetings, especially at mosques only for women's rights and the values of womanhood. 2511 sermons and 8 Khutbahs were given on violence (Martı, 2015: 57). Moreover, on the protection of family and the prevention of violence against women, 16,500 personnel were educated and taught, and assigned to the different regions in Turkey (Martı, 2015: 58). These numbers, which are taken only from 2014, exemply the intense activities of Diyanet.

embraces and performs his social roles internally, more or less, than the influence of external social conditions ... Religion provides an endless source for punishments and rewards.

OKUMUŞ, 2006: 18

Therefore, the transformative position of Diyanet in society needs to be observed because it gives meaning to the occasions and domains of Islamic lifestyles. Diyanet also influences individuals' sensibilities, so it deems itself as a mechanism to prevent the exploitation of these sensibilities in the name of religion and God on the basis that *those who have the true knowledge have a responsibility to guide society, especially in critical times. True religious knowledge should be shared and disseminated* (Khutbah, 12 September 2014). Foucault (2014: 91) asserts that "religion ... binds the individual to and through obligations of truth". "Religious obligations of truth" are implemented as cultural and traditional practices through the institutional authorities (Foucault, 2014: 92). Although Foucault is discussing Christianity, his ideas are applicable to the case of Islamic principles, which seek to bring the obligations of truth more completely in line with social practices. I assume that social practices based on traditions and cultural habits have somehow a religious background, which is significant when examining the directorate logic of Diyanet in order to apprehend the hierarchy of religious obligations in the context of daily life. On this point, Foucault says that the secrets to happiness and salvation are also built on the promises of truth, provided that true actions and acts are examined by the conscience, as well as through rituals, procedures, and processes that manifest the truth to others (2014: 92).

Regarding the impact of religion through cultural and traditional practices, Foucault draws attention to the importance of (social) memory in order to return to specific behaviours, conduct, and thoughts by recalling rules and principles for a better social order (Foucault, 2014: 99). For conservatism and traditionalism, religion is the most important reminder to find the truth in history in order to transform society, form subjects, and rationalise institutions. Through the codes and rules of religion, subjectivities are reconstructed to remember "the errors committed during the day serves to measure the distance between what was done and what should have been done ... [*so*] the subject is nothing more, essentially, than the intersection between rules of conduct that must be remembered and the point of departure for future actions that should conform to this code" (Foucault,2014: 99–100, emphasis added). Upholding truth(-telling) is possible to decode the knowledge-power sources that direct us to what is true and what is false, and to realise it in social practice "as a weapon in relationships between individuals ... as a means of modifying relations of power among those who speak, and finally as an element within an institutional structure" (Foucault, 2014: 29).

Therefore, as specified earlier, I select some monthly journals of Diyanet and some Friday Khutbahs to illustrate the discussion. I seek clear statements and expressions in them because I examine religious and traditional references in order to pinpoint the common thread of governmental rationality. There are some open statements about the woman's behaviours and about manhood, for example. I cite them where appropriate. In order to bring what Diyanet states in its own publications to the fore, my initial aim is to discuss its institutional mindset, which reflects governmental rationality. Therefore, this book does not aim to open true religious knowledge for discussion. Instead, it is an attempt to explore the analytical relations between the influence of state-centred Islamic principles and the construction of everyday life rationality.

In what follows, it will also be critical to cite implementations, reports, and educational booklets in order to widen the perspective from which to examine post-2002 Turkey's transformative rationality. Indeed, Diyanet has signed protocols with various ministries.[5] To illustrate, in 2011 the Ministry of Family and Social Policy (Aile ve Sosyal Politikalar Bakanlığı – ASPB) collaborated with Diyanet to disseminate traditions and manners to the next generations. In order to produce the problematisations of government, the state needs to access the problems of individuals regarding family relations and reasons for divorce. To do so, Diyanet provides special training to personnel[6] on how to counsel individuals and families. For example, the ASPB hosted family consulting services between 2008 and 2013 with the aim of preventing the demise of the family and reinforcing the maternal status of the woman. This is why some of its publications related to the pre-and post-marriage process and family-life skills shall be worth referring to.

The qualitative analysis, national action plans, publications, and annual reports, along with international agreements on gender equality and violence, are additionally supported by quantitative data sourced from various research companies. The quantitative data provides me a holistic perspective on the changing lifestyles and values, as well as statistical information regarding

---

5 For example, in 2009, Diyanet signed a protocol with the Ministry of Health (Sağlık Bakanlığı – SB) in the fields of early marriages, women's health, violence, social psychology, and so on. Between 2008 and 2013 with the Ministry of National Education (Milli Eğitim Bakanlığı – MEB) Diyanet focused on the establishment of prayers schools and education for girls (Mutluer, 2014: 13).
6 Between 2002 and 2012 the ramping rate of Diyanet's personnel was 60%, and the collaborations impacted this rate (Mutluer, 2014: 32).

the reasons for violence. In addition, the party programmes of the AKP, the speeches of political actors, and selected news items about gender-based crimes are consulted in this book. Finally, various legislation and regulations shall be significant in understanding official administration, and I benefit from these where appropriate.

In light of my selected materials and sources, this book is not solely about the gender question and women's rights in Turkey focusing on the 2000s. Rather, it intends to explore the rationality of government through which womanhood has been regulated, conducted, and instrumentalised in order to reconstruct new subjects under the AKP's power regime. The data employed to answer the guiding questions outlined above have been selected for the critical light they shine on the governmental description of womanhood and the analytical reasons for the rise of gender-based violence.

5   Structure of the Book

I begin by outlining the normative sexual behaviours regulated by virtue and moral values. Exploring the discipline of the body and the regulation of sexuality in line with these virtues and values, Islamic performances of heteronormativity particularly draw attention to the imagined population, which desires to transform the gender regime, and to impose specified idealisations onto social norms. In this chapter, I aim to shed light on the intimacy of the female body and the woman's sexuality, which religious order purports to bring into harmony through the practices of the youth and the woman. Self-discipline and public surveillance on the female body need to be focused on in order to understand how the sexuality of the female body and womanhood are regulated according to Islamic principles. Therefore, I use veiling as a regulative and transformative tool through which to discuss key Islamic principles in the upcoming sections. Virtues such as shame, temperance, and chastity have been carrying a message that dictates how the woman should present herself in public, and how the woman herself can protect her body by being aware of the sexual connotations associated with her nature. In addition, reproduction, (religious) marriage, and gender roles are reduced to fit in conservative life forms. More importantly, all these regulated fields regarding the female body and her sexuality gain further instrumentality, through which political and economic goals can easily produce, govern, and conduct individuals and the population.

In the following chapter, I focus on the family unit. The family provides a secure life – a fact which is expected to be internalised by the woman. The fact is that the woman's life, in a way, becomes the family. The concept of the family reminds the female body of her womanly identity. Therefore, a woman gains her 'womanhood' through her motherhood and wifehood. Along with this female identity, womanhood is regarded as the major actor of the continuity of family life. In line with this, perseverance, loyalty, and sacrifice are codified as the features of ideal womanhood. In a way, womanhood is instrumentalised to protect the family unit by missing or ignoring all real problems in it. In this context, happy marriages and happiness itself point to the consent of the woman regarding family life and her duties. Moreover, legislative and religious regulations regarding motherhood and marriage display that the strong family structure is only dependent on the self-actualisation of the woman, which is intrinsically concealed in pain and inequality due to patriarchal gender relations and the violation of women's rights. Most importantly, the family as a life sphere of womanhood opens up a discussion on continuity and change in the construction of state identity in Turkey.

In the next chapter, violence as another life sphere of womanhood is examined. I set out the brutal and explicit violence against women by providing statistical information about the reasons and numbers for why and how women are abused, raped, and killed. Additionally, some media news about gender-based violence shall be shared to show how violence against or 'the death of the woman' are justified as the hand of 'masculine sovereignty' in the public and private spheres. Likewise, my aim is to understand and uncover how the 'regime of truth' has permeated into our daily lives by deeming violence as a disciplinary and regulatory technique of power. What I am tracing is how gender-based crimes have become a reality for the woman in Turkey. It is reasonable to ask why and how fears and unfairness are turned into the risks of being a woman. On the one hand, women's rights are expanded. On the other hand, risks and warnings based on statistics are produced to show 'the problem of violence in society'. Thus, it is clear that the politicisation and depoliticisation of violence appear as an unwillingness to eradicate problems even though effective solutions are there to be implemented. In the scope of this chapter, violence has a meaning beyond patriarchy or cultural habit, and this is evident in politics. In this chapter, I address violence as the disciplinary and regulatory apparatus of power.

The final chapter describes neoliberalism and womanhood in terms of the risk society, precariousness, poverty, and female employment. Capitalism has been built upon a neoliberal individualism concealed within cooperative responsibilities. Furthermore, bodies are commodified, becoming human capital governed according to emotions, risks, happiness, and social prestige. In this context, gender justice challenges the content of gender equality by means of collective responsibility and the complementary duties of gendered social roles. A healthy and secure life is tied to moral, religious belonging and family life. In other words, falsified womanhood and the uncontrollable female body define moral disaster and social problems (and possible risks). However, women's empowerment is also at stake in competitive neoliberalism, as well as Islamic conservatism. Accordingly, individuals are expected to govern themselves, but the result has been quite the opposite; in the Turkish case, neoliberal governmentality takes advantage of religious and traditional sensitivities as disciplinary and regulatory mechanisms, which provide fields of authoritarian intervention. Womanhood and the female body constitute fields of intervention that make societal restrictions and control mechanisms felt. Namely, biopower creates an economy of power targeted at maximisation and optimisation. The main concern here is the maximisation and optimality of the human body and its gender for well-defined targets. Under the AKP power regime, the female body and gender categories recognise the sovereignty of power within disciplinary and regulative practices. At the end of this chapter, the female subjectivity of post-2002 Turkey will reveal the multiple faces and roles of Islamic neoliberal governmental rationality.

6   Concluding Remarks

I attempt to come up with a response to the question of Islamic neoliberal subjectivity because the constructive elements of womanhood provide a clue as to Islamic norm impositions on individuals and corresponding to moral boundaries and conflicts. Across the life spheres of womanhood, the woman meets us as a vital constituent element of social and political transformation in post-2002 Turkey.

In this respect, I aim to contribute not only to Foucauldian literature by drawing attention into Islamism and womanhood in contemporary neoliberal rationalities, but also to the debates about the vulnerability of the woman and about violence by analysing and deciphering the transformative influence of conservative values through the instrumentality of the female body and gender identities. In order to make the changes in post-2002 Turkey understood, I deal with Islamic principles as a constructive component of this great transformation. While I clarify its effective influence on subjectivities in the context of knowledge-power relations, I argue that the fact of neoliberalism destructs the main intention of pure religious salvation. In fact, the stimulation of religious values and traditional sensitivities can not protect women and children outside of the peaceful discourse of religion. Therefore, this book aims to shed light on what the promises of change and regulation since 2002 could not achieve and why they could not protect women.

This book offers a way to analyse key unspoken aspects of womanhood. I consider that the new truth regime in Turkey is intrinsically rationalised by religious and traditional values. Additionally, instead of bluntly putting forward the gender question in Turkey, this book prefers to move on the problematics of the government with womanhood in order to uncover the modes of governmental thinking regarding individuals and the population. Eventually, the strength of the conservative society is in its promise of a more reliable and trustworthy living space on the other side of the risk society, which neoliberalism always longs for. However, factors such as reliability, trust, and risk remain intertwined; thus, I believe that womanhood as a governmental domain provides critical insights to evaluate the relevant religious motifs within the neoliberal rationality of government.

In line with this, I do not intend to describe the current questions by referring to religion, so never discuss religion here outside the context of questions of gender and gender-based violence in a given society. My aim is simply to articulate other possible ways of seeing and thinking on the correlative and conditional equation involving sociopolitical transformation, gender, the woman, crimes, public peace, values, virtues, and neoliberalism by taking advantage of the perspective of governmentality, just as Rose, O'Malley, and Valverde suggest in their joint article, entitled *Governmentality*:

> Every practice for the conduct of conduct involves authorities, aspirations, programmatic thinking, the invention or redeployment of techniques and technologies. The analytical tools developed in studies of governmentality are flexible and open-ended. They are compatible with many other methods. They are not hardwired to any political perspective. What is worth retaining above all from this approach is its creativity. We should not seek to extract a method from the multiple studies of governing, but rather to identify a certain ethos of investigation, a way of asking questions, a focus not upon why certain things happened, but how they happened and the difference that that made in relation to what had gone before. Above all, the aim of such studies is critical, but not critique – to identify and describe differences and hence to help make criticism possible.
> ROSE ET AL., 2006: 101

CHAPTER 2

The Closed Circuits of the Woman's Sexuality and *Temperate Seductiveness*

One of the Friday Khutbahs clearly states that *soul and body need to move in harmony and collectivity; otherwise, imbalance appears as a main reason for difficulties because God does not like those who overdo* (06 March 2015). The tone here tries to invoke 'true' unity between pleasures and sex, which depends on social control and self-discipline. From this point on, this chapter aims to examine these controls and discipline mechanisms based on Islamic principles, through which the woman's sexuality is explored in the context of behavioural restrictions and intimacy. Through the lens of governmentality, Islamic principles produce specific virtues for subjects in order to reconstruct the ideal sexuality of society and its associated behaviours. Virtues such as shame, chastity, modesty, and docility converge in the matter of honour, which provides sophisticated technologies not only to conduct the woman's sexuality but also to reconstruct a gendered population through individual responsibilities of the female subject.

Taking the undiscussable principles of religious knowledge together with the neoliberal journey of Turkey, I conceptualise the regulation and control of sexuality as a biopolitics of Islamism in order to look into the discipline of the female body, whose strategic position between population and subjects needs to be specifically emphasised. Islamic virtues and values are highlighted in order to uphold the consent of the woman. It is believed that *the woman is heroes of compassion, strength, and perseverance, and these features are God's giving nature of the woman. This nature is implemented by protecting innocence and chastity. That is the reason why the woman needs to realize its nature in order to look out for moral and religious structure. Woman and man should struggle against our desires (nafs)* (Sarısaman-Yıldırım, 2015: 55–57).

Therefore, consent indicates the will to be an ideal Muslim woman with social practices. Additionally, the consent to be virtuous sheds light on the operable usage of honour, which enables me to discuss female docility and the male-dominant gender regime in a critical vein. Furthermore, this biopolitics of Islamism paves the way to explain gender relations reconstructed in post-2002 Turkey through new technologies and mechanisms of control of the female body. Thus, the gender regime pre-2002 should be briefly mentioned in order to make the distinction clear for a better understanding of the new

'Islamic' constructive elements of heteronormativity against 'republican' virtues. This comparative reading of Republican and Islamic virtues leads to a factual question on womanhood. No matter if the woman gains an Islamic or secular identity in accordance with state objectives, the reconstruction of womanhood through self-esteem and social morality is problematic in terms of restrictions on her own sexuality and bodily control.

Correspondingly, regarding the political, social and economic development of new truth regime in post-2002 Turkey, the arguments and debates are tied essentially to female bodily performances. The changing practices and boundaries of intimacy need to be challenged here in order to emphasise the politics of sexual control by questioning public life and the 'intimacy' of the public. With this question in mind, we come to see that *the line between intimacy and freedom* highlights *consent* (Sarısaman, 2015: 55–56). It is believed that *the demands about sexual freedom morally and structurally destroy the life itself.* Indeed, *'the woman'* should be described *according to her nature*. It is said that the woman is *the keystone of the society, the touchstone of family*. The woman is *an equilibrant in family relations* and *a must for her children* (Sarısaman, 2015: 56–57).

Thinking these virtues and tailored roles in the context of the intimacy of the female body and her public visibility, there is no place but a home for a woman. Just to illustrate, being a woman in suburban areas of Turkey means being unable to go out alone. In case of any sexual attacks or other 'possible dangers' by the public, the responsibility belongs to the woman herself. The woman should stay at home. No matter if she wears revealing clothes or not, 'they' are looking at her because 'public space' means that a woman searches for a relation. Women in rural areas have not already been going out at night without a man but systematic religious suggestions after 2002 extend the scope of intimacy on the grounds of the woman's own goodness and public peace (Toprak, 2008: 80). The crucial point here is that this scope has been extended to sexual connotations of woman's behaviours, clothes, and even accessories. In addition to these connotations, religious expectations and prohibitions want to see a gendered order based on Islamic living. In line with this, mixed-sex education or mixed-sex public institutions reveal the fact that the state is the main mechanism to regulate gender relations and conduct womanhood through sexuality by producing and providing the required knowledge and biopolitical authorities according to Islamic necessities.[1]

---

1 To illustrate, there are books about sexuality and gender relations that the municipalities have been delivering. *Marriage and Sexual Life* (1999), whose author is Asım Uysal, is among them. Asım Uysal is thought to be able to make a competent image in terms of being in

As these books are prepared out of necessity for knowledge, all details regarding sexuality can be found: *Homosexuality, masturbation, female anatomy, orgasm, oral sex, contraception, restrictions and times, adultery, exhibitionism, jealousy between the spouses, mixed education, and advises and suggestions regarding conflicts between spouses* (Uysal, 1999). All the details are specified. There are many of this kind of sources provided by municipalities, ministries, the Presidency of Religious Affairs in the same 'enlightening professional language'. For example, the book *Marriage and Sexual Life* suggests that *a man should get married to a woman who grew up in a religious family. A virgin woman should be preferred rather than a widow because the virgin knows only her first man, feels love and loyalty to her first husband. Moreover, there are different moralities between a virgin and a sexually experienced woman. If possible, a fertile woman should be preferred. In brief, the woman should be religious and a virgin, and have a family and honour* (Uysal, 1999).

Pointing to these suggestions drawing upon religious knowledge, I do not intend to discuss the reliability of these books in the context of 'real' Islam.[2] I do not seek the most reliable religious response to the woman's sexuality, either. What I point out is that these books and many state mechanisms have been working as biopolitical authorities to enlighten people by spreading knowledge in line with Islamic values. I just consider that some virtues are associated with ideal womanhood through these biopolitical experts and authorities. For me, that is obviously problematic due in particular to the following three reasons: i) If actors and state mechanisms are closely following these knowledge requests, it indicates that the sexuality of the woman is under political reconstruction in order to manage gender roles and the population. ii) The rules and discipline are built on the woman's sexuality. In other words, the woman has no chance or choice but complies with rules and values based-on male-dominant knowledge. iii) Patriarchal repression concealed in religious virtues tries to persuade the woman that pain and suffering are her gender-based faith.

---

charge of sexual life and Islam as he studied Science of Islam (*İslami İlimler*). Everything about him is reliable at face value, so there is no reason to prevent curious people from seeking to satisfy appetite for knowledge regarding *the secrets to a happy marriage, its prohibitions, classified information and top secrets regarding sexuality, consanguineous marriages, spouse selection, cleaning and hygiene, beautifying of the woman and temperance, parfumé usage of woman* (Uysal, 1999).

2 According to Asma Barlas, many contemporary Islamic studies saw that the status of women and gender roles are "a function of multiple factors, most of which have nothing to do with religion" (2002: 2).

In order to analyse this from a broader perspective, I think that the initial attempt is to read the chastity, honour, virginity, shame, and modesty in the context of self-esteem and respect. These virtues find their own meanings in bodily acts, and behaviours, which are implicitly bound up with the woman's ability to control and hide sexual desires and pleasures. Thus, as *intimacy is about personal borders and limits,* it needs exploring and tracking the meaning of this sentence: *Intimacy emerges where chastity* (iffet) *and shame* (hayâ) *complement each other* (Khutbah, 20 May 2016).

1 Islamic Virtues on Woman's Sexuality

By categorising post-2002 Turkey as the governmental rationality of not only high politics but also everyday life and daily relations under AKP rule, I principally draw attention to new mechanisms and practices based mostly on religious knowledge. My intention with this is to identify the changes within the continuities. The changing norms on the female body and the discipline through sexuality illustrate the critical points about womanhood through which I try to come up with the rationality of regulative mechanisms and agencies for a discussion. Needless to say, this perspective prompts me to focus on the rising panoptic interest in the woman's sexuality in post-2002 Turkey. What I mean by the panoptic interest is the public concern and panic about the fact of sexuality, which has produced daily surveillance, moral guardians, and sexual offences by means of the sexuality of (idealised or excluded) womanhood. These concerns and fears over sexuality are placated by usually religious responses and traditional references given by political actors and biopolitical authorities. Possession of the religious responses gives individuals the authority to pass judgments about whether given behaviours and choices are wrong or right. However, this is not simply seen as dogmatic prejudices emanating from traditional or local knowledge because Islamic knowledge addresses the truth of God.

Therefore, for Islamic knowledge and Islam,

> the Quran is the divine Word, kalâmu Allah, the universal logos, pure idea. The Sunna of the Prophet is the practical model, the ideal behavior that conforms to the sacred word; behavior embodied in a living being, of course, but which, though historical, is nevertheless the privileged echo of transcendence. In Islam, tradition is an ideal cultural set of rules. To conform to them strictly ensures that we are in the ways of God. Departure from them is tantamount to straying error.
>   BOUHDIBA, 2008: 2

In light of the decisive power of religious knowledge, the truth initially deals with the female body in order to construct its social belongings and normality. That is to say, developing an identity according to Islamic principles requires correct clothes and finery, proper social behaviours, and Islamic performance. However, 'how' to cover the female body and 'how' to activate the woman's sexuality have to be responded to with a rational explanation to make more persuasive why Islamic principles pay attention to the control of the woman's sexuality and her body politics. Obviously, customs and manners are ready to firmly control the female body. In a manner of speaking, the woman's sexuality is an everlasting public case in that it is connected to the moral and physical health of society. Therefore, the woman's sexuality is restricted, and sexual freedom is entirely out of the question within the Islamic lifestyle (İlkkaracan, 2014: 12–13).

In fact, defining the female body and assigning specific behaviours to it constitute the essence of gender relations. As for post-2002 Turkey, these gender relations are regulated with the help of complex mechanisms in reference to the public order,[3] which is built upon the persuasiveness of religious knowledge.[4] However, taking a closer look into these complex mechanisms, the harmony of public and private order must operate emotions (and self-perceptions) in order to make transformative power successfully proceed on the failures of past discursive practices. The transformation itself must give a reasonable excuse or critique about previous political experiences. The critiques and new directions build the new truth. This truth needs the knowledge to increase its persuasiveness. Religious knowledge, thus, provides absolute knowledge based on the will of God. Therefore, motivated by *Ilmihâl*, which states Islamic principles, I point out to issue of *balance* in order to start a better analysis by retrospectively unpacking falsified discursive practices.

To put it simply, *this balance is about the public order, about relations between man and woman, even about the connection between politics and the newborn. This balance is so fragile that the deviation of (sexual) tendencies* (temayül)

---

3 In this regard, rape is not seen as an attack against a person, but it is a public nuisance. The increasing rates of rapes and other pre-marital sexual relations are evaluated within the public question with respect to the Islamic life order (İlkkaracan, 2014).
4 The knowledge related to homosexuality is very limited within the resources I reviewed. What I just can say is that it is firmly forbidden and seen as a deadly sin. The Prophet Lût (Lut or Lot) and his community may be known for a parable in the Quran, which is about homosexuality and God's wrath on homosexuals (Bouhdiba, 2008).

is directly connected to the social body (toplumsal bünye) (Ilmihâl, Vol. 2: 70). Furthermore, *unbalanced relations need limits and rules in order to prevent the intemperance, which is the major reason for moral depravity*. In this context, *nakedness, impudence, and shamelessness are about intemperance through which individuals would grow away from social conscience and common sense*. Therefore, *to veil the female body should be regarded as a balance and temperance between* (gender) *relations in order to protect public life in general, and particularly both the woman and man's honour. This balance carries the gendered bodies to the healthy family life* (Ilmihâl, Vol. 2: 70–71). If so, a "balanced society produces balanced sexuality – and not the reverse" (Bouhdiba, 2008: VII).

It is seen that the female body must be covered for two principal reasons: First, *some organs would be religiously forbidden (haram) for the man's gaze because the uncovered body would be sexually tempting and that would make a man sin (outside of marriage)*. This means *the tempted man would be a detriment to the public*. Second, *the veiled female body minimises the vulnerability of the woman against assault* (Ilmihâl, Vol. 2: 72). This last point should be highlighted once again in order to show how veiling or lack of veiling would have a sexual connotation and even denote a sexual invitation. Likewise, balance and temperance should be clearly seen in behaviours, selected clothes, even wearing accessories and perfume because there is a vital nexus between the notions of disobeying God, awareness of nakedness, and shame (Bouhdiba, 2008: 10). This shame does not only come from a rudimentary desire to avoid the public or to cover naked parts of the body, but it is also a mechanism generating the combined effects to perform multiple mechanisms. These multiple mechanisms clearly make social reward and punishment possible along with religious and traditional parameters, assembled for the honour of the self and community.

The Khutbah states that *shame (hayâ) and modesty are the most basic virtues of Islamic morality. Freedom makes a woman into a sex object, and intemperance and obscenity are the results of shamelessness and impudence, plus the result of lack of education regarding Islamic morality. Shame and modesty are life itself but modern life lacks the feeling of shame* (Khutbah, 22 August 2014). *Shame, modesty, and manners should be shown to any existence of the creator* (Khutbah, 28 June 2013). However, it would be good to reiterate that if shame and modesty are emotions gaining their meaning with bodily acts, it is obvious that "emotions are associated with women, who are represented as 'closer' to nature, ruled by appetite, and less able to transcend the body through thought, will and judgement" (Ahmed, 2014: 3).

To illustrate, Bülent Arınç, ex-head of the Turkish Assembly, used the example of the woman's laugh to illustrate the problem of behavioural intemperance:

> The issue of shame is so important ... Shame is beautiful. If a woman had it, shame would become more beautiful ... Where are the women that are going red in the face, bowing their heads and turning their eyes away when we (*the men*) look at them?! What the Hadith says is that *if she does not feel shame, you can do whatever you want* ... A woman should be chaste, she should know what is religiously forbidden, she should not laugh loudly, and she should *avoid tempting behavior* ...
>
> CNN Türk, 28 July 2014; emphasis added

It seems that shame (hayâ) is a politically useful tool to remind the individual how he/she should feel about him-/herself. The feeling of shame allows observing it on the body, as well. Feeling shame is about which we have done is bad or wrong (Ahmed, 2014: 103). Furthermore, following Ahmed (2014: 104–107), there are two interrelated results of shame. First, it allows the person to recognise the failures through the reactions of witnesses. Second, it pushes you to rethink and reform your actions by means of covering or hiding. Obviously, there is a paradox, which actually gives functionality to shame for moral development because in order to display the consent to cover your failures or something bad regarding your actions, you need to be marked by the witnesses, who are responsible for the reproduction of social norms and particularly the norms of sexual conduct (Ahmed, 2014: 104–107).

Islam categorically forbids all behaviours and acts that lean towards adultery and 'wrong' sexuality. It is suggested that *the woman should keep herself clean* and *she should dress up only for her husband* (Uysal, 1999). Further, *flirting causes sexual provocation*, which means that *the woman playing with love looks like children who whittle. Like children, the woman mostly gets hurt. Nothing happens to the man, while the victim becomes the woman in this love game. That is the reason why marriage is required* (Uysal, 1999). Even the woman's voice and her scent are included in these prohibitions because of their possible sexual incitement. On the other hand, all these strict restrictions set the woman free in front of her husband. It is stated that the *woman needs to be very seductive for her husband while she definitely protects her honour and chastity apart from her husband* (Uysal, 1999; İlmihâl, Vol. 2). I call this *temperance seductiveness*. As is seen, the woman's sexuality is not entirely ignored but it is trapped within illusive borders in the name of balance and temperance. To do so, the woman is expected to know which kind of life she deserves by being aware of her nature. That is to say, she conducts her bodily acts and behaviours according to her virtuous choice to have a respectable lifestyle.

The Turkish language itself defines and classifies the female body according to its virginity. For example, the hymen is the 'girlhood/ maidenhood' pellicle (kızlık zarı) in Turkish. When the hymen is broken, the girl (kız) becomes a woman (kadın) – no matter how old she is. In this context, being a 'girl /maiden' (kız) means sexual purity and asexuality of a woman (Özyeğin, 2009: 104, 110). Her gender role and sexuality begin with her broken virginity. Thus, virginity and social honour are two important obstacles to gain sexual liberation because the hymen signals an internal and external authority and personal responsibility (Özyeğin, 2009: 109; Cindoğlu, 1997: 253; Parla, 2001: 67). Sexual purity represents the honour of the family and moral purity of community. In other words, "this honor is defined by the behavior of its womenfolk. Honor is lost as a result of female misconduct. Women thus carry the burden of safeguarding group identity and group honor" (Özyeğin, 2009: 11).

Since sexual purity is about the values and quality of life, sexual freedom is not regarded as the individual choice of a woman. If a woman behaves against her purported nature by insisting on her sexual freedom through her bodily acts and active sexuality, this is seen as a sort of negative behaviour against society as a whole. Indeed, the link between virginity and social morality makes one feel guilty about sexuality. Therefore, the woman's shame due to active sexuality stems from showing respect to the family and social order. This point lies in the fragility of the woman's position in that she may be pushed out of the social order for participating in unsanctioned sexual relations. This being a normative case, the law and medicine are also employable under the heading of 'virginity examinations' to prove the *true* womanhood of virgin woman (Cindoğlu, 1997;Özyeğin, 2009; Parla, 2001).

Indeed, life and desire are tied to one other in order to maintain reproduction. Eroticism, in this sense, is a fundamental bond to keep immortal life within the sexuality that is "diversity in unity", "affirmation and complementarity" (Bouhdiba, 2008: 12). This sacred representation of sexuality brings existential meaning because sexuality places in the heart of life, and through sexuality, man gains meaning in the divine world as well (Bouhdiba, 2008: 13). However, regarding the eroticism of the female body, which is accepted as a seductive object in this context, sexuality of a woman is marked by virginity and is reduced to the blind side of man's sexuality, such that the woman should avoid seductive behaviours towards the man.

Islamic rationality also defines how to be an ideal woman-subject, and how she performs her social identity in pursuing a better Islamic life in this respect. If I narrow down these idealisations to Islamic womanhood, it is expected that the Islamic woman herself should take control of her body by being aware of her womanhood, which means covering the body, hiding emotions, and controlling any seductive behaviours. Actually, Islam as a religion suggests unity and totality in life, including sexuality and the sexes. This unity and totality seek out the harmony intended by God in society as well as between the sexes. This unity is about the separation of the sexes and their union and their mutual adjustment by insisting on being masculine and feminine for the reconstruction of ideal manhood and womanhood (Bouhdiba, 2008: 30–32).[5]

Sex is the critical factor to determine the different mechanisms and regulations towards the woman and the man to prevent chaos in society (İlkkaracan, 2014: 18; Mernissi, 2014a: 41–42). The woman's sexuality may be destructive for public and private life (Mernissi, 2014a: 40). Therefore, marriage is not only about personal demands and choices imposed by norms but also it has to do with the will of God in order to explore "sacred representation of sexuality", which is composed of Islamic social practice between eroticism and the sacral (Bouhdiba, 2008: 5). In this sense, *marriage is a self-training to conserve the disposition and to edify womanhood and manhood within their gendered responsibilities building around disciplined pleasures.* Thus, *religious bans are the precautions for a more peaceful inner world and a better society* (İlmihâl, Vol. 2: 127–128). Otherwise, according to Islamic principles, *the punishments against* (gender-based) *offences are not major solutions to protect the woman from the sexual abuse.* First of all, *the emotions should be trained, there should not be tempting gaze and word, and the veiling should be used* (İlmihâl Vol. 2: 129–130).

It seems that in order to prevent possible sexual provocation by the woman, there is no specific gender hint to be able to guess whom these warnings hold to be accountable. Obviously, veiling and tempting behaviours invoke the truth of the woman's sexuality. According to Islamic principles, the female body itself is inciting and it should be particularly controlled for a better public and family order. This control confines the woman and keeps her under control through taboos, which legitimise restrictions and even death on behalf of honour. Thus, womanhood is conducted by a series of reasonable fears: fear of her own active sexuality, fear of God, fear of man, fear of taboos that engender insurmountable norms and fear of being excluded in civilised social life. In the end, all these fears make the woman cautious about her sexuality and nature. For the woman, coping with this fearful life becomes bearable by rendering these restrictions as the pride of shame and modesty.

Indeed, there are two points I want to stress:
– Sexual freedom and woman's rights are ultimately tied to population. It can be well observed that heteronormative sexuality proceeds on manhood by highlighting the economic and moral usage of female sexuality.

---

5   It is relevant that "homosexuality is seen as a challenge to the order of world as laid down by god and based on the harmony and radical seperation of the sexes" (Bouhdiba, 2008: 32; see also Foucault, 1998).

In other words, it is expected that the woman should protect her virginity until marriage in order to prevent possible deviations, as the inability of a man to control his desires is taken-for-granted.
- Sexual freedom is regarded as the main reason for deviancy in society. I think that the solution suggested by the authority is to review the gender regime according to political rationality. Pınar İlkkaracan (2014) begins her edited book, called *Women and Sexuality in Muslim Societies*, with two important questions: How is sexuality built in Muslim societies? Moreover, what are the contributions of women to this construction? (İlkkaracan, 2014: 7). According to İlkkaracan (2014: 7–8), the regulation of sexual behaviours and of sexuality itself varies with political, socioeconomic, religious and cultural conditions, which play a critical role in forming pleasures and life. Furthermore, she argues that the Islamic (far-) right fits the woman's sexuality into the heart of its politics to control society through sexuality (İlkkaracan, 2014: 7–8). The most important point İlkkaracan emphasises (2014: 7–8) is that political Islam or the Islamic right politics needs a strategic domain, which is usually the female body and womanhood, in order to strengthen its seizure over society and lifestyles. In other words, the power of control over individuals and society intrinsically necessitates the woman's sexuality that provides not only variable mechanisms but also a manoeuverable domain to realise Islamic right politics.

Islamic governmental power regulates life and classifies individuals through the woman's sexuality and control. Therefore, the female body and the woman's sexuality are not left with the woman-subject, but the body and sexuality are, in a sense, publicised by entrusting the woman to society, her family, husband, father, brother, and the safety of the man in general (İlkkaracan, 2014: 7–8). For this, I argue that Islamism gains and reinforces its sovereignty in this view that renders the female body as *res publicae*. Therefore, the woman politically turns into a vulnerable object that needs protection and security always. This argument forces me to re-think the biopolitical components of sexual control and surveillance that can always easily apply religious discursive practices and performances for political, social and economic necessities.

Similarly, cultural values govern sexuality in terms of the gendered performances of the sexes. Therefore, punishments and rewards provide inevitable domains of intervention and regulation against the wrongdoings and failures of bodies in line with social and moral values because performances of bodies are public actions, which are subject to public surveillance and control. This is why true gender identity is the actual regulatory mechanism in society (Butler,

2002). For that reason, one way or another, "patriarchal control over women's bodies has been reproduced through honor and shame" (Cindoğlu, 1997: 254), and the male members of the family and community are seen responsible for the woman's purity in that context. This protective male culture is actually related to social recognition in need of protecting the woman's sexual purity (Cindoğlu, 1997: 254).

Accordingly, the woman's choices regarding marriage and sexuality are a topic of concern to the family and community. Her purity is reproduced and redefined according to a male-based order. As stated earlier, virginity cannot be reduced only to the existence of the hymen and personal choice to have it broken, but it is a social phenomenon (Cindoğlu, 1997: 254). This is why there are punitive mechanisms to prevent premarital sexuality. Therefore, *marriage* is employed to *prevent moral deviation. The premarital sexuality* causes *the rise of immortality, prevalent delinquency.* Namely, *the security of society* is seriously disrupted by unblessed sexuality (Uysal, 1999).

Mixed sex occasions and flirting do not help to tame sexual desires; on the contrary, the social encounters of woman and man pave the way for *exploiting the female body* because the man has always other seductive ways in which there are no *sexual restrictions to satisfy his desires.* For example, *prostitution and cohabitation bring about new pleasures to the man, even if that is considered abnormal. The (sexual) freedom of the woman causes the man to look for his authority elsewhere.* That is to say, *the tendency of the man towards drug addiction, patronising prostitutes, criminality, or seeking sexual adventure is the fault of the woman of easy virtue and the way it undermines the man's authority. The losses of being single are depicted as spiritually and bodily ill youth, who suffocates in mafia, prostitution, human trafficking, pornography, mass adultery, sexual harassment, child abuse, illegitimacy, and the other sexual tastes* (Uysal, 1999).

Thus, one of the Sermons about adultery and prostitution underlines the significance of having a family and marriage not only for having well-mannered individuals but also for building a morally strong society. According to this Sermon, strong morality ensures social norms and reinforces the development of societies (Şentürk, 2013: 281). This virtuous recipe for a strong society including a string of values leaning on the woman's sexuality forms the political and economic veins of the gender regime in post-2002 Turkey.

2   The Imagined Population in the New Gender Regime

2.1   *Islamic Heteronormativity and Its Performances*

Gender is about woman and womanhood (Scott, 2010). As the concept of gender neutralises and objectifies emotions regarding the woman and her body, gender relations are seen in the natural relations practiced by woman and man. Around these gendered roles, the sexual and social differences between woman and man are discussed and featured in reference to especially the biological skills of the woman so reproductive skills and motherhood are tied to the woman's chores at home in the name of her gender duties. However, the concept of gender points to the reconstructive elements of the sexes in a cultural manner beyond the domestic duties and performances of the woman. Therefore, gender is a category of the population, so it burdens a social role and certain responsibilities assigned to the sexed body. The use of gender categories is an emphasis on the system of relations that is not directly determined by sexuality although it is entirely related to the sexes (Scott, 2010: 115–116). Relying on Joan Scott's approach to the notion of gender, gender has an integral analytical relation that should be separately examined in two dimensions: i) Gender is the main way to reconstruct and recognise the power relations acting on the sexes. ii) Gender produces reconstructive tools of social relations and subjectivities. In this way, the organisation of social relations and the changes within them become subjected to changes in who holds the power and how subjectivities represent power relations. Proceeding on the answers of questions related to gender, cultural, religious, traditional symbols, and representations meet us in complementary and contradictory ways in which the meanings of femininity and masculinity categorically have been redefined. In the end, the normative standpoints of the contradictory and complementary constituents appear as sovereign in the name of social compromise (Scott, 2010: 127). With this social compromise, gender is strengthened within the structural relations of politics and economic (Scott, 2010: 128).

In another critical vein, Judith Butler claims that idealised gender roles pave the way for new forms of power relations embedded in hierarchical heterosexual practices. There is collusion between sexual hierarchies and the strength of gender because gender roles are the result of any performances developed by sexes. Namely, the "gendered stylization of the body" is actually internalised features of the socialised sexes by the subjects, so gender is an array of bodily acts in line with expectations (Butler, 2002: VII–XXIII).

Gender is, therefore, a question of representation of the woman as a political and social subject. In other words, the legitimacy and visibility of political subjectivity shape normative language surrounding how to be a true woman.

Therefore, Butler does not suggest that gender is seen as a cultural output because gender categories prompt discursive and cultural tools to practice politics upon natural sexes (Butler, 2002: 3–16). Thereby, gender and heterosexuality accompany each other to reinforce acceptable desires solely between woman and man by excluding other sexual orientations. That is to say, the gender order refers to a peace order in accordance with social norms. Similarly, gender disorder means the collapse of unity based on sexes and sexual roles, which also denote unmanaged desires (Butler, 2002: 23–30). Ultimately, Butler wants us to see that gender is a social performance of repeated acts, whose consistency needs heterosexist pressure concealed in the regime of masculine policing towards idealised gender performances (Butler, 2002: 43–44). As such, the woman's performance becomes an indispensable element to highlight gendered division and relations because religio-cultural and political norms constitute how womanhood should be through her female body and social behaviours. Saba Mahmood (2001: 214) thinks that sexual virtue points mostly to feminine norms that form ideal womanhood and her bodily acts. For example, shame and modesty are regarded as the values of a virtuous woman. To perform these values, the woman is expected to veil and behave modestly.

Thus, gender is an agency with the articulation of rules, responsibilities, and performances in accordance with the constructed identities and categories. Gender as an agency gains a transformative and disciplinary effect instructing individuals on the heterosexual way of living (Butler, 2002: 185–187). Sex is a mainstay to produce norms and to regulate bodily performance, so gender roles and relations provide a measurement by which to judge the quality of bodily acts (Butler 2002, 2011). This is why discursive practices create sexual markings, and some symbols increase sexual eroticism. The body with social and gender roles becomes a sign of risks and rewards through its agency (Butler, 2004b: 26). It seems that performances in line with social values need bodies to redress the balance between morality, gender, and politics. For this, Butler says, "focusing on ostensible lack of agency signified by the veil or the burka, not only misunderstands the various cultural meanings that burka might carry for women who wear it, but also denies the very idioms of agency that are relevant for such women" (2004a: 47). Apparently, veiling is the best sign to recognise the woman as a part of her public performance.

Similarly, sexual pleasure and eroticism are the tastes of paradise that should be experienced in Islamic heteronormative marriage for reproduction on the earth (İlkkaracan, 2014: 17). Going a step further, it would be good to say that sexuality and sexual control rebuild subjectivities and then these subjectivities supervise the heterosexual requirements of their production. Therefore, sexuality is not only about satisfaction, but also it is about self-realisation

(Imam, 2014: 81–82). Norms and rules are necessary to be able to determine who marries whom and in which manner. Sexuality is always inspected (Imam, 2014: 81–82). When needed, the policies and agencies aim to make sexuality an operational technology in order to manage birth control, reproduction, motherhood and the like. In order to use the technology of sexuality, discourses should be regularly and continuously practiced in a heteronormative way. Traditions and experiences have a strong impact on life and particularly the life of woman, which means that the duties of womanhood are shaped in daily life practices. In this vein, Islamic-right politics seeks to construct a threat against Islamic values as an excuse to increase pressure on sexuality and its branches surrounding individuals in everyday life. Through the woman's sexuality, the Islamic right seeks to exclude new counteractions such as feminism and the women's movement (Imam, 2014: 83–86). For Abdelwahab Bouhdiba, the matter is not whether sexuality is part of the sacral or whether the sacral itself is the part of sexuality, but the fact of the matter is that "the social may profit both from the majesty of the sacred and from power of libido" (Bouhdiba, 2008: VII).

This lays bare the fact that Islamic-right politics directs a religious route in which the woman's sexuality is always immoral; and the woman's demands, behaviours, and clothes can be easily labeled as a social disaster deserving more control and also sexual abuse as a disciplinary punishment. On the other side of the coin, Islamic-right politics aims to strengthen interest in womanhood within the limits of wifehood and motherhood (Imam, 2014: 86). Islamic-right politics wants to see performances of the female body in a worldly asceticism (Imam, 2014: 87). Besides veiling codes and visibility, the Anatolian woman, for example, is cultural production, who is expected to perform unconditionally, sacrificing herself for her family and nation.

The sorrow of the woman, which is actually pain because of patriarchal pressure, is exalted and nowadays politically used in order to compare the categorised womanhoods by the woman's pervasive choices. The woman's own will is ignored and demands for equality are seen as selfishness. Islamic-right politics idealises a womanhood that suffers a lot and endures difficulty without complaint. In addition, the endurance of the female body is appreciated by Islamic-right politics. Asexual womanhood is represented in order to make the woman focus on their basic social and economic roles. Such an aim is also concomitant to restraining the man's uncontrollable pleasures for the good of the social order. It is expected that the reconstruction of asexual womanhood makes easier political and social control, which come to prominence during the discussions about reproduction and relevant issues (Imam, 2014: 89). Therefore, *marriage and sexuality are brought under control by wedding. Marriage is based on a corporate contract so sexuality without this marriage contract is seen as adultery, which is the root of all evil in society* (Khutbah, 10 July 2009). Obviously, it is believed that the body belongs to God and living out of what God confirms is out of the question even though Islamist feminists reject the Islamic demand of a community-based life because of subjective interpretations of the religion. In any way, sexual freedom is forbidden for both the woman and the man, and it must be activated in a heterosexual way.

In this vein, if a heteronormativity is established on the basis of honour/shame, virginity as a regulator of sexuality reconstructs society by means of punishments and rewards. The performance of womanhood gains her an identified gender role through the disciplinary reconstruction of womanhood, wherein the female body is rendered as a 'woman' through reminders of her virginity. Comparing to the female body, the male body does not have this kind of sign, i.e. there is no bodily equivalent to the hymen that transmits the gender role onto the male body (Abu-Odeh, 2014: 254–255).

When we take virginity as a sign of the gender performance of the woman, three semantic fields – the vaginal, bodily, and public – appear in order to regulate and ban the (sexual) freedom of the woman (Abu-Odeh, 2014: 255–256). That is to say, virginity is loaded with abstract and concrete cultural practices and meanings during the smooth transition from a young girl to woman (Abu-Odeh, 2014: 255–256). Hence, the axes of marriage, virginity, and masculine protection show me the route to understand Islamic heteronormativity and its relevant performances. The body needs to be understood as a mediator of dress and behaviour (Bordo, 2004: 309). Likewise, the regulative mechanisms on the body provide a domain to reconstitute subjectivities. Bodily discourse can, thus, be a political and social indicator to display who is subjected to power (Bordo, 2004: 310–312).

Indeed, Islamic principles clearly address body politics in order to produce Muslim identity and morality, particularly through the defined womanhood. When culture, nationalism, the state, and other social and economic belongings come into play in modern times, religious body politics becomes reproduced and legitimised within new parameters of change within the continuities. One of these continuities is the fact that the female body should be kept under control no matter what the motivation is, which would tend towards either identity construction or public salvation.

Islamic-right politics concentrates on womanhood as an identity and the woman's sexuality in the context of two different points. On the one hand, womanhood is constructed within the family. For this, the woman's pleasures and sexuality are strangled in morality and sin. On the other hand, the woman's maternal skills are driven forward (İlkkaracan, 2014: 20–21; Imam,

2014: 86). This being the case, Islamic principles describe the performance rules for the sexes in a gendered way, in that *the gender roles should be clear in order to directly distinguish which of them is woman or man. Namely, the man should not wear a necklace that belongs to woman's accessories, just as a woman should not wear trousers or a hat. From shoes to hairstyle, the woman should be seen as a woman* (Uysal, 1999). Obviously, there is a religiously strict body politics here based on heteronormativity. I suggest that we need to understand these restrictions and regulative suggestions in the context of the Islamic body politics and justice of the gender regime.

2.2 Contouring Gender Justice

Family order is the hub of sexual life, taken in inner satisfaction, sexual pleasure, and reproduction, which are composed of the common activities of woman and man. Nevertheless, these Islamic principles point out that *pleasure itself is not the aim; otherwise, irresponsible sexuality causes idleness, which is the basis for lack of compassion, hostility, conflicts, and inexorableness in public. In addition, sexual freedom brings various physical and mental illnesses. Therefore, marriage is a religious duty for public and private order* (İlmihâl, Vol. 2: 124–125). As Abdelwahab Bouhdiba states, there is "the dialog with Being and dialogue of the sexes", which "punctuate our daily lives" (2008: 2). In parallel with this, the social one plays a catalyst role to combine religious practices and the means of sexuality in kind of three-part dialectic, which implies that economic and cultural factors deliberately become involved in domestic ethics in order to adjust the religious and sexual values for the survival of society (Bouhdiba, 2008: 2). This survival ability of society depends on the strength of norms and God's messages about marriage. According to Islamic principles, there are two sexes, which are expressed through the gender roles of manhood and womanhood. Both roles complement each other by performing their duties in the public and private sphere.

As already noted, gender is not only an identity, but it is an agency to change gender relations and transform the gender regime through reconstructed gender categories. In this sense, bodily acts and practices show to what extent the individuals comply with the dominant norms without resisting. In this sense, feminism is seen as a danger for society, but the transformative power of the woman makes feminism more dangerous because the transformation of woman means the transformation of society (McNay, 2000: 4–9). Therefore, it is understandable why feminism is excluded during transformative times because it is defined narrowly, as if all misfit and unmanageable women conspire together in the name of feminism and equality. However, gender as an agency makes clear the link between the symbolic and material dimensions of power through bodies and acts (McNay, 2000: 26). This is ultimately about the woman's sexuality, and its relation to the spheres of power.

According to Islamic principles, *even the voice may cause unrest* (fitne) (İlmihâl, Vol. 2: 319–320), so *the woman's priority ought to be home and with the children. Man is the head of the family* (reis), *wherein he is responsible for order, including having the woman well in hand*. However, it is thought that *feminism degenerates these values by means of discourses of human rights and equality. Obviously, justice and structure should have a religious and moral basis* (İlmihâl, Vol. 2: 321–324). It means that *feminism is seen as a thought process that was destructive to the social order as outlined in religious principles* (İlmihâl, Vol. 2: 478).

The nexus between sex and pleasure can be understood by responding to the question of how to regulate sexuality because the established mechanisms of sexuality bring us the pleasures of the gendered sexes that should be channelled to the benefit of the population as well as for the individual. It is also arguable that this nexus is the main source of the differentiated gender regimes that need to be explained according to the changing mentality and mindset at the time of transformation. The change regarding post-2002 Turkey not only refers to the new governmental rationality and mechanisms in the way of a more religious society but also denotes a multifold transformation with the help of political actors and agencies, including the female body, womanhood, and the woman herself.

To do this, *the family is important to teach gender roles according to the sexes. The internalised role is realised with religious perception and practices, and secularisation would crash some religious practices with its lifestyle promised* (Albayrak, 2016: 54–55). Nevertheless, it is accepted that *both woman and man are human beings, so they are equal; however, this equality should be in terms of justice. Islam legitimises inequality according to differences in the sexes, races, possessions, and wealth, but is against the misuse and abuse of these God-given differences* (Okumuş, 2009: 34). It is *divine justice* that considers *duty and obedience necessary, as articulated by gender and social roles. Corresponding to divine justice, a woman needs to demonstrate absolute commitment towards her man, and she should be willing to do her duty in the family* (Okumuş, 2009: 36).

Along the lines of patriarchal sensitivity, morality produced new control mechanisms and expectations for the woman in the early Republican period. This new gender regime highlighted the civil rights of the woman in the family(Türkmen, 2009: 133). However, these new rights did not lighten the woman's domestic load; in contrast, new public duties imposed an additional burden on the woman's shoulders to promote modern Republican values. Likewise, in the post-2002 power regime under the AKP, the new image of the national woman implicitly speaks to social justice by pointing to the just division of labour for man and woman.

In any case, patience is enforced as an important virtue of ideal womanhood, which "invokes in the minds of many the passivity of women" against the injustices, difficulties and gendered burdens and duties (Mahmood, 2001: 220). Suffering and living without complaint is a constitutive virtue of gender justice, which needs to be internalised by the woman. Additionally, patience in the face of difficulties brings self-esteem to the woman (Mahmood, 2001; Cooper, 2008). There are many ways to depart from virtues binding at the end to woman, sexual politics, self-esteem, and lifestyle. Even if inequality is at stake in relations between man and woman, it is clear that motherhood is seen as a privilege on the part of God (Cooper, 2008: 40).

It is believed that the woman has more advantages than the man with regard to God. There would be even a religious analogy between God's power to create and maintain life and the woman's role to found a family and reproduce. Therefore, woman-mothers have a primary and essential responsibility on behalf of God as the carrier of morality and mediator of divine law (Cooper, 2008: 40). Gender relations are the naturalisation of sex categories, and gender with its instrumental meaning provides a way of organising life (West and Zimmerman, 2004: 167). Therefore, the solutions to the problems related to the family and gender justice point out *the education of the woman because the woman should be able to develop her problem-solving skills and strategies without divorce. Divorce itself is not only to dissolve the family, but it means idle and uneducated children.* Therefore, *the long suffering and tenderhearted Anatolian woman* should raise *awareness* through the transition of traditional and experiential knowledge against *the loss and damage of divorce* (Koytak, 2004: 18–21; Demirkan, 2007: 47–49; Beder-Şen, 2005: 53–54).

Overall, the patriarchal forms in biopolitics desire to have a useful body equipped with strong emotional and physical empowerment rather than the intelligible body (Bordo, 2004: 320). I argue that Islamic patriarchy adjusts itself to biopolitics by recasting the issue of gender equality in contemporary neoliberal governmentality through gender justice (Aslan-Akman, 2013). It seems that marriage is the guarantor of gender justice enabling family norms and the roles of the sexes. In addition, marriage regulates property and procreation rights (Young, 1996: 257–258).

Gender justice denotes the assemblage of practices that are ultimately bound to the norms of judgment (Jones, 1996: 83–85). Gender justice proceeds on the identities and social roles that have moral and complementary reciprocity in the private and public domains. The norms bring justice into practice meaningfully with respect to these categorical differences (Jones, 1996: 85).

Intimate relations are regulated by gender justice, in which the responsibilities of the gendered sexes are distributed according to norms (Jones, 1996: 85–86). Therefore, if I contour gender justice in terms of Islamic norms and patriarchy, four important points are worth bearing in mind in order to rethink gender justice and female subjectivity with neoliberalism and neoconservatism in the final part of this book:

i. Woman, man, and all creatures are equal on the side of God; and there are natural differences between the groups of God's creatures. That is to say, each one is created for a specific duty for the social body. Like organs, the groups of creatures play a vital role for the goodness of society, and this is actually divine justice.

ii. The woman is equipped with maternal skills and emotions. Her body and duties are sacred, and justice wants a woman to have a family and children. Otherwise, the different demands of women cause social as well as gender injustice.

iii. In order to determine gendered duties and fairly divide heterosexual labour, marriage is a mechanism to bring to light the sexes, gender categories, norms, and rules of social order. Justice is defined in a microsphere between family and community relations.

iv. Justice includes both punishments and rewards in line with accomplished or failed gendered missions. Norms and traditions shape a judgemental ground on which the "conduct of conduct" between man and woman operates gender categories in the name of divine justice.

3 Intimacy in Public or the Intimacy of the Public?

The public means the social, economic and political participation of free individuals regardless of their identical symbols and roles. In Turkey, the public is used for the transition of power relations through female subjectivities. For a Republican and neoliberal modernisation of Turkey, secularisation and Islamisation are best embodied on the female body to transform the society and individuals. Therefore, the public visibility of the woman in Turkey needs cautious attention to see the liberties and limits of the gender regime, which is a direct reflection of changing power relations from Kemalists to political Islamists (Çınar, 2008: 892). In other words, the "public sphere not as a coming-together of critical-rational individuals that form organizations and then confront, resist and challenge the state, but rather as a domain whose contours are drawn and redrawn by the state" (Cindoğlu and Zengirci, 2008: 794). The public sphere is, then, the state's agora, in which the ruler and ruled have a standpoint around the norms of the woman's behaviours and the intimacy of her bodily existence in public.

Alev Çınar insistently draws attention to the public sphere as "a disembodied voice" and as "a regime of visibility produced through media and state-mediated discourses" in order to examine "the production of the public subject and the appropriation of gender in the Turkish public sphere" (Çınar, 2008: 894). With the transformation of modernity from the early years of the Republic of Turkey to contemporary neoliberal Turkey, the transformation of intimacy was at stake in legitimating the public image and practices of the woman (Türkmen, 2009; Göle, 2016). While modernity develops mechanisms of self-awareness, Islamic lifestyles force the limits of modernity in tandem with social and political demands. To exemplify, the body is used as a flag in order to redefine the images of Islamic or secular identities. Kemalist modernization replaced the intimacy of the veil with the intimacy of chastity and solemnity (Türkmen, 2009: 132–133; Cindoğlu, 1997: 255).

As for the Islamic transformation in post-2002 Turkey, the intimacy of the female body according to Islamic principles forms the intimacy of the public through the public gaze by extending the private and redrawing moral boundaries in the public. In this context, the public gaze is a constructive function as a reminder of public norms and standards (Çınar, 2008: 904). Islamic transformation envisions an Islamic public order within a moralised society, so moral hygiene and veiling are two important carriers of the Islamic society project (Türkmen, 2009: 135; see also Aygül and Öztürk, 2016). It does not mean that the woman has to cover her head in post-2002 Turkey, but still, the *flag-body* needs a public meaning with veiling and other symbols, in accordance with the identification and foundation of the Islamic order.

The anti-westernization of Islamic critiques paves the way for alternative Islamic practices in order to rescue and emancipate woman from the exploitative public order in company with women themselves (Türkmen, 2009: 135). The Islamic project based on a moralised society and individuals problematises the boundaries of intimacy. By instrumentalising the intimacy, control of the female body and the regulation of womanhood gain legitimacy, and through these controls and regulatory mechanisms, the Islamic project gives its message to society (Türkmen, 2009: 137–138). Thus, policing the female body and bodily performances prompt daily surveillance and strengthen the public gaze on the woman as disciplinary and security tools of the Islamic social order.[6]

---

6 In order to clarify this point, I want to indicate 'the intimacy of the collective' in aiming to illustrate the contemporary Islamic order. Neriman Polat, a visual artist from Turkey, organised her own exhibition entitled "Collective Privacy". At the exhibition, her work based on

3.1 To Veil or Not to Veil

Islamic discourse separates the spheres as private and public. Obviously, the private and public spheres have a gendered context and meanings; that is, "the public domain is for men and the private for women and children" (Cindoğlu, 1997: 254). As mentioned earlier, the woman's sexuality is dangerous for society so modern gender norms in Turkey deliver control of female body and the woman's destiny to the man (Cindoğlu, 1997: 260; Arat, 2000: 113). This proves that the modernisation of Turkey has been built on traditional gender roles.

With regard to the fact that the female body and womanhood have been always employed as an agency during both secularisation and Islamisation times in Turkey, the sexual control of the female body is questioned in terms of Islam's idealised womanhood by comparing and challenging with the state feminism of Kemalist secularisation. With the secular social order, the structure of intimacy and its meaning are changed by re-defining what is public and what is private. Although it is questionable whether intimacy and the public represent two different spaces, discussion through these kinds of dichotomies does not help to recognise the demands for new forms of the public. To their needs, the different woman's identities ask for a public equivalence to gain recognition and mobility. In this sense, an accessory or turban as a religious or ethnic habit may come into question.

Furthermore, in Islamic principles, mixed public order is a question, as far as we understand from the religious sources. In other words, the relation between woman and man is reconstructed and regulated by religious prohibitions. It is believed that the woman carries her sexual potentiality with her whole body, including nose, eyes, mouth, arms, legs, and all visible parts. That is why, Fatna Aït Sabbah claims that Islam sees the woman as omnisexual, i.e., her body is entirely sexual (Aytaç, 2015: 129). The will to have and control this omnisexual body brings competition between men. Therefore, the easiest way is to keep the woman away from the public, which may be found plausible in aiming for the woman's safety and public peace. In line with this, the rules of marriage regarding marital ages, polygamy, marriage with a fostered child, and temporal marriage have far-reaching scopes with regard to sexuality itself rather than

---

"the hasema series", aimed to uphold the changing meaning of privacy -I call it intimacy- and its influence on the collectivised behaviours of women under a control society (Arik, 2012: 26–27). The headscarf or the covered body makes it convenient to recognise the intimacy among women as well men because "the discourses over the headscarf allow the emergence of spaces of violence where the female body can be acted upon in terms of its physical integrity, sexuality, and mobility" (Arik, 2012: 26–27). In a way, the sexual connotations of female bodily acts come together in order to signal the common values of the public.

family life (Aytaç, 2015). In order to teach girls their gender roles; assaults, gossip, or social confirmations arise in her consciousness regarding her gender duties by hearing and feeling "you are a girl" (Abu-Odeh, 2014: 257–258).

Accordingly, public visibility is related to the man's permission for the woman's mobility. This permission would be seen as a performance of the man because he has control and disciplinary authorisation for the woman's own good. To put it simply, the man protects the woman from other men. This means that womanhood and the female body create a domain for the fight of masculine power. Therefore, it has been said that "gender peace" would be possible if the public could be composed of only men (Abu-Odeh, 2014: 259).

In order to protect social order, it is expected that the woman should show consent for the public sovereignty of the man. This means, *instead of flirting and temporal satisfaction; sexual, physical and spiritual happiness should be targeted* (Uysal, 1999). *Lack of intimacy causes marital infidelity so destroys families* (Khutbah, 13 May 2016). Therefore, the *consciousness of intimacy should be taught according to the gendered nature of the sexes. Moral discipline is the feeling of shame and modesty towards behavioural failures because of intemperance, low-cut dresses or bodily acts* (Khutbah, 02 November 2012). In this sense, the scope of marriage has to do with the desire to push the woman into private life. Namely, marriage and chastity are mechanisms to regulate the woman's sexuality (İlkkaracan, 2014: 21).

However, it seems that the scope of intimacy moves further beyond the secular functions of marriage. For example, Süleyman Demirci, the former head of the Promotion and Media Department of the AKP, says that "a woman without a veil (headscarf) is like a home without a curtain. A home without a curtain is either for sale or for rent" (Hürriyet, 11 March 2011).[7] In Mr. Demirci's statement, the emphasis on veiling reminds us that the issue of intimacy leaves an open door to discuss and extend the meaning of veiling since his statement points to a very blatant sexual connotation of unveiling the body. This shows that the necessity of confinement to home and veiling are not the same things even though they meet each other at a similar thought axes. Just as veiling should not be an obstacle to the woman's participation in social life, it is also problematic to see unveiling visibility as a sexual invitation.

In Islamic patriarchal settings, veiling is regarded as a unique solution to prevent sexual harassment and attacks. Nevertheless, it should be noted that the visibility of the Islamic woman in public makes their intimacy public as

---

7 According to the same source, Demirci resigned from his position and left the party following a warning from fellow party members due to public pressure (Hürriyet, 11 March 2011).

well. This visibility of intimacy provides an opportunity to uphold the limits and deficits of the public for Islamic identity. While the modern world has been trying to find a solution for identity problems on the way to a more democratic and egalitarian order, intimacy in public is still constructed by male-based norms and control (Berktay, 2012; Aytaç, 2015;Göle, 2016). For this, religious knowledge provides the required concepts to rationalise restrictions toward the female body.

The personality and individuality of the woman is compartmentalised into the roles of being one's wife, daughter, or mother. If the woman wants something outside of these gendered roles, it is believed that all society is imperilled. Likewise, the bodily acts and behaviours of the woman cannot be set free because her freedom connotes disobedience and indiscipline, which is dangerous for society. Moral degeneration is associated with "the woman" and "her body" (Berktay, 2012: 128–130). Therefore, veiling and community life are rendered the exclusive remedy to make the woman able to participate in social life because the religious confirmation of her omnisexuality leaves no other features and content regarding womanhood. With the virtues and values backed by religious knowledge, a veiled female body gains sacred meaning as well as social pride, while different visibilities are otherised in public (Berktay, 2012: 130). This otherisation causes sexual violence and harassment because the strict prohibitions against the bodily visibility of the woman do not allow debate over difference in a liberal context.

Fatima Mernissi (2014a: 33) approaches the woman's sexuality from a different perspective. For her, the woman's sexuality is active and has its own energy, which is regarded as an instinct in the Islamic context. These instincts do not have good or bad meanings; however, they appear when the social faith of the individual is at stake. That is to say, the conditions determine your good or bad behaviours, and the orientation of bad or good feelings are entirely under the individual's own charge. For example, sexual pleasure can show up either as a violent attack or a desire for the continuation of life. The bad or good use of pleasure is the individual choice (Mernissi, 2014a: 33–35). According to George Murdock, paraphrasing Mernissi, there are two societies: in the first group, the bans and taboos regarding sexuality are internalised; in the second group, precautions such as temperance or veiling are employed (Mernissi, 2014a: 36). Therefore, the woman is always active sexuality and needs control, confinement and pressure mostly in eastern societies, in contrast to societies where the sexuality is regulated by means of love, loyalty, and self-esteem (Mernissi, 2014a: 37). In both ways, it is clear that the woman has pleasure and desires like the man.

The increasing visibility of the woman in public is contextually the most important detail pointing to the issue of intimacy. Obviously, Turkish modernisation has directly attempted to reform religious rules and forbidden practices. Therefore, modernity and the modern Turkish woman surely played a significant regulative role in order to reconstruct family-society relations by means of stimulating emotions such as, love, healthy generations, a strong nation, loyalty/infidelity, intimacy, and shame in the place of the religiously forbidden, which was totally based on the confinement of the veiled female body, and her submissiveness to male-domination for the sake of God (see Sancar, 2014). It resulted in changing the social structure, and the fear of God was replaced by the fear of losing honour, fear of humiliation and exclusion. With the help of *modern* social norms, classifications, and codes, a woman's sexuality and her gender role were reconstructed and controlled in parallel to above-mentioned emotions. To put it more clearly:

> Under modern conditions, a woman will not feel honorable if her love does not include sacrifice, while a man will demonstrate his by providing for his family. A woman will show her love to her family and country by controlling her own sexuality while a man will do so by being prepared to die for family country and honor.
> SIRMAN, 2004: 54

Obviously, the fact of a Kemalist paradigm unsettled Islamic morality on the intimacy and invisibility of womanhood. This paradigm thereby got the woman started as the carriers of secularism, the witnesses of civilisation and pioneers of westernisation (Göle, 2016: 30). Accordingly, I need to repeat a vital argument now and then: The conflicts between modernists and Islamists are embodied in the female body and the woman's mission by focusing on the intellectual and emotional development of the nation. Both of these were mainly constructed with an eye to governing society by dividing it into gendered sexes. However, the AKP transformed *society* into *population*, stressing its own idealised womanhood and Islamic morality by constantly referring to family, reproduction, and the related issues of the intimacy of the female body, women's behaviours, and sense of belonging. I argue that the female body and womanhood are the main instruments of Islamic neoliberal governmentality. Additionally, this enables the power regime to permeate anywhere through its sexual control, which has actually shaped the AKP's transformative governmental rationality by dividing the population into absolute gender categories.

It is crucial to reassess this transformation in the context of a changing gender regime in Turkey because the observation of gender(ed) relations at different levels and domains lead us to identify the perpetual conflict between Islamists and Turkish modernists. Furthermore, zooming in on the reconstruction of gender relations makes the ongoing economic order comprehensive in the context of new right discourses and neoliberalism. The power regime under AKP rule and its interventions in *life* converge in a two-fold explanation: The first deals with the shifting boundaries (or meanings) between intimacy and religiously forbidden in particularly referring to woman's liberation and visibility as a problematic result of Turkish modernisation after the fall of the Ottoman Empire, which was based in religious law. In a similar manner, the religiously conservative side of the AKP insistently points out the intimacy of gender relations and the feminine body by signalling religious duties and by serving as a reminder of ideal womanhood. On the other side, the economic and political rationality of the AKP, which would be the second explanation, needs to be taken into account in the context of modern neoliberal needs that offer an analytical perspective to understand the discursive practices of political actors and other agencies for a better and stronger country.

Indeed, in the early Republican period, the woman somehow had to get used to seeing her unveiled bodies in the public. Then, the woman quickly learned the *dos* and *don'ts* in the public and private alike. Instead of women's rights, the woman's look and visibility were subject to the decisions and regulations of male bureaucrats. Obviously, the reforms for a better modern society opened the way to a gender regime in the name of the Republican woman's liberation and the morality of a nation, as Nükhet Sirman asserts:

> In the context of the transformation from empire to a nation state in Turkey, ... nationalist discourses were not simply about change in the political order, but were also about inventing a new social and moral order. Gender and the family took the leading role in shaping the way these discourses were formulated. The effect of these new discourses was to produce nothing less than a new gender regime in Turkey that was suited to the structures of a Republican regime.
>
> SIRMAN, 2006: 41

This transformation did not aim to change religious subjectivities, but it forced the modern belonging of the Muslim woman to be reinterpreted in the context of her national duties by producing new norms revolving around honour. This was intrinsically substituted for the religious prohibitions on the woman's sexuality. In other words, this transformation brought the woman's sexuality and her body under cultural surveillance and control instead of the religiously forbidden (Kandiyoti, 1987: 335; Türkmen, 2012: 131). The woman was encouraged to gain political consciousness, and the especially middle-class urban woman was supported to enter new fields of activity in public spheres. Besides, legal steps regarding the civil code and marriage definitely strengthened the position of the Turkish woman within the family. However, regardless of religious or traditional rules, male honour has always been important in Turkey and is enshrined in Islamic culture as well. It actually addresses the purity and chastity of all women. Faced with this reality, respective structural changes for the empowerment of women were defined on the basis of traditional and political aims in order to rationalise the political and public status of the woman without leaning on sharp critiques of religious dogmatism (Abadan-Urat, 1986; Göle, 2016).

It is clear that secular modernity, beyond the political goal, worked as a regulative mechanism on the female body in an attempt to produce new feminine subjects, expected to be aware of their duties not only for their nuclear family but also for the nation. This radical transformation inevitably caused a social rupture in society and produced its own repressive mechanisms along the way to a more modern, more secular and more open-minded society towards public visibility of the woman. As a result, under Kemalist paradigms, the inclusionary discourses necessarily pointed to unveiled, modern, secular, and well-educated successful women, while the exclusionary discursive practices played upon Islamic signifiers as an indication of backwardness, provinciality, and lack of education in order to strengthen this modernity project.

However, two issues still need to be discussed; they are firstly the paradox of being "emancipated but unliberated" despite "westernization" (Kandiyoti, 1987), and secondly the often-ignored reality of Islamic demands based on the boundaries of intimacy between man and woman (Göle, 2016; Kandiyoti, 1991). I would like to point to the unliberated woman once again in order to highlight the fact that patriarchal power relations and male domination existed before 2002 as well. Needless to say, these gendered relations of dominance are worth questioning and speculating on in order to shed light on the oppressive face of modernity.

Indeed, the Islamic revival in Turkey appeared through the existential and identical questions of individuals as the inevitable results of oppressive Kemalist modernity. Namely, changing social relations in the 1980s forced individuals to look for new identities and meanings based on their own culture (Özdalga, 2015: 61–62). Therefore, the culture- and identity-seeking efforts of some believers in Turkey has materialised in the Islamic movement, which has flourished especially among young Islamic women who demand the freedom to wear the headscarf in the public sector.

More interestingly, educated and modern veiled women have paid attention not only to the deficits in the Kemalist modernity project but also the Islamic interpretation of women's position in society, which obviously goes hand in hand with patriarchy and male domination (Göle, 2016;Özbudun, 2016;Sancar, 2014). No doubt, Islamic young women's problematisation of different Islamic interpretations was a good yield of modernity that highlighted individual concerns, rational questions, and free choice. Educated Muslim women sought to hold their social, economic, and political rights without having to remove their headscarves whilst studying at university or working in the public sector. Thus, the fact of oppressive and aggressive intervention on religious signifiers such as the headscarf became the breaking point at which the AKP– even today – began rationalising its discursive practices and exclusionary discourses against secular lifestyles and choices. This is also the lens through which I argue that the headscarf under AKP rule has gained its main regulative meaning in the name of solidarity with those excluded under the old regime. However, this is the same mechanism employed to identify chaste women, believers, purity, docility, and morality. The headscarf again became the veil of female intimacy and sexuality in the power regime under AKP rule. In brief, it is the symbol of the Islamic society project against the "state feminism" of the Kemalist regime (Sirman, 1989: 2).

In different words, the political struggle around the headscarf highlights the "deprivatisation of religion", which describes well the increasing reference to religious sources for conservative ideals and intimacy at the state level (Ravazi and Jenichen, 2010: 833; Buğra and Savaşkan, 2014: 14). In the fifth chapter of this book, I shall discuss this by looking at religious conservatism and neoliberalism together, but for now it is enough to note that religion or religious values are directly related to lifestyles and public order instead of being confined to the private sphere as a liberal aspect.

In Turkey, although use of the headscarf is a religious choice, it becomes the symbol of political conflict between Kemalists and Islamists, positioning the woman beside her headscarf. In line with this, I argue that not only the headscarf, but also other visible forms draw the private into the public. In Turkey, the headscarf is an ideological and existential symbol; dress codes also serve this purpose (Arat, 1998: 123). To protest the headscarf ban, women had carried their rights to freedom of religion into the public. They aimed to deconstruct the Kemalist perception that visibly Islamic women should not attend universities (Arat, 1998; Çınar, 2008; Göle 2016; Türkmen, 2012). However, human rights and democratic boundaries discharge the ideological bans and restrictions; having been explained by simple fears. The democratic and liberal expansions change the meaning of public dress codes, and religiously political change brings about a major change in the life of the woman (Ravazi and Jenichen, 2010: 835). Nevertheless, communal norms and customs, civil rights, and also demands pointing to 'the woman question' seek to find new meaning to public and private (Arat, 2000: 107–108). There was always careful emphasis on "the traditional" in order to provide the woman easier integration into modern practices during the early republic Turkey (Arat, 2000: 108), but ultimately Islam has always been the "traditional religion of the majority" (Arat, 2000: 109).

With the promise of "being different from the West", Turkish modernisation actually made its way in which the "authoritarian faces of modernity" and "modern interventions of masculinity" intersect at the prosperous domain of the production of oppressive gendered practices (Sancar, 2004: 204–205). It means that Turkish modernisation itself did not herald gender equality; on the contrary, it created new feminine subjects who were expected to dedicate their lives to the nation in parallel with modernisation, mostly related to the 'visibility' of unveiled women in public. In this context, the temptation of the woman's sexuality has always been an explanation for why she should stay at home. When she appears in public, this may cause both man and woman to sin. However, the temptation emanating from the nature of the female body cannot be prevented even if she is totally secluded, since that very seclusion elicits an interest in the forbidden and the unknown (Aktaş, 1991: 254).

Therefore, veiling actually refers to a prudent measurement of how and when to be seen in the public. This measurement changes according to the cultural and moral values of the times, so the veiling is about social rather than religious rule (Aktaş, 1991: 255). According to Saba Mahmood (2001: 217), cultural and religious symbols or accessories provide a "practical context" in which the meaning of symbols is differentiated and couched in governmental rationalities. This is why, shyness and veiling symbolised backwardness in the Kemalist regime (Arat, 1998, 2000) while unveiling signalled the emancipation of woman from male authority (Mahmood, 2001; Kandiyoti, 1987; Parla, 2001). In contrast, Islamic revivalism challenges the Kemalist paradigm, and instead locates the 'emancipation of woman' through religious signs and symbols in general, and through public veiling in particular. After the Islamic revivalism of the 1980s, Islamic practices and religious knowledge-authority started to reconstruct the meaning of veiling as a sign of the woman's self-discipline, thereby excluding idea of male control in discourses on veiling. It is explained that veiling and shyness are virtuous and the public practice of these behaviours are a matter of a woman's choice.

The neoliberal transformation in the 1980s, on the one hand, opened the way to realise new religious and ethnic identities, as well as individualism;

on the other hand, this realisation revealed particularly Islamic identity with special reference to the global integration of the local, that is, Islamisation (Özyeğin, 2009: 103). Meanwhile, different aspects of "liberal gender ideology" were encouraged by media images of the woman's right to sexual freedom (Cindoğlu, 1997: 255). Gender liberation backed by neoliberal transformation advertised sexuality as if it were not a taboo or rule by getting far away from the daily lived realities of both Kemalism and Islamism (Cindoğlu, 1997: 255). Through the awakening of Islamisation in Turkey with the complex relationship between the local and the global, virginity progresses beyond its meaning, being employed as a norm as a reminder not only of the red lines between gender relations but also of the differences between the global values of the West and the local values of the East. I think that the inimical separation of the West and the East within the context of cultural and religious values, as it were, needs to touch on the honour of nations, states, and men by perpetually talking about 'how' the woman should be. In this context, the possessions of womanhood ranging from human rights to virginity help to mark and reproduce the identical values of the states. Richard Sennett put this remarkably:

> Decoding means you take a detail of behavior as a symbol for an entire character state. Just as, say, the color of a scarf or the number of buttons undone on a blouse may symbolize a woman's sexual looseness, so small details of appearance or manner can symbolize a political stance.
> SENNETT, 1978: 238

Therefore, premarital sexual relations become related to the rotten values of the West, which highlights the harms of individualism on the heteronormative family order and public peace due to sexual harassment. Looking at the issue of virginity through the lens of secular values, it is surely no coincidence that well-educated young women in Turkey are more open-minded regarding sexual freedom and virginity norms (Özyeğin, 2009: 104). However, it does not mean that the schooling and education of woman are major reasons of immorality related to sexual freedom. Just as in Islamic practice, issues of the woman's sexual freedom are constructed as problems, the solution to which becomes confining the woman into the private sphere. In this sense, even schooling becomes a controversial public issue on the grounds of protecting the intimacy of the woman. Furthermore, well-educated women are even seen as "active violators of virginity norms" (Özyeğin, 2009: 104). No doubt, this point is specifically worth questioning in a different context, however now I think it is more important to say that the norms generated from the female body provide major operable discursive practices not only to conduct the woman as a category of the population but also to regulate the personal and collective identities through honour, rotating the woman's sexuality from the West to the East and vice versa.

The concept of honour is a complex issue in the definition of the new Republican woman, who, with the lifting of her veil became on the one hand a symbol of liberation from Islamic law, while on the other hand was still being held to Eastern moral values through the reinforcement of virginity norms. The new ideal republican woman was an " 'enlightened' mother in the private sphere as well as a 'masculinised' public actor" (Özyeğin, 2009: 105–106; see also Kandiyoti, 1991); in other words, Turkish modernisation retains traditional components of womanhood in order to preserve the ideal of asexual and paternalistic mothers.

Religious and traditional values were attached to the female body in the same way but the public visibility of the woman increased the worth of her modesty and shame in a different context (Özyeğin, 2009: 106; Cindoğlu, 1997: 254). This differentiation in the context of patriarchal control is discussed through questions of "state feminism", which by itself sought a "gender consensus" by imposing gender norms upon the paternalistic nationality of the Republic (Özyeğin, 2009: 106; Cindoğlu, 1997: 255). Nevertheless, the upsurge in Islamisation with neoliberalisation created gaps in state feminism regarding women's questions by converting all good changes regarding womanhood into losses of modernisation in a very deductive sense, thereby reinforcing the idea that the woman belongs to the private sphere. It seems that women are still "under the hegemony of the public, and of men" (Cindoğlu, 1997: 254).

Nevertheless, it should be seen that in the 1980s the driving force behind Islamist women's enthusiasm about being more visible was the motivation to unite women around the same gender issues, these being honour killings, domestic violence, civil codes, and human rights (Arat, 1998; 2000; Özyeğin, 2009). Feminist activism started to have its own discourses and responses against gender discrimination and ignored the personality of the woman. This increasing awareness of women's questions eventually addressed the issue of virginity and its control in the form of virginity tests (Özyeğin, 2009: 106–107). Even though talking about virginity is very humiliating, to push the female body into the authority of medical knowledge is doubtless destructive to the preservation of personal identity and sense of self. Thus, virginity examinations were regarded as an illegal practice with the intense effort of feminists in 1990s Turkey (Özyeğin, 2009: 107). In fact, applying for virginity examinations was recently outlawed, but the structural necessities through which virginity examinations are somehow rationalised still represent the kind of control mechanisms that lead towards 'veiling' the woman's sexuality.

Correspondingly, the woman needs to determine the limits of intimacy in order to fulfil her public requirement and other daily necessities (Türkmen, 2009: 139). If power needs the systematic continuity of discursive practices in the same logical frame as womanhood and sexuality, the woman-subject and the female body are an important domain for the repetitive activities of power. Therefore, the Islamic lifestyle does not have numeric values, but ingrained practical values without coercion. Regarding intimacy and the sexual connotations of the female body, Islam has several principles and guidelines, so virginity is not only a bodily activity but also is an important part of the Islamic image of veiled womanhood (Türkmen, 2009: 142–145). To conclude the issue of veiling and virginity, the new gender regime of post-2002 Turkey intends to generate covered and conserved bodies as a reliable signal of sexual purity, and therefore the honour of the woman and the intimacy of the female body in these transformative times. In general, the representation of the headscarf is directly related to the political atmosphere and political norms, which influence cultural norms in Turkey. Thus, the matter of the headscarf is the hub of "the norms governing what the Turkish state stands for" (Cindoğlu and Zengirci, 2008: 795).

3.2 On the Political Representations of Women

The gender perspective of the AKP can be evaluated as a reduction of the woman's representation and participation in the parliament and politics, however not as a symbol of achievement or liberty. The rise of various women's visibility on the political and social platform on behalf of the AKP cannot be interpreted as a religiously accepted public visibility; nevertheless, it exists to emphasise women's duties in society as mothers, wives, and so on, by making suggestions and recommendations to women, families, and children. These platforms play a kind of mediator role between micro- and macro-politics for womanly issues. The women in question generally do not come from an Islamic tradition, they are well-educated and self-confident. However, it is vital to remember that the visibility of well-rounded women has gone hand in hand with the AKP's stance on family, marriage, and mothering (Ayata and Tütüncü, 2008: 382–383). Ayata and Tütüncü's work sums up the role of these women very well: "AKP leadership places women at the heart of the culture, which is deemed essentially different from European civilisation. Thus, it invites women to return to the family nest, instead of seeking political status and power in the public sphere" (Ayata and Tütüncü, 2008: 383).

In other words, the representation of women serves as an explanatory mediator of the AKP's perception and politics. Particularly, women convey the will of the AKP to tackle women's problems[8] by providing knowledge from women themselves regarding their problems (Çitak and Tur, 2008: 456). The party encourages the women to establish civil organisations to maintain educational activities regarding the sexual and economic exploitation of women, good motherhood, and good family management (Çitak and Turk, 2008: 456–457; see also Bayraktar, 2011).

The activities of Women's Branches under the AKP umbrella addresses their important political role in spreading party power into micro-spheres and opening new domains for intervention and change. Therefore, it is crucial to understand that conservatism and practices of Islamism find their instruments through the public presence of the woman, which sets post-2002 AKP's government apart from the other political periods in Turkey. I argue that as a disseminator of knowledge, the woman becomes the core of this Islamic transformation through the emphasis of 'problematic womanhood' and the moral values underlined by the state.

Accordingly, the 1984 article on *Fascism and Women* written by Şirin Tekeli states that the woman's removal from social life brings about its own politics. Entirely removing the woman from social life is not possible, but with wage politics and harsh working conditions, the woman becomes forced to stay at home. In parallel with this, the exalted family values are employed to remind the woman of her duties towards the children, household chores, and other domestic work. According to religio-cultural values and expectations regarding family life and womanhood, the public and private sphere are politically regulated by the fact that men have always been in the dominant position. In a way, the woman learns to be obedient because of her family duties (Tekeli, 1984: 420–429).

In this sense, Barbara Brooks's argument for the definition of woman provides an interesting perspective to reinterpret the collaboration of women, especially in neoliberalism. Brooks says that woman as a gender category refers to female subjectivity, whose content and context are moulded in cordial relation to the solidarity of sisterhood (1999: 4). This solidarity is based on the accumulation of knowledge about the nature of the female body and constructive elements of womanhood (Brook, 1999: 7–8). I think that the

---

8   There is a general impression regarding women's sincere support for the AKP, which is that it extends from the party leader Recep Tayyip Erdoğan's interpersonal skills, such as sincerity, honesty, charisma, and the like. In addition to his family life, his problem-solving skills in pursuit of the better economic development and welfare of the nation for well-beings of population are found attractive and reliable especially by women (Çitak and Tur, 2008: 457). I think that this is related to an ingrained sensibility among women regarding male protection.

representation and the soul of sisterhood tell the heterosexuality firstly to the woman. Through the woman's heterosexuality and relevant gender duties, the values gain political and social meaning in public and in private. Therefore, the public representation of the woman is mostly related to the behaviours, symbols and the configuration of the ideals in Turkey.

It would be good to open a bracket here for Islamist feminists by differentiating them from other feminist movements in Turkey because they see the problems both in the Kemalist patronising of modernity and also the Islamist interpretation of the woman (Aslan-Akman, 2013: 113). More importantly, the political acquisitions of the Islamist feminist movement in Turkey are represented by symbols and especially the headscarf. According to how Diyanet, as a "bureaucratic agency of state", describes "appropriate secular gender codes", it is clear that the politics of Islamism aim to build an Islamist order (Aslan-Akman, 2013: 116–119). However, as we understand from the Merve Kavakçı case,[9] the use of the headscarf in parliament was objected to due to its perceived defiance against the state.[10] This parliamentary crisis in 1999 put a lid on the escalation of the headscarf issue as a crisis of the secular order since a new political page would be turned in 2002. From the 1980s until the late 1990s, as the increasing visibility of Islamist women started to cause conflict with secular sensibilities, the representation of women in politics became a particular source of tension. With the Merve Kavakçı Case, then, political Islam reached the next phase in becoming a direct source of counter-power to the Kemalist establishment. By 2002, Islamist power had successfully achieved state-power by associating itself with notions of democracy and liberalism.

Until the presidency of Ahmet Necdet Sezer expired in 2007, the headscarf ban became the main political tool of Kemalists to gauge public opinion. The 2007 election of the AKP's Abdullah Gül as the new president caused a public outcry in part because his wife, Hayrünnisa Gül, was veiled. There was much speculation over the seeming paradox of how, in the context of a ban

---

9   The ban on the headscarf restricted its use in state institutions and organisations, including students and collegians. It was lifted in 1981 and with the rise of political Islam and Islamic activities, but reinstated on 28 February 1997 as a part of an event known as the Turkish Military Memorandum. With the 28 February Decisions basically based on the protection of secularism, the Welfare Party, which would form the constitutive ground of AKP, was closed and the Virtue Party immediately was founded. Merve Kavakçı, as a woman deputy of the Virtue Party, dared to enter parliament to take the oath of allegiance to the principles of the Republic and secularism, only to be summarily dismissed and her status as deputy rescinded.
10 Ex-Prime Minister Bülent Ecevit reacted to the entrance of veiled Virtue Party deputy Merve Kavakçı with these words: "Here is not the place to challenge the state. Please put this lady in her place" (Star, 31 October 2013).

on headscarves in political life, the first lady of the Republic could occupy the presidential residency, Çankaya Köşkü, in Ankara. With macro-level high politics witnessing such discussions, its repercussions could be felt at the micro-level. Especially university students suffered from the headscarf ban, which I find unfair and quite anti-democratic. However, the point here is that the issue of the headscarf clearly shined amongst other political agendas in special reference to the unfairness of the Kemalist order, which thereby became an essential political re-constitutive element of post-2002 Turkey. It is crucial to understand that the unfairness and exclusionary order of the Kemalist regime was concretised by the female body, and thereby the political representation of the woman was reduced to the visibility of the headscarf, instead of her individual voice on political and social problems. Therefore, the headscarf and veiling are political symbols.

Subsequently, the headscarf was again on top of the agenda of parliamentary discussions in 2008. With the AKP's second election triumph in 2008, Prime Minister Erdoğan said more openly, "Given that the woman wears the headscarf as a political symbol, can you call it guilt? Can you impose bans on symbols? Where in the world is there such a ban on freedom? This is related to another (*hidden*) problem. We know it very well" (Hürriyet, 14 January 2008). Finally, in 2013 the headscarf ban was lifted in most public institutions and organisations with the help of the democratic initiative process. Judges and public prosecutors were granted the right to wear the headscarves in 2015, police in 2016, and members of the Turkish Armed Forces in 2017 (140Journos, 1 March 2017). Additionally, four veiled deputies joined the Turkish Assembly in 2013. These numbers increased in the 2015 General Elections – first in June, followed by a snap election in November – twenty-one and twenty veiled deputies,[11] respectively, became parliamentarians. Additionally, the increasing number of veiled deputies shows women's struggle to enter the party administration from below by gaining experience in the Women's Branches, which are the "real heart of politics" (Çitak and Tur, 2008: 458).

Observing this history of the headscarf in Turkey, I am reminded of the words of Richard Sennett:

> An institution can rule as a single font of authority; a belief can serve as a single Standard for measuring reality. Intimacy is a tyranny in ordinary life of this last sort. It is not the forcing, but the arousing of a belief in one

---

11   It should be noted that the rate of female deputies in parliament has never passed over 20%. (http://ka-der.org.tr/kadin-istatistikleri/).

> standard of truth to measure the complexities of social reality. It is the measurement of society in psychological terms. And to the extent that this seductive tyranny succeeds, society itself is deformed.
>
> SENNETT, 1978: 338

The headscarf became an obvious political marker for Islamic identity. It invokes intimacy, secrecy, and privacy, which determines the meaning of the institutionalised public. With the institutional representations, the headscarf and the veiled woman visually represent the gender regime of politics. Inevitably, the idea behind these institutional representations becomes disseminated to the society through female bodies in order to form a more conservative culture. For this reason, Diyanet as a bureaucratic agency of the state plays a vital role in the transformation of culture by teaching and refreshing religious and traditional norms (Aslan-Akman, 2013). To be more effective, Diyanet hired and educated women at the provincial level in order to raise religious awareness of pious womanhood to transform the gender regime. With the Diyanet's guidance, women began organising their lives according to moral and religious principles. Similar to the discourses about the stability of high politics, the micro-stabilities regarding relations and family life were prioritised during times of transformation.

To keep the basic units such as family and social order stable and non-chaotic makes transformation easier to achieve. Therefore, the representation of the headscarf is an efficient signifier to convince the society of the rightness of the mainstream gender order because the headscarf as a political domain has its own struggle and history beyond that of the Islamist feminist's struggle. It is an identity now and it seems that the achieved political arena targets the seizure of the cultural and social arena in order to govern power relations at a high level. If gender refers to the cultural idealisation of womanhood, the power relations through the representations at high politics find their way in which interpersonal relations take a shape in line with what political order shows (West and Zimmermann, 2004: 153–165).

In Turkey the woman is confined to the political world of symbols although the feminine body and womanhood are the very essences of the political structure and gender regime (Direk, 2009). According to the form of these representations, some bodies are excluded while others are included.

3.3 Policing Public Morality

Morality has two faces but both of them serve the man. On the one hand, there is public morality and family order that seek the ideal woman. This ideal womanhood is an instrument to reconfirm the man's power. On the other hand, as the exalted man's power cannot come in contact with the ideal woman, he buys the satisfaction of his pleasures from another woman, humiliated and excluded by the man in the same patriarchal setting (Mernissi, 2014b: 104–105). Obviously, this is elusive, but if we rethink it within the context of heteronormativity, virginity as a virtue of purity not only signals herself-respect, it is also of particular interest to the man because the woman's asexuality comes to an end with the man. Therefore, the protection of virginity and its control generate a social concept, which further creates four changing dynamics based on mixed sex living. Namely, spatial models, and institutional, economic, and psychological changes, may arise from heteronormative relations built on religiously gendered roles (Mernissi, 2014b: 106–109).

This clarifies that "the changing the emphasis from the physical reality of virginity to the morality of virginity is central to ... sexual modernity: 'virginity is not between the legs; it resides in the brain'" (Özyeğin, 2009: 109). Additionally, "the parameters of the Kemalist project of modernity were drawn around puritanical sexual morality regarding women ... A strict morality which linked male honor to women's control over their own sexuality prevailed" (Arat, 2000: 116–117). I consider that it would be better to consider these changes as demands of modernity and the conflicts of Islam with modernity instead of framing it as 'daring to lose virginity'.

It needs to be realised that the woman's sexuality is regarded as a public question, so gendered spatial models need to be positioned according to the gendered necessities. For example, accepting in advance that the woman's mobility in public space should have limits, that mobility needs to be regulated so that the sexes can be kept apart (Mernissi, 2014b: 109). Veiling would thus be a technique of bringing women into public space; however, this does not change the fact that the woman is pushed into living her own intimacy. Fatima Mernissi emphasises the "always fresh collective-memory" loaded with the results of unmanageable sexuality, such as prostitution, rape, abuses, and attacks (2014b: 109). This collective memory provides traditional and empirical knowledge to legitimise control and justify the woman's exclusion from public. This is realised through constant reminders of the ways in which the woman's freedom to move in public space also represent her freedom from social norms.

The marginalisation of this misfit woman reconstructs the perception of the insecurity of public life, which reinforces the expectation that the ideal woman stays at home whilst the man earns and copes with the difficulties of public life. When outside of the family, loneliness and insecurity come to the fore, and this in a way directs the woman towards family life by means of marriage.

Therefore, moving beyond the religious symbols such as veiling that were turned into a counter-political mechanism against modernity, the body politics of Islamic rationality and its sexual control mechanisms need to be elaborated through the virtues of ideal womanhood in questioning the comforts of modernity. It is said that *intimacy education begins with the woman.* The equilibrium is simple: *the mother conveys the necessity of intimacy to the child through the feeling of shame. The consciousness of intimacy is mandatory so as to decrease sexual harassment* (Dönmez, 2014: 16–17). For this religious approach, Sara Ahmed also remarks well in line with my argument:

> Women, if they are to have feminine respectability, must either stay at home (femininity as domestication), or be careful in how they move and appear in public (femininity as a constrained mobility). Safety here becomes a question of not inhabiting public space or, more accurately, of not moving through that space alone. So the question of what is 'fearsome' as well as who should be afraid is bound up with the politics of mobility, whereby the mobility of bodies involves or even requires the restriction of the mobility of others. But the production of 'the fearsome' is also bound up with the authorisation of legitimate spaces: for example, in the construction of home as safe, 'appropriate' forms of femininity become bound up with the reproduction of domestic space.
>
> AHMED, 2014: 70

To illustrate this in a broader sense, many cities in Turkey have put 'pink buses' into practice to eliminate sexual attacks and harassment on public transportation. One Civil Society Initiative began a campaign entitled "We Want a Pink Bus". One of the male members of the initiative explained the intention of the pink buses: "A mixed journey may be also preferred but it would be better to provide a private pink bus to make women's journey more comfortable. Indeed, it draws intense interest" (Diken, 5 January 2018). The pink buses were actually opened up for offer after a young nurse Ayşegül Terzi, was attacked on a bus by a man whose defence was that "her way of sitting was obscene. I told her to sit *correctly* in the passenger seat. She hinted at me with her gestures and mimicry to show that it was none of my business ... I could not tolerate this and then ... It was involuntary, a reflexive act. I do not think that I'm in the right, but I do not find the woman's sitting position right either" (NTV, 26 October 2016).

The young nurse, Ayşegül Terzi, described the same incident in the following terms: "I needed extra income, so I did overtime after normal office hours at the hospital. After I completed my shift, I took the bus to go meet my father, and I was sitting in an empty seat on the bus ... I was listening to music ... Suddenly I was attacked ... I didn't understand what happened to me ... I don't remember anything after that ... When I opened my eyes, I was in the hospital"

(NTV, 26 October 2016). For the same problem, apart from the battered woman, the perpetrator man and the civil society initiative one way or another show the same confidence about the source of the problem and its solution, which always points to the necessity of gendered public spaces for the benefit of the woman. While Ayşegül Terzi had not understood what happened to her on the bus, the proposed solution for her protection, and the protection of women from all walks of life, were effectively an admission of her 'wrongdoings'.

Both the logic of civil society and of the man on the street are represented in the same rationality in promising to 'comfort' the woman by taking advantage of 'patriarchal creativity in producing different forms of violence against the woman'. The moral guardians should be debated here in the context of the social, political, and economic motivation of masculine protection, which takes its power from 'the wrongdoings of woman' with reference to religion and traditions. Therefore, I call attention to, "the emphasis of values, truths and norms that will allow survival *slides easily into a defense of particular social forms or institutions*" (Ahmed, 2014: 78, emphasis original). It seems that the intervention of the state and civil society lead ordinary people in daily life to intervene in a similar way. However, there is a pointed failure to recognise the necessity of many women to work. Therefore, I argue that confining the woman to home-life is a 'luxury desire' of conservative politics because it is often impossible to make the woman economically dependent on the man under neoliberal precarity. Otherwise, economic stress and violence spring up.

That is to say, while neoliberal conditions promise a precarious life for both the man and the woman, it is not simple to separately regulate the gendered spheres in public because the economic and political public spheres, correspondingly, need to be reconstructed and economically well-organised. After the example of the young nurse Ayşegül Terzi, it is obvious that the young population in Turkey urgently needs opportunities for earn an independent income. This is about surviving. However, it is sufficient to say that the social harmony based on Islamic principles renders two-faced reality, whose conditions are changeable according to class, political, and gender relations.

Knowledge-power relations generate new forms and styles through modernity. Referring to the weakness of human nature, social regulations have been generated in terms of the true behaviours and values in public (Haeri, 2014). Nevertheless, veiling is not only one form to demonstrate good morality because a new conservative woman is modern and keen on showing her chastity and modesty by means of her maternal roles even if prohibitions and rules are produced by the segregation of gendered sexuality (Ayata and Tütüncü, 2008). To put it more clearly, the transformation of the public proceeds on a lot more male-based rationality, taking advantage of the Islamic control of social harmony. This new transformative power tries to reconstruct social intimacy and morality through those who were left vulnerable according to this purported social harmony. Creating and showing these woman-victims also means to transmit the rational flow of daily life. Therefore, as the example of pink buses shows, there are two options provided for the woman's comfort in the public. She is free to choose pink bus or mixed municipal bus, but the results of the 'wrong' choice reinforce conservatism and traditional roles to the detriment of the woman (Shalhoub-Kevorkian, 2014: 208–209).

Breaking the confidence of the modern woman forces her to seek out new self-technologies to exist in public. Veiling is a solution among self-technologies but one that stimulates feelings towards marriage and family life that are exactly the appropriate solution to balance out public life in order to take the consent of the woman regarding a home-centred life. In either way, the woman's bad experiences are transformed into a social phenomenon through which the events are discussed in the context of social losses. The woman, her body, and her behaviours are cross-examined by norms. The social reaction is expressed against the woman instead of the man, and this situation leaves the woman guilt-ridden. Therefore, public life embeds the woman in two moral dilemmas, these being respect and shame (Shalhoub-Kevorkian, 2014: 218–224).

For Islamic morality, *the moral consists of divine capabilities and divine predisposition.* This means that *acts are not signs of good morality, but good morality is based on bodily performances as a reflection of the inner world* (İlmihâl, Vol. 2: 493–494). Looking at the matter of Islamic morality from its philosophical base, *good morality and bad morality may easily appear via bodily acts. The moral value of acts is deemed to be good if the intention to do something consists of will, conscience, and compassion* (İlmihâl, Vol. 2: 495). *Following the promises of Islamic morality brings salvation and freedom against the governance of desires. Allah (God) knows everything, and we need to listen to what he suggests to us. Islam leads us to good morality and wants us to be in harmony* (müsâmele, uyuşma) (İlmihâl, Vol. 2: 496–500). *The nub of this harmony is truly constituted by individual conscience and public conscience* (İlmihâl, Vol. 2: 500). It seems that religious knowledge points to the fact that an individual cannot break off the public and become disconnected from its flow. Noticing the interwoven relations of public conscience and individual conscience, religious knowledge suggests the realisation of our existential reasons on this earth. Indeed, realising existential reasons gives the individual problem-solving ability and thereby eternal peace.

To recap this topic of the woman's visibility and sexuality, the woman herself ought to understand that she needs to remain out of public view for the sake of the social order. By consenting to the control of the man, she realises her intimate duties towards her husband and children. Therefore, I suggest that control mechanisms, surveillance, taboos, and restrictions revolving around the woman's sexuality are only the reality on the observable service. Thinking of sexuality itself with the public conscience helps to uphold the impasses where power is intrinsically concealed. Even if it is impossible to unbind these impasses, it goes without saying that power, one way or another, desires to continue its own dominance. The discursive practices form the external face of power encounter us because there are

> 'public' places where standards of dress and conduct were expected. Not only could authorities inspect and judge citizens, but parents could scrutinize and criticize children and families could evaluate each other. At stake was more than the simple imposition of a moral code under the threat of punishment, more than blind obedience to an arbitrary set of doctrines. The existence of a space of regulated freedom depended upon the generalization of a set of ethical techniques for self-inspection and self-evaluation in relation to the code, a way of making the feelings, wishes, and emotions of the self visible to itself, a way in which citizens were to problematize and govern their lives and conduct, tofind a way in which, as free subjects, they could live a good life as the consequence of their own character.
> ROSE, 1999: 227–228

To illustrate, Ankara, the capital of Turkey, witnessed an announcement at its Kurtuluş metro station in 2013 that went, "Dear passengers, please act in accordance with moral rules". The immediate reaction from the passengers was such that metro system officials were forced to explain that "the warning was given to young people who were seen behaving improperly in the security cameras" (HaberSol, 22 May 2013; Hürriyet, 25 May 2013). Before this event, a kissing couple on the bus in Istanbul was dropped off by driver because, as he said, "this is not a sex bus" (HaberSol, 24 April 2011). Both events were summarily protested by dozens of couples kissing in high-profile venues.

Taking these similar events in different cities into account, what I am interested in is how the above-mentioned sayings in religious sources spot the target and first reform the reaction of the authority and then produce the behaviours of like-minded people. Obviously, there is always resistance to pressure and control. However, what is crucial is the legitimation of transformative and re-constructive power by securing the order for the purposes of public peace and moral values. Obviously, there are different reactions to similar cases. For example, a bus driver in İzmit found the passenger's reaction against a mini-skirted woman unjust on his bus. According to the news, the passenger warned the driver about the woman because she might cause an accident during their intercity journey. The driver, with the support of the other passengers, rejected the man's warning, saying, "We cannot intervene because of her mini skirt ... Turkey is a free country" (Hürriyet, 14 July 2018). Such reactions are characteristic of the social individuals and venues where each event took place, and they further illustrate the mechanisms and instruments of power, which provide clues to the reasons for intervention. Kissing in public is taken as a sign a lack of shame, modesty, and chastity because it would be destructive to social harmony. The actors of such events point to a social failing in need of correction (Foucault, 2003b).

All in all, public morality produces fears and concerns that stimulate control and surveillance towards the female body and the woman's behaviours. The interventions and the public gaze have always had a reasonable explanation in terms of public peace and requirement of modesty within the human relations (Özyeğin, 2009: 112; Cindoğlu, 1997: 255). The public gaze and self-monitoring should be deemed as the most important technologies to reconstruct subjectivities. The public gaze seeking the honour of a woman in the street could be called new panopticon (Türkmen, 2009: 153). Alev Çınar (2008) also addresses the public gaze in the reconstruction of subjectivities, labelling it through not only the authoritative voice of the power regime but also its forms of visibility.

4   Concluding Remarks

When I try to re-read all these Islamic principles, which particularly refer to female body and sexuality in the context of patriarchal, political, and economic power relations, I realise an equation with multiple variables, which is set to social harmony and justice for differences. No doubt there are deep theological explanations and Islamic philosophy regarding social harmony and justice. However, depending on daily life religious knowledge from sources everyone can easily reach, I find it necessary to challenge some facts regarding the visualisation of womanhood, the woman's sexuality, and her body that have been, in my understanding, systematically reinterpreted according to the interests of time and politics.

"Islam means submission" (Mernissi, 1991: 55). No matter if a leader makes mistakes, injustices, and reprehensible acts or not, it is strictly forbidden to challenge the leader so that order is not put in jeopardy (Mernissi, 1991: 55). Obedience and submission are more than following social norms. They are the essence of the Islamic social contract in order to save and protect the society and state. Like all liberal social contracts, the essence of the Islamic social contract constitutes ideal identities that should be internalised to make the individual one's own guardian, as well as to transmit one's values to the social body. The daily practices are important to break the ignorance towards religious knowledge. However, the intellectual capacity and existence of wise authorities do not have to be over there to check true behaviours and acts in terms of the reliability of Islamic knowledge because having good morals is the most significant factor in carrying and transmitting reliable religious knowledge (Mernissi, 1991: 59–60).

The submissive role of the woman and the rules on her sexuality are related to her religious and social duties. As her docility and modesty go hand in hand with her sexual control and chastity, she becomes more virtuous to internalise her shame and intimacy for the benefit of society. This is her gendered role, tailored by Islamic principles. Man, unconditionally, is her authority. Therefore, thinking this authority in terms of inequality causes misinterpretation of God's justice, which desires to keep social harmony and balance between differences. That is the reason why I call Islamic order an equation with multiple variables ultimately targeting balance and temperance. However, it also strikes me that if woman and man represent different variables in the equation set to social harmony, the woman's contribution to this equation is increased in value by sexuality. Therefore, I think that it is easiest and least risky to count her sexuality as zero or meritless in order to increase the political and social weight of the man's control in the furtherance of social harmony.

The power within the hierarchical relations is important to recognise for the sake of public peace. Power strengthens itself with its control mechanisms and objects such as the woman because the woman's body is available in order to legitimise its interventions and produce discursive practices stimulating individuals to care about the woman's sexuality and relevant norms.

Correspondingly, heterosexuality as a vital parameter of the gender regime is a result of the above-mentioned submissiveness. Gendered sexes are suggested for family life and public peace due to the damage associated with irregular sexuality. In a society, behaviours and connotations are sexually regulated by taboos on bargaining places reinforced by "social silence contracts" (İlkkaracan, 2014: 17; see Kandiyoti, 1988). Homosexuality is an example of a social silence contract in Turkey. Nobody wants to exhibit knowledge or curiosity about homosexuality. Prostitution and brothels are also subject to silence contracts and are rarely talked about. Their existence may be a reminder of the woman's disobedience, so may be used as a cautionary tale of unmanageable sexuality. Fatima Mernissi puts it well when she says that "Islam does not have problem with sexuality itself, but with woman. Woman may be interpellative for sin and she disturbs the order" (Mernissi, 2014a: 52). In this context, marriage is a mechanism to manage sexuality and the honour of the family/community. Therefore, family is an institutional output of marriage.

Like womanhood or gender, the family is employed as an agency to balance the consent of responsibilities towards authority and the social structure. More importantly, the family marks the line between intimacy and the public, plus relevant correlations. The understanding of intimacy emanates from state control prevailing to public control. The act of state forms daily public life in the same Islamic line. Deriving from the intimacy principles of Islam towards the woman's sexuality and her body, public control over the woman turns also towards intimacy by creating "homosocial publicity" for the woman's comfort and public peace (Özyeğin, 2011: 158–159). The merits of homosocial publicity try to set out the map for how to live and sit separately as woman and man. However, the problem in the mixed-living style and intimacy of the public is not as easy as proposing 'pink buses'. Hence to realise intimacy in public is to notice the intimacy of the public, which unequally and unfairly discriminates, excludes and marginalises the woman not only from the public but also from her own intimacy by controlling it instead of her (Türkmen, 2009).

Granting the Islamic and feminist critiques about the commodification of the woman's body and rights, I finally emphasise that discourses about the woman's sexuality are "structurally produced, share similarities to narratives produced in other social contexts, and take a very local and nationalized form" (Agathangelou, 2004: 29). This means that the commodification of the female body and sexual relations are the consequences of a social, historical and political articulation of narratives and popular discourses embedded in songs, stories accompanying capitalism, and consume culture. Sexual pleasures inevitably develop the desire industry, which objectifies, for example, migrants, domestic workers, secretaries, and high school girls for being more seductive and opportunist than anything (Agathangelou, 2004: 30, 135). Thus, the exploitation of the woman is always worth highlighting, but we should not turn a blind eye to the fact of economic and political interest upon sexuality either.

CHAPTER 3

The Sacred Family Portrait
Balance, Uniformity, Patience and Piety

Recep Tayyip Erdoğan, as the most important political actors in Turkey, has strongly suggested that families have at least three children, saying, *"one means loneliness, two means rivalry, three means balance and four means abundance"* (Hürriyet Daily News, 03 January 2013; NBC News, 08 June 2016). Just as in 2007, he underlined a vital relation between a *strong family* and *strong society* in his 2011 election manifesto and called on *every member of the nation to mobilise* in pursuit of a *great nation, great power* (AK Parti, 2007; 2011; 2012). In order to have strong families, all state institutions from the Ministry of Health to the Directorate of Religious Affairs have started to provide counselling and training services by promulgating the state rationality to even the smallest neighbourhood unit (AK Parti, 2012: 34).

For the AKP, as *"a conservative democrat party"*, the family is valuable, and the aim of the AKP's social policies is *"to protect and support families that are the strength of our community and builders of our future"* (AK Parti, 2012: 32). All these goals surely repeat the woman's duties to family and nation. Ahead of the 100th anniversary of the Republic in 2023, it is heralded that *"assistance for balancing work and family life will be provided. Childcare assistance will be given to mothers, and opportunities for children to be placed in private or public day-care will be created"* (AK Parti, 2012: 34). Obviously, promises in the context of the woman's empowerment have been stated in election manifestos and the annual development programmes, but the gaps and challenges between neoliberal modernity and conservative democracy have been filled by religious and traditional references in order to motivate the woman on the way to uniforming a great nation.

From a different angle, conservatism manipulates the gendered hierarchy, and this may fit into neoliberal rationality as well. Rationalised hierarchies of gender categories open up a way in which gendered consciousness and responsibilities of woman and man stimulate self-governance and self-control according to the tailored roles. For example, sexual freedom, which is actually related to population, is regulated by conservatism through which sexual austerity and contraception ultimately amount to having an honourable life and self-esteem (Hughles-Rinker, 2013). In other words, conservatism impairs freedom of sexuality by codifying it as selfishness, hedonism, and irresponsibility.

Instead, commitment, love, and particularly maternal feelings are regarded as the virtues and values on the way to a good and safe family life (Brown, 1995: 9, 25).

New parameters and codes for the reconstruction of womanhood should be here described and idealised with didactic references for good motherhood and a sacred family life. On the other side of the coin, true womanhood paves the way for 'normalised' exclusionary practices. For example, Turkish President Erdoğan has said that women without children are *"incomplete"*, and this incomplete womanhood is due to a denial of femininity (Independent, 6 June 2016). Furthermore, in order not to have children, contraceptives are also left out of the Muslim family structure according to Mr. Erdoğan's statement:

> I will say it clearly ... We need to increase the number of our descendants ... People talk about birth control, about family planning. No Muslim family can understand and accept that. As God and as the great prophet said, we will go this way. And in this respect, the first duty belongs to mothers.
>
> THE GUARDIAN, 30 May 2016

Therefore, the departure point of this part shall be from the interwoven relations between the state, the female body, and the family. Drawing the linkage between them, womanhood as an agency produces its own mechanisms and becomes a target in order to govern the family and produce new subjectivities. It is expected that entrepreneur mothers should bring up entrepreneur subjects, but this re-generation points to a new neoliberal rationality of government, which needs to be apprehended first by the woman herself. This is because during time of transformation, the values of identities and roles are carried from private to public by the duties of idealised womanhood (Rottenberg, 2014: 151; Fraser, 1989: 123).

In the previous chapter, marriage was framed as a disciplinary mechanism of sexuality to optimise the sexual relationship between woman and man. In this chapter, I prefer to separate the concepts of marriage and family from each other in order to uncover the veins of family relationships, which are actually in elusive cooperation. The aim of the family and the nub of relationships have a dynamic character, which prompts codes and norms, especially in times of transformation. With the help of the docile and easygoing woman, traditional family practices build a big family from common values. Moreover, in these big family relations, traditional and religious practices turn into knowledge transformation from woman to woman (Doğan, 2017a; Iskhanian, 2014). Home is a cultural domain in which discipline and management are at stake in producing true care, true motherhood, and the true housewife. Therefore, gendered works related to the family, and the home may be rationalised by pointing to efficiency and family economy (Navaro-Yaşın, 2000).

That is to say that the family, as the smallest unit of society, has had a key role in reconstructing womanhood and manhood, and in the reproduction of new subjects since time immemorial. All duties associated with womanhood and manhood serve a purpose for the reproduction of good subjects. Especially in conservative societies, gender and social roles are constituted according to their social functions to reproduce and duly bring up new subjects regardless of the personal expectations of parents. This would be a reason why conservative societies stress family/community life, instead of highlighting individualism as in recent modernity practices.

In parallel with this, the family in Turkey is a gendered structure that idealises the sexes according to their socio-cultural roles. In other words, this idealisation sets its sights on an imagined nation based on the sexual division of roles, whether according to secular tenets or Islamic. In particular, womanhood has been depicted and also narrated with reference to the (desired) normal. The new truth, without being far from moral and traditional control on the female body, galvanises new norms and rules for transforming order. Therefore, Turkish modernisation from the early days of the Republic to the present time has been framing family life and gender roles with idealised womanhood in the private and public sphere, from the micro to the macro level. This yields two results: i) Idealised womanhood evokes more than the individuality of a woman, whose existence is domesticated within the community and family relations. ii) This idealisation of gender roles is based on sexual and inegalitarian relationships engrained in the family. Therefore, moving beyond her reproductive skills and sexual duties, being an ideal woman is a mission to verify the fact of who is the authority. This micro-verification of statehood within family relationships identically constitutes the state itself. Concisely, family as an autonomous field empowers the state to monitor the population and makes it possible to impose norms on women and children for the sake of moralisation and normalisation (Bell, 1993a: 393).

Therefore, this chapter aims to unfold the rationality of the power regime in post-2002 Turkey by placing womanhood in the relations between high politics and daily life. These relations are clearly power itself, for which ideal womanhood justifies struggle against the reflection of counter-womanhood because the truth – idealising a single form of womanhood – always desires to win and be rewarded. In order to ease the tension between the differences, a two-fold functionality of family is employed: i) Family life is filled with safety, risklessness, and happiness, especially for women and children. The aspiration to have a family is used as a force to keep women and children under control with the false promise of freedom. ii) Family is a source of honour, cultivating self-governable subjects for a good nation and bright future. However, on the other side of this polished coin, family connotes intimacy and obscurity, which would theoretically be stated as control and surveillance on the female body. That is why a family with marriage, divorce, and the role of the woman therein needs to be discussed to clarify regulations and norms, which claim to be protecting the woman and family against social disorder. Vested womanhood through motherhood and wifehood legitimises codes and norms of family life with the help of social rewards or punishments. So to speak, the image of a patient, loyal, and suffering mother and wife highlights the enshrined merits of womanhood. Hence, with religious knowledge and traditional sensitivities, the family constitutes a second life sphere of womanhood for post-2002 Turkey.

Before extending this discussion, it is necessary to say that it is about building a female identity, which gains operable function, especially for post-2002 Turkey. In this chapter, along with the regulations, speeches of political actors, and religious references about family, motherhood, marriage, and divorce; exploring the themes of governmental rationality about the family, as expressed in exalting the features of ideal womanhood and family values, allows me to describe these interventions in the context of norm imposition.

1   Understanding the Family in Its Cooperative Manner

The family is generally seen as the core unit of society regardless of what individuals expect from it. However, apart from its usual definition, the "family is a location where production and redistribution take place" (Hartmann, 1981: 368). In order to realise biological and social production within the family, the family should be thoroughly understood by identifying the place of the woman therein. The features of the family and its functions intrinsically imply the role of the woman and its function in the family. In a way, the woman is a security lock for family strategy (Sancar, 2014: 146).

The public service ads of the Ministry of Family and Social Policies in 2011 provided remarkable insights about the place of the woman in the family by constantly highlighting the importance of the family especially for the protection of risk groups, including elders, women, the disabled, and children. Along with these public service ads, some specific statements are more hearable to draw attention to the function of the family, portraying the mother, father, grandmother/-father, and children within a framed story, within which we are led to believe that the state never allows anybody to get lost because Turkey is a big family.[1] In addition, supporting and protecting groups at risk helps to produce the values through which the state can develop and stand against threats. Specific emphasis on traditions as a healthy road to the future is presented to identify the social and gender roles of the woman within family relations (Günaydın and Özdoğan, 2014: 61–72).

Indeed, the modern Turkish family with the Republic of Turkey was at first raised on the shoulders of the progressive family head (*aile reisi*). This new ideal father as a performative actor helped the social revival of modernity by keeping both the continuity of tradition and the changes of the contemporary world under control at the same time (Özkan-Kerestecioğlu, 2014: 13). While the religiously unaccepted requirements of modernisation blamed the woman for her integration into modern lifestyles, the new progressive father of modern Turkey approaches relations between woman and man by reminding his daughters of the family honour (Özkan-Kerestecioğlu, 2014: 14). In a way, the woman was in the hands of the old man (Berktay, 2012: 108). Therefore, the authority of a national father was needed to keep the woman under control and surveillance and to prevent her from being seen as a growing threat to the family, where the demise of paternal authority has been always the case in point (Özkan-Kerestecioğlu, 2014: 14).

As Aynur İlyasoğlu and Ayşe Durakbaşa (2001: 195) state, the " 'required and sufficient degree of modernization' over women's bodies, behavior and social conduct" was provided by modernist men. Thus, with the role of the father or this male authority, the ideal family was described as a "modern", "national", or sometimes "happy" family, and sometimes like nowadays, it has been described as a "sacred" family in post-2002 (Özbay, 2014: 109–110). Power according to its own rationality produces a model for an ideal family with the help of population and general social policies. This is an analytic explanation as to why family values go hand in hand with national aims as a first step towards national solidarity (Berktay, 2012: 104; Sancar, 2014: 210–211).

The modern and national family of the early Republic of Turkey desired to have gendered citizens who need to be reproduced through national service. The number of children was a way of demonstrating patriotism. In the 70s and 80s, fertility was discouraged by modelling a happy family, including mother, father and two children (not more). In that context, 'happiness' was related to quality of life. A family with two children was deemed necessary for the welfare of the state because the educational and individual quality of

---

1 Foucault defines this sense of the big family in terms of extended family relations and friendship in which *soul services* function as protection and compassion embedded in national and traditional affinities (Foucault, 1997c: 98).

new subjects was more valuable than its quantity. In post-2002 Turkey, the ideal family has been reconstructed through discourses on the "sacred" family (Özbay, 2014: 109–110; Berktay, 2012: 116–117). For Ferhunde Özbay (2014: 110), the notion of the "sacred" family is not related to nostalgia at all.

Like Özbay, Fatmagül Berktay argues that sacred family values are neither traditionalists nor anti-modernist, but as many have said, it is a "post-modern reaction for a specific modernism in an Islamic third world" (Berktay, 2012: 117). According to Berktay, there are traditional and religious references for pre-capitalist family life, but actually the "sacred" family is the contemporary result of globalisation. As Ayşe Buğra (Özbay, 2014: 110) claims, the "sacred" family is a culturally conservative and economically neoliberal dream. In the same critical vein, Berktay draws attention to "the new sacred" which is produced by "working on traditional and religious materials" (Berktay, 2012: 116). According to Berktay, "patriarchal family crises" require the family to be repaired against the destructive flexibility of globalisation with the help of "God", namely quelling attempts to counteract patriarchal inequality (Berktay, 2012: 116). Moreover, religious references attribute natural values to gendered duties. Hence, the family and relevant belongings promise salvation from the quicks of globalisation.

The new Turkish family of the early Republic believed that "family as the first cell of the state is 'the source of national morality and cooperation'" (Özkan-Kerestecioğlu, 2014: 16). Looking at the sacred family of post-2002 Turkey, cooperation and morality are still worth emphasising, but religious references point out that the family is *a life source* and *life itself is an exam. The sons of Adam and daughters of Eve take the brunt of the moral and material difficulties of life together* (Martı, 2014: 7–9). This means it is a *multi-tasking exam*, whose questions are *changeable according to role* (Martı, 2014: 30). In a sense, the existential reason for the family is about divine responsibilities towards society beyond national motivations. This does not mean that the state and nationality are not important anymore. Conversely, state and nationality gain more significance in order to draw attention to the belongings with tradition and religion. However, the manifold transformation in post-2002 needed a characterisation to convince people of the sacredness of the family reinforced by nation, religion, tradition, motherhood, and children. All these elements of culture constitute sacred belongings in order to underline the rotten values and degenerated lifestyles as a threat against family cooperation, in which care relations in the mother-father-child triangle build on moral responsibility for society beyond concerns over kinship relations (Foucault, 1980e: 172–174). This moral responsibility is subjected to protection and the reproduction of life itself independent of individual expectations.

Sara Ahmed also remarks on this point well:

> The reproduction of life – in the form of the future generation – becomes bound up with the reproduction of culture, through the stabilisation of specific arrangements for living ('the family'). The family is idealisable through the narrative of threat and insecurity; the family is presented as vulnerable, and as needing to be defended against others who violate the conditions of its reproduction.
>
> AHMED, 2014: 144

Eventually, power desires to transform individuals by voluntarily bringing them under the sacred family roof. In order to make the desired new subject, power mechanisms are projected, and hopes for the family as a societal and state institution are pinned to this project. The expectations juxtaposed in the final declaration of Family Conference in 2010 are worth remarking on, in particular the opening speech of Aliye Kavaf, the former Minister of State for Women and Family:

> We believe that the structure of the natural family is *based on the marriage of man and woman* for the healthy, productive, and well-being of new generations ... We care about *religious motivations*, which play a major role in the protection of the whole family, and we support that all cultures and religions develop common strategies. Accordingly, we criticise the underestimation and non-legitimacy of religious marriage ... We consider it necessary to implement *all kinds of measures to reduce divorce based* on the protection of the generation ... We argue that every nation *must return to its spiritual values* that make it a nation and that the family must be restructured in response to the inevitable consequences of modernity, such as urbanisation, industrialisation, migration, wars, epidemics, and selfish individualism ... We support policies and projects that prevent abortion and increase the declining birth rates ... We demand that adequate measures be taken *against homosexuality and domestic incest*, and we *work together* to prevent *these diseases* that threaten every society.
>
> BIANET, 8 December 2010; ÖZKAN-KERESTECIOĞLU, 2014: 18–19, emphasis added

Regarding the noteworthy points of her speech: i) The definition of family is necessarily heteronormative. ii) Its institutional function is legitimised and regulated by religion, law, and tradition. iii) The driving force of a stronger family is religion, which is a plausible obstacle against divorce. iv) In addition to education and training programmes on family life and roles, homosexuality is also comparable to incest. More importantly, homosexuality is seen as a disease by the state actor responsible for the woman and the family. A common struggle is summoned against homosexuality. Naming homosexuality as a disease and aiming to minimise divorce rates bring regulations and preoccupations because ultimately *marriage is not just two people coming together, but also a means of collectively building society* (Martı, 2014: 12).

The neoliberal rationality of the power regime under AKP rule seeks to find the operating parameters of gender because gendered relations between man and woman, as well as peripheral sexual orientations, are not only the core of power relations but also the main determinant of internalised social roles. As Wendy Brown emphasises, "gender can be conceived as a marker of power, a maker of subjects, an axis of subordination, without thereby converting it to a 'center' of 'selves' understood as foundational" (1995: 40). As may be known, (neo)liberal rationality does not force individuals to be something, there must be voluntarism; individuals should consciously and freely choose to comply with social roles and rules that are framed within the (neo)liberal discourse clearly based on family, community, maternity, heterosexuality and the explicit sexual division of labour (Brown, 1995: 143–144).

However, in the age of biopolitics, (neo)liberal feminine and masculine subjects are "divided ultimately by reason (objectivity) and passion (subjectivity)", and they are "bundles of power, rather than effect of power" (Brown, 1995: 145). This means, male-based order and subordinated woman are the reconcilement of individuals with the promise of warmth, safety, and protectiveness within the family order by pushing an insecure life and dangers into loneliness and singleness (Brown, 1995: 149–150). Put a different way, the family is a unique legal unit in order to regulate and conduct individuals and populations according to everyday needs. It is somehow the only way to reach and socialise individuals and cultivate self-existence for themselves and society.

Against the differences concealed in different identity politics and civil society, the family develops community relations with the aim of "collective responsibility" (Berktay, 2012: 117; Rose, 1999: 228). Given what Diyanet says, the relationship between individual and society, and the relationship between individual morality and social morality are the same because morality always targets society, which is constructed by *collective responsibility, pure goodness,* and *blessing* (Okumuş, 2007: 17–18). In order to prevent badness and evil, *social corrective and chastening mechanisms* are employed on an individual because one individual mirror, actually the family, social life, politics, and economics (Okumuş, 2007: 17–18). Islamic morality aims to protect the individual and society by envisioning and constructing a future. Obviously, there are already fixed reasons and signifiers regarding bad morality: *extravagance* and *intemperance, selfishness, dispute,* and *disunion, lack of corrective mechanisms* (Okumuş, 2007: 17–18). The family is a disciplinary place for "the hegemony of a universalizing and collective identity – nationalization of a racialized identity – that disciplined and unified those within its territory against external enemies" (Nadesan, 2008: 21).

Tracing the trajectories of changes to the "modern, national" and "sacred" family, it would be good to raise the argument that modernity itself has continuity, but that the patriarchy embedded in modernity is always changing. The position of woman illustrates this change very well, such that if modernity (or capitalism) wants to see more women in the public sphere, patriarchy accordingly adjusts itself to its needs (Ahıska and Düzkan, 1994: 148). Likewise, post-2002 Turkey's modernity prefers to see the woman in the private sphere. The belonging of the woman is built on family values; however, the family first needs to be cleansed of the secular habits reinforced by the welfare state of the 1970s and the neoliberal transitions of 1980s. There are dramatically rising discursive practices about strong religious-conservative family duties. All these discursive practices are politically reconstructed by adequate mechanisms and norms in order to first convince the woman to return to the family and to manage family life. In addition, it is the return of the woman to the husband and father's authority in the name of safety and security. Some mechanisms such as religion provide a path to the pressure of the man by rationalising the control and restrictions put on womanhood using religious knowledge. This makes the family, womanhood, and the female body just the operable instrument for religion to govern patriarchal individuals composed of homogeneous groups.

Regarding Turkish modernisation, gender relations and the position of the woman form an area where two contradictory politics – the fear of the resemblance to the West and enthusiasm of the nation for being an organic modern unity – intersect (Bora, 2010). Namely, there is no break from tradition and religion with Turkish modernisation of the Republic, but unsettled power relations need to be resettled (Bora, 2010). These new power relations point actually to the new gender regime. However, it is claimed that the reconstruction of gendered power relations brings modern forms to the intimacy of sexual and social relations, so the family loses its importance. I think that this kind of counterargument against the pre-2002 family is wrong because Turkish modernisation is entirely family-centred (Sancar, 2014: 21; Aytaç, 2015: 113).

It is argued in Diyanet publications that with the demise of the family the matter of being a woman or man loses its meaning. Accordingly, it is said that the family *is a school*, in which all members and especially women have key roles for *permanent life education*. In addition, the Western family, leaning on modernity, minimises *the gendered division* between woman and man, which is regarded in a kind of lifestyle. *A happy, successful, and healthy society* must take the family in priority without ignoring different sexed roles because *family* itself is *the source of discipline and order* (Ceceli-Alkan, 2004; Özbuğday, 2004; Beder-Şen, 2007). Family provides a traditional control on forbidden relations. Additionally, married life between two sexes provides not only an internal regulation on couples but also conduct mutual emotions with respect to each other (Foucault, 1997d: 53; 1997e: 91–92). In a way, the family becomes the place of surveillance and power on the individual (Foucault, 1980f: 152).

Therefore, for Diyanet, the family is a *revival field* (Koytak, 2004: 21). *If the family is the core of society in order to preserve the culture, the mother is the essence of the family and the carrier of the characteristic core of that culture. The mother has a key role in teaching the culture to the next generations. For education, the mother comes first, the father takes the role of assistant because womanhood is the accumulation of experiences, which are the main source of life knowledge, for example on how to overcome conflicts and difficulties* (Demirkan, 2007: 48–49). Given that the state teaches this culture and social norms at schools, motherhood gains public responsibility as the first teacher of children in the school of family.[2],[3]

No society rejects the idea that family is the bridge between individual and society. It has *traditional and universal duties*, ranging from the biological and financial to protection and education. Furthermore, having a family provides a *prestigious and social statute*, in addition to *helping occupy leisure time and*

---

2 In Turkish, there is a proverb which could be translated into English as 'Man makes houses, woman makes homes'. Originally it states in Turkish that 'the nest is made by the female bird'. Its meaning is about the training and schooling function of family, which is carried by mothers.

3 According to Wendy Brown (2018: 124–126), the woman is naturally regarded as responsible person for family and its internal organisation, which impacts the public too. She calls this as a kind of privatisation that can go hand in hand with neoliberal governmentality. For her, as the gendered division is sharpened, the idea of community-based society in terms of a big family image is empowered too. This develops the idea of public motherhood through volunteer mothers and volunteer families to empower family values. In this vein, single mothers and children without families are seen as social problems for similar reasons, which are related to responsibilities of the woman and her freedom (Brown, 2018: 124–126). Namely, there is no direct action to build a big family because voluntary organisations and civil society take responsibility for solving problems (Ishkanian, 2014). Therefore, civil society and public institutions prepare special programmes and training programmes to teach the couples and especially women how to function in their gender roles in the name of family values, child education, elder care, and even how to cope with and eradicate domestic violence (AK Parti, 2007, 2011).

learning tolerance with a mother's affection and father's compassion (Demirkan, 2009: 10–11; Özbuğday, 2004: 14–15). The subject gains its sexual, political, and economic identity according to religious principles and cultural sensitivities in the family. However, the family is not only a unique domain where codes and norms are re-produced, but it also conveys these to the next generation through family and community relationships. Family provides a *semantic field*, surrounded by basic religious knowledge in order to prompt paradigms, strategies, and ideals for *life management* (Koytak, 2004: 19). Surely industrialisation, urbanisation, and employment bring about changes in the family; however, the influence of religion and culture on the family during neoliberalisation should be noticed as well (Vergin, 1985: 574). According to the understanding of Diyanet, the family is a requirement both for individuals to manage their life and for the state to regulate daily life in order to standardise the population.

Meanwhile, it is wrong to say that the Western family or 'modern family' is egalitarian and freed from patriarchal relations. It is also wrong to claim that there was a bad family structure in pre-2002 Turkey. In contrast, family always occupied an important place in a cultural and political sense, no matter if there are secular liberals or conservative Democrats in power (Berktay, 2012; Özbay, 2015;İlyasoğlu and Durakbaşa, 2001). Moreover, womanhood has been always employed as an agency in professional life and socialisation in order to promote modern styles in housework chores, household activities, eating habits, organisation of rituals, visiting and hosting (İlyasoğlu and Durakbaşa, 2001: 200). In addition to this, the family has been always a mark of social status within community relations. All groups within the nation ultimately compose a big family in that community relations promote mutual aids and solidarity (Vergin, 1985: 574; Aytaç, 2015: 28,120).

On the other hand, the image of a great national family causes discursive practices and surveillance to each of its members. Şerif Mardin conceptualises this as "neighbourhood pressure" in order to explain the fact that "everybody monitors each other in Turkey" (Radikal, 24 May 2008). The neighbourhood, or I would say community mindset (cemaat kafası), consists of individuals who move together in accordance with common values. For Şerif Mardin, in order to share such commonalities, "to look" is important to learn what is good, beautiful, and nice that Islam seeks to find out.[4] Looking or monitoring

---

4   The social body is a total of multiple relations in which the economy of discourses and practices disciplines bodies as well as regulates population (Foucault, 2003a: 24, 245, 252). These extended family relations in the name of kinship or neighbourhood create the social field to gain (self-)surveillance and (self-)policing by conducting and correcting each other (see also Foucault, 1980c; 1980g).

is the core of neighbourhood pressure by controlling woman-man relations on the plea of the family's honour and neighbourhood's values (Radikal, 24 May 2008). Similarly, Deniz Kandiyoti, in her seminal study entitled *"Emancipated but Unliberated? Reflections on the Turkish Case"*, draws attention to the "corporate control" of female sexuality, the psychological effects of sex segregation, and features of the female life cycle (1987: 325):

> The corporate control over female sexuality becomes strikingly evident in the large number of different individuals who see themselves as immediately responsible for ensuring women's appropriate sexual conduct. Parents, siblings, near and distant relatives, and even neighbors closely monitor the movements of the postpubescent girl, firmly imprinting the notion that her sexuality is not hers to give or withhold. This is clearly apparent at the critical juncture of the choice of a marriage partner. Although a woman's personal attributes do play a role in whether she is considered marriageable, it is ultimately her family's responsibility to see to it that a suitable match is arranged. In the past, and currently among the less permissive strata of society, this has kept multitudes of women from competing against each other on the free market for sexuality and marriage. Against this background, the equation of love with marriage, notions of romantic love, and images of marriage as woman's ultimate fulfillment find less fertile ground on which to flourish. Emotional attachment is often expected to develop after marriage. The degree of emotional closeness, actual or expressed, in the wife-husband relationship is variable.
>
> KANDIYOTI, 1987: 325–326

For Kandiyoti (1987), corporate control brings strong-same sex bonds in the name of sisterhood (bacılık) and solidarity as well, which is perceived as liberation by women. Additionally, this sisterhood not only produces knowledge regarding good womanhood but also provides an opportunity to strengthen family and community networks. The woman is an important social actor with access to new knowledge about the private sphere, which is why the woman and womanhood became a focal point. In other words, community life, constructed by Islamic belongings, needs a woman's knowledge and experience to understand what is going on in family life. Through this womanly contribution, political actors, state institutions and other religious activities confidently emphasise the problems and the ways out. On the other hand, the woman can learn religious knowledge from mosques and religious groups. Then they educate their own children and find their own ways to solve family problems on their own. Additionally, the woman's knowledge is important for religious officials in order to realise the problems entrenched in the most hidden and closed places of society, i.e., family (Martı, 2013: 34).

Therefore, I consider that womanhood is a social activity and an agency in family cooperation to transform society with the help of knowledge regarding the private sphere. To do this, mosques and religious communities play a vital role in establishing local networks and power. With all that, Şerif Mardin and Deniz Kandiyoti provide us an analytical framework through which the political agenda on some topics finds its own meaning in the context of family cooperation.

From this point of view, I directly proceed to some critical agenda topics underlined first by political actors:

i) Student-houses were blacklisted by Mr. Erdoğan:

> It's not clear what is going on in these places. They are all mixed up, anything can happen. As a conservative democratic government, we have to intervene. In these places, there is intelligence received by our security forces, the police department and the governorates. Acting upon this intelligence, our governors are intervening in these situations. Why are you annoyed about this?... Mothers and fathers cry out, asking 'where is the state?' These steps are taken to tell them that the state is here.
>
> HÜRRIYET DAILY NEWS, 5 November 2013

Student houses and cohabitation are criminalised by the intimidating attitudes of neighbours who fear the obscurity of what is going on therein. Not only premarital sexuality but also an ordinary student life are pointed to as threats to the family. University students and youths are shown as abnormals and a social disease who need state intervention to be managed and regulated. Such state interventions prompted a strong reaction from the people; in fact, even though the family and social values have always been significant in Turkey, under the conservative AKP rule, this structural and emotional unit was thought in need of transformation as a signifier of acceptance of the new hegemonic lifestyle. This 'desirable' lifestyle was even touted "as an opportunity to fight terrorism" according to Interior Minister Muammer Güler, who backed Mr. Erdoğan's statement on the student houses (Deustche Welle, 15 November 2013). Mr. Güler discussed the purported ills of student life and youth through the lens of the 2013 Gezi Park Protests, which had resulted in a forceful intervention by the state:

> Terrorist organizations utilize the relationship between male and female students to gain support from youth in schools and universities ... No one knows what is happening in these living spaces – all manner of dubious activities could be taking place.
>
> DEUSTCHE WELLE, 15 November 2013

Through the student houses and the high-profile counteractions of young people against political and social interventions, the state draws a red line through the private and public spheres using the structures and values of the family. A person may be excluded from public life according to his/her lifestyle and choices. More importantly, the public power of individuals is politically eroded by enclosing people within the family for security purposes. Therefore, it is crucial to notice that explicitly supporting and implicitly suggesting family life in a moral, political, economic, and social sense is a way in which terrorism and criminalism can be taken under control. Therefore, the family is converted into an ideological signifier pointing out a standard lifestyle, approved by religion, tradition, and more importantly the state. Ultimately, *lifestyle is putting values into practice* (Bayraktar-Karahan, 2015: 7) because "the access of truth is reachable with a particular way of life" (Foucault, 2014: 127).

ii) Referring to the Gezi Protests, Mr. Erdoğan criticised the leader of one of the opposing parties for his reaction related to an alleged attack against a veiled woman with a baby. Mr. Erdoğan claimed that Devlet Bahçeli, the leader of the nationalist MHP, could not understand the social pain regarding the news because "Mr. Bahçeli [who has never married] does not know what family or having children is. He does not have this kind of fight" (Haberler.com, 22 February 2014). The overblown nature of the reporting on the incident notwithstanding, here it is worth stressing the exclusionary discourse because of the social sensitivity bound up in the idea of family life. A healthy family life becomes framed as a precondition for compassion, and thereby a solution to crime and moral degeneration.

iii) Like Şerif Mardin, I think that regulations over alcohol consumption should be analysed in the context of neighbourhood order and healthy family life. Instead of drinking in public areas, it is permitted to drink at home or venues licensed to sell alcohol (BirGün, 28 April 2017)Mr. Erdoğan states more clearly what is expected from the ban on alcohol consumption:

> If you will drink, just drink. We are not against this. But we are not allowing this in certain places and at certain hours – and within 100 metres of mosques and schools.
>
> HÜRRIYET DAILY NEWS, 28 May 2013

Like with student houses, here the private and public spheres are bisected by a focus on family and neighbourhood values, and the restrictions on alcohol consumption cannot be reduced only to religious sensitivities. Nevertheless, through such religious sensitivities and 'sacred' values, there is an obvious struggle to rule over public space and public services, so alcohol consumption rather signals ownership of public space.

Along with these juxtaposed examples from the daily political agenda in Turkey, the power regime under AKP rule has had a strong desire to draw attention to the rotten values resulting from Kemalist modernity in order to legitimise the required transformation of power relations in politics and society. According to Diyanet, *modern morality does not judge lifestyles and values because free choice itself is important, no matter if these choices are (religiously) meaningful or not. However, tradition seeks to find meaning and purpose in the life course so freedoms can be restricted if this restriction brings meaning and content to personal and social life. To do so, the mother and father are key figures leading new family members to a life based on the guardianship and guidance of God* (Çekin, 2009: 13–15).

In a way, 'good' choices and a desirable life are taught in the family. While Diyanet attempts to solve questions and problems about the society and individuals by emphasising family life and gendered relations, I argue that Islamic-neoliberal rationality in Turkey clearly tries to categorise individuals according to their private and public choices, and existential forms, in order to manage social and political transformation. Additionally, I consider that family values determine the risks of public life and the risks of individuals. In other words, the different lifestyles and form of public visibility within the drawn lines signal risky areas of the public and unacceptable areas of the private, by producing knowledge about who is reliable, who is dangerous, how a woman should behave, with whom it is good to get married, why family is necessary, and how family relations should be. Conservative family values change the definition of risk itself, especially for women and for marginalised populations, including homosexuals, unmarried cohabiting couples, sex workers, and so on.

What we witness in Foucault's texts is that, beginning in the eighteenth century, two technologies of power were established. The first was disciplinary power, which centres on the body, produces individualisation and serves to render it more and more docile not out of selfish desire but as a result of attentively calculating a feature of power in order to extract greater efficiency and profit. The second technology, that of biopower, is focused not on the body and its life, but on life for life's sake in the sense of mass effects on the population (Foucault, 2003a: 249). To put it simply:

> The theory of right knew only individual and society, disciplines knew individuals, their bodies in practical terms ... New technology of power is not exactly society nor individual-as body. It is new body, multiple body, a body with so many heads, cannot be necessarily counted. Biopolitics deals with the population as political problem, that is at once scientific and political, as a biological problem as power's problem. This is the time of biopolitics.
>
> FOUCAULT, 2003a: 245

As a contribution to his lectures at College de France, Foucault begins with a clear definition of biopolitics. Biopower, according to Foucault, is "the sets of mechanisms through which the basic features of the human species became the object of a political strategy" (Foucault, 2007: 1). Firstly, he calls attention to the mechanisms of power that are not in any way a general theory of what power is. The important point of what he proposes regarding these mechanisms is related to the function of power rather than its definition. That is to say, power can be found by looking at the answers of where and how, between whom, or between what points, according to what processes, and with what effects (Foucault, 2007: 2). It seems clear that power, as described by Foucault, is omnipresent and not held by a single individual or institution.

The mechanisms of power are twofold: On the one hand, they are an elemental part of relations. On the other hand, these mechanisms are the reason for and result of these relations, which re-exist around hierarchical subordination, coordination, technical identities, and chain effects. That is to say, all these relations and tactics reinforce the mechanisms of power with the guidance of knowledge (Foucault, 2007: 3).Rose and Miller (1992: 181) bring our attention to the fact that knowledge as to how we manage our family life, business life, our morality, and friendships turns into a virtue which gives clear 'successful' or 'failed' outputs. The state, in this context, is not the ultimate decision maker to determine the clear-cut models of state intervention. Therefore, it has to do with the governmentalisation of the state bringing about the formation, evaluation, and development of acts and events regarding problems of the social body, health, crime, poverty, and family life by "requiring some measure of collective response" in cooperation with (*bio-*)political authorities (Rose and Miller, 1992: 183).

Based on the risk analysis of our lives, entrepreneurship and self-entrepreneurship come to the fore. In order to promote knowledge about this, all sources based on religion are kept ready and reachable anywhere we can look and read. To illustrate, the ministries' and Diyanet's information booklets instruct us on *how to know whom we should marry* by highlighting that *flirting is not a solution to knowing someone*. In addition, it is suggested that a *prospective woman or man should be well-observed*. It should be asked *whether he or she behaves respectfully towards his or her family, honestly at work, friendly towards others*. There are specified suggestions, for example, if *the family* does *not consent to a marriage*, couples should not do it. *Relations between families* are important as well. The family *does not depend on luck so love should be of secondary importance* (Kök, 2016: 23–25; Akçay-Civriz, 2017: 17; Martı, 2013: 14–17). Likewise, the Ministry of Family and Social Policy publishes booklets with guidance on pre- and post-family life, and the duties of different aspects of marriage, such as *Life Skill in Marriage, Family Management, Family Economy, Family Law Guide, Marriage and Health* (Deniz and Göral, 2012 Canel, 2012a, 2012b; Alpaydın, 2012; Bilgiç-Selman, 2012). In order to practice this guidance, many details are provided for scenarios ranging from violence to the performance of the woman in the family. These guides are given to local governments, law enforcement agencies, NGOs, and universities. The emphasis on *life management* points to *the team-amity of couple*s.

What we are meant to learn from the publications of these state institutions is how to overcome the challenges and difficulties of family life; in effect gender-based problems are normalised in the name of saving the institutions of marriage and family. We are warned that starting a family life is not a toy to be handled by confused, love-drunk couples. It needs effort, patience, and dynamism to maintain it. In parallel with this approach, Mr. Erdoğan once stated, in a speech given to young women at Mevlanakapı Girls' Dormitory:

> Do not put marriage on the back burner. When you meet your destiny, take your decision. However, do not be too fussy, or you will leave the rose garden empty-handed
> BIANET, 14 July 2014

Likewise, Ahmet Davutoğlu, while he was the prime minister, encouraged young men to establish families:

> The state will pay one year for our young people [*men*] who find work for the first time. This is encouraging for employers. Now that you have your job, your salary, your food. What's left? A spouse! We want the people of this land to be blessed, we want to reproduce but at the same time we want to be a workforce. When you say you need a wife, you will go first to your mother and your father, Inshallah [God willing] they will find a good wife for you. If you do not find your future wife, you will contact us (*i.e. the state*).
> HABERLER.COM, 22 October 2015, italics added

Taking these two statements together, the paternalistic approach of the state clearly appears as a 'matchmaking service and contact point for marriage'. Additionally, while the role of the man as breadwinner is explicitly described, the woman – as object to his subject – is implicitly called into the home for the reproduction of the workforce. These quotations are usefully thought through using Gülnur Acar-Savran's concept of "hybridized Islamic patriarchy" (2011: 270). Patriarchy does not have a unique face to describe the oppression on the woman, so its various faces should be explored along a continuum of change unity and its dialectic (Acar-Savran, 2011: 266). Especially in Turkey, where different cultural and religious communities live together, national development needs to carry customs and traditions by embracing mostly Islamic social expectations, regardless of what is actually believed. Therefore, the social reflections of these above-mentioned statements are warmly welcome by every side of society.

My recent attempt to pinpoint cooperation between private and public is notably crucial to understand the family in a neoliberal context, hand-in-hand with Islamism, individualism, intimacy, and conservatism. The crucial point here is that focusing on the family from the perspective of governmentality sheds light on the neoliberal rationality that maintains its influence in market-society relations. Let us see what Veysel Eroğlu, the Minister of Forest and Water Management, said:

> We will mark the 100th anniversary of the foundation of our Republic in 2023. Turkey is among the world's 10 largest economies. You all have grander goals. Fatih [Sultan Mehmed II] conquered Istanbul at the age of 21 [in 1453]. When the 600th anniversary of the conquest of Istanbul is celebrated, these young people will carry our flag even higher. Target 2053! Another target is our newborn children. Sultan Alparslan won a major battle on Friday, August 26, 1071. When our sons celebrate its 1000-year anniversary, Turkey will be a global power. That is why we say to the mothers, instead of singing a lullaby such as 'sleep and grow up' or something like that, rather 'my son, grow up, target 2071, this glorious flag will rise to the top!'.
> SPUTNIK TÜRKIYE, 16 May 2018

This is the populist discourse directed at prospective families. Here the question is how a conservative politics, whose ground colour is Islamism, can take advantage of the family by convincing people to support its pure neoliberal goals. On this point, Wendy Brown posed a question that I also want to ask: "How does a rationality that is expressly amoral at the level of both ends and means (neoliberalism) intersect with one that is expressly moral and regulatory (neoconservatism)?"(2006: 692). For ordinary people, there is no financial profit in being a citizen of *the world's 10th largest economy* because poverty and welfare dreams must move together. For Wendy Brown (2018), neoliberalism is a normative rationality uniting the people against public power; individual families can thereby be understood as the building block of a nation or society, each singly built, in line with desired norms. The family is encouraged to be a unitary and unified social structure while the public individual fades. Meanwhile, for Brown, the family is rendered as a lifesaver by gaining and attributing sacred values to it, especially when the market is disrupted by financial and social crises. To put this into practice, especially womanly values are employed to expand the rationality of the power regime within the family (Brown, 2018). However, there is still a crucial question to be answered: How is the woman-subject motivated to join national development projects? According to Berktay, the question of how subjectivities are motivated develops in line with the question of how the subjects forget their own self-interest and benefit (2012: 118).

In line with Berktay's answer to the construction of subjectivities, I also assert that subjects are motivated by emotions. Even though state power persists according to its own interests by creating and narrating historical events as a glorious revival of the Turkish nation in the context of global development and market relations, it seems that actually no rational person is influenced by the market profits of high politics (Berktay, 2012: 118). In this context, again special attention to Sara Ahmed's seminal work entitled *The Cultural Politics of Emotions* needs to be highlighted in order to examine how subjects are governed by emotions:

> Emotions and bodies are associated with femininity and racial others. This projection of 'emotion' onto the bodies of others not only works to exclude others from the realms of thought and rationality, but also works to conceal the emotional and embodied aspects of thought and reason ... The 'truths' of this world are dependent on emotions, on how they move subjects, and stick them together.
> AHMED, 2014: 170

Obviously, new political rationality is built on two different triangles: family, state and economy; and emotionality, rationality, and personal interest, respectively (Aytaç, 2015: 89). These two overlapping triangles provide a persistence and sustainability of power everywhere. Accordingly, from Jeremy Bentham's concept, Foucault analyses the mechanism of the Panopticon by emphasising its instrumental context, in which disindividualised power reappears on bodily acts and gazes (Foucault, 1995). Power is in circulation with the help of norms, emotions, belongings, and statuses. In this sense, family/community relations build a new social prison wherein "the more numerous those anonymous and temporary observers are, the greater the risk for the inmate of being surprised and the greater his anxious awareness of being observed. The Panopticon is a marvelous machine which, whatever use one may wish to put it to, produces homogeneous effects of power" (Foucault, 1995: 202). The taming influence of the social panopticon through family and community relations becomes a central domain in order to uphold the reasons for moral degeneration and to generate driving forces for the development of the nation. The assemblage of mechanisms of the panopticon is related to disciplinary mechanisms of power through the gazes, surveillance, guarding of mother and father, rituals and other social interactions are distributed to individuals, locations in a different way. Therefore, it is of great importance to understand the family in its cooperative manner.

In line with this, Diyanet also gives the central domain to the family. The young population already exists, but has no motivation to participate in the production process because this generation does *not know its culture and values to strengthen its bonds with society and nation.* Diyanet argues that modern education and global doctrines *motivate* youth with *personal interest by ignoring their contribution to general social benefits.* This situation influences not only the unemployment rate in society but also *moral emptiness*, both of which can be learned within relations and conflicts in the family (Çiftçi, 2009: 6). Dwelling on the question of how subjects are motivated to join national development programs, womanhood gains its vital meaning by motherhood and wifehood.

2   True Womanhood and Unmanageable Fields of Government

"The true" is generated by falsifying. Likewise, true womanhood is produced and employed by describing wrong womanhood in public speeches and official publications. Obviously, new cultural language, imposing correct codes of conduct, has taken the place of political language (Bora, 2014: 56–57). Under the roof of the progressive fathers of the early Republic, "true" womanhood was brought up as the daughters of the *paternal*-Republic,

> because fathers were far more educated than mothers, and they were the representatives of modernity in the household, their influence and

support in the shaping of new women were very important. The social milieus they provided in the household were shared by their daughters and very much valued.

ILYASOĞLU AND DURAKBAŞA, 2001: 197

In a similar vein, as Fatmagül Berktay states that national consciousness was awakened by national actors seeking a civilised way to cultivate the "ideal woman" (2012: 106). The national fathers took responsibility for the modernity project, but the woman should be well-educated without demanding freedom outside the moral limits and boundaries in modernisation (Berktay, 2012: 106).[5] Therefore, the "new woman" of the early Republic was described "modern but virtuous" in order to determine to what extent modernity and tradition should be merged with new womanhood (Bora, 2014: 60–61; İlyasoğlu and Durakbaşa, 2001: 196). The modernity of the early Republic did not promise liberation for the woman. Like today, "the area of clothing and body care was also where women could challenge the father's or the husband's authority over their bodies" (İlyasoğlu and Durakbaşa, 2001: 199). Likewise, oral history studies with early Republican women illustrate that "new women" of the early Republic were intelligent, smart, hardworking, strong, honest, and self-sacrificing for being good mothers, wives, and housewives (Bora, 2010: 60–63, İlyasoğlu and Durakbaşa, 2001: 200–201).

National solidarity was a driving force to encourage the woman to participate in public life, but she should not forget her family duties. The new woman of the early Republic was sacrificing to her family life as well, but the context was different; namely, the woman was expected to manage her public integration and representation in parallel with successfully managing her family duties (Berktay, 2012: 109). Thereby, under the fearful shadow of the "patronage father", a modern Turkish woman was built by republican virtues, such as "virtuous good wives, dedicated mothers and modest housewives" (Cindoğlu, 1997: 255). Therefore,

> 'familialization' was crucial to the means whereby personal capacities and conducts could be socialized, shaped, and maximized in a manner that accorded with the moral and political principles of liberal society. The languages of the regulatory strategies, the terms within which they

---

5 With modernity, the extended family tradition shifted authority from father to brother (Berktay, 2012; Sirman, 2005; İlyasoğlu and Durakbaşa, 2001;Sancar, 2014; Kandiyoti, 1987). The daughter of the father surely would grow up to be the modern woman of the Republic with the title of the wife or the mother of privileged modern men.

> thought of themselves, the ways in which they formulated their problems and solutions, were not merely ideological; they made it possible and legitimate to govern the lives of citizens in new ways. In doing so, they actually brought new sectors of reality into existence, new problems and possibilities for personal investment as well as for public regulation. If the familialization of society worked, it was because it both established its political legitimacy and commanded a level of subjective commitment from citizens, inciting them to regulate their own lives according to its terms.
>
> ROSE, 1999: 128

It is clear that when the culture constructs the woman in tandem with politics by taking advantage of her natural skills and moral norms, the life and politics benefit from these natural skills by producing new roles and meanings. Motherhood, for example, serves as a category. I think this specific category needs to be evaluated with reference to population, instead of individual status. It is said that "new technological strategies for monitoring corporeal and dividuated (data-defined) populations, coupled with the imperatives of accountability and security, lead to new panopticons of surveillance" (Nadesan, 2008: 215). However, the family is a taken-for-granted domain to reproduce subjects, to teach moral values, and to bring them up as good and hardworking 'citizens' for the well-being of the population and nation. To do so, politics and culture aim to stimulate the woman through motherhood by raising the question of security and risks out of the family. The love and loyalty of the mother become instruments of power in order to bring to light the safety of the family, and to prevent potential criminal subjects from growing up with a lack of maternal love and concerns. This point is important to explore that motherhood offers an ambivalent angle as 'dispositifs' of security.

2.1 *The New Definition of Womanhood*

The general enthusiasm about traditions and family cooperation, one way or another, found its correspondence in society because motherhood is brought to the fore in a magniloquent way, as if womanhood could gain its virtue through motherhood alone. Given that womanhood as a gender role is achieved with marital status, true motherhood needs a sophisticated performance measured by reproductive skills related to motherhood, pregnancy, abortion, contraceptive methods, and caesarean section. Running parallel with this, the emotional investments involved with being a true woman are exalted and rewarded by social assessments and happiness. This would be depicted in ways such as *crowned* womanhood (Piyade, 2014: 20).

When reading state regulations on the woman's sexuality and reproduction in the context of neoliberal governmentality, as Foucault points out, it is seen that there are not only restrictions on sexuality and the traditional social order, but are, as Nancy Fraser suggests, an "emancipatory promise" (Aslan and Gambetti, 2011: 130). The emancipatory promise is the learned helplessness to cope with micro-dominations and interventions in hopes of having social protection and security along with subjection to the norms of society (Fraser, 2012: 12–13). In a way, economic and political necessities lead individuals to voluntarily obey the rules to achieve or reach emancipation, which is actually restricted freedom for civil society and individuals intrinsically representing the market and self-entrepreneurs of this market (Dardot and Laval, 2013). That is why understanding neoliberalism through the lens of Foucault helps us consider the reconstruction of gendered, racialised, or classed subjectivities (Larner, 2000b: 19–20). It seems that the restructuring process of subjectivities enables us to see that a woman's subjection in itself is not the result or expectation of biopolitics, but aims at governing, regulating, and conducting the female body through reaching the internal world of the woman. For this, Ruth Miller is incisive:

> If we place sexual and reproductive legislation at the center of subject formation, and understand political activity as biological passivity – then we need to re-think this analysis. Rather than understanding men as the norm and women as artificial facsimiles of men, it makes far more sense in a biopolitical framework to understand women as the norm and men as their copies. It is the womb that has become the predominant biopolitical space, it is women's bodily borders that have been displaced onto national ones, and it is women who have taken the concept of consent to its logical conclusion.
> MILLER, 2007: 149

The matter of consent is to unsettle our perceptions and our acceptances regarding everyday expectations from the woman's bodily performances. The woman's bodily borders are placed in the private sphere, that is, family. Her borders must be protected for the sake of the social honour of the man as well as the nation, which are actually gendered forces of biopower, pushing the woman into dark confessions, meaningless tediousness, and facile existential questions (Leite, 2013: 10). In brief, the woman and her relations are accepted as commodities and therefore their bodies are constructed as objects of control (Leite, 2013: 10).

On the one hand, consent is necessary to be a good mother; on the other hand, the emotions against the other should be reconstructed in order to formulate neoliberal necessities in the context of risky society and questions of security. For this twofold expectation from the woman as a national project, "compassionate mothers", who seek security for their children, are emphasised. These mothers are expected to provide security by applying for specific conservative discourses revolving around family and societal values. They are security moms, as a new element of a neoliberal female subject (Grewal, 2006: 27). The idea behind the context of "security moms" should be clear: The security of public realms belongs to the state, but in the private sphere mothers are responsible for bringing up good subjects for the security of the nation.

As a neoliberal output, the state does not promise to protect everyone. Therefore, leaning on religious practices, the mothers – not women – are exalted and sacralised regarding their responsibility to support social security. That is to say, even if women themselves are not protected, they are used as security dispositifs to govern subjects by telling them how bad the public and external world is. With motherhood, the neoliberal aim seeking the development of self-security mechanisms finds a way to prevail in the internal worlds of individuals. Additionally, motherhood serves as a great governmental apparatus of disciplinary and sovereign power with the help of religious and traditional meanings of reproduction and its domestic position (Grewal, 2006: 28–30). Mothers are basically the mentors of not only the physical growth of their children, but they are also responsible for the internalisation of gender roles and other social duties:

> From a variety of political sources come suggestions that there are crises of "self-esteem", drug use, eating disorders, bodily mutilation, suicide. While some of the same considerations are raised in regard to boys, the discourse around the girls is alarmist and crisis-laden and thus creates a moral panic that represents parents and especially mothers as protecting subjects.
>
> GREWAL, 2006: 33

With easy access to the internet, the neoconservative imaginary of family and society is under threat because of terrorist attacks, gays, lesbians, and feminists, who are regarded as deviants. The discourse of safety became a very effectual governmental apparatus in order to stimulate especially self-care technologies (Grewal, 2006: 35). Mothers become surveillance (Grewal, 2006). On the other hand, the gendered logic of masculine protection wants to see submissive women and children under men's authority at home (Young, 2003: 2). Even if the mother is defined as an entrepreneur and the family itself is based on teamwork, the persistent problem is that womanhood is always reduced to motherhood. Therefore, discussions about reproduction, motherhood, and family are not restricted to high politics. Furthermore, TV series/programmes, news about marriage, family, and motherhood have played a key role in showing how to be a woman, and the different criteria of womanhood as to what makes good female subjects because

> the family was an ideological mechanism for reproducing a docile labour force, for exploiting the domestic labour of women under the guise of love and duty, for maintaining the patriarchal authority of men over the household. The notion of the family as a voluntary arrangement – entered into out of love, suffused by positive emotions, naturally wishing to have and to cherish its children, the site of self-realization for mothers and of mutual regard and protection of family members – was an ideology that disguised the oppressive relations within this intimate sphere, and the social and economic coercion upon women to enter into family life and motherhood.
> ROSE, 1999: 26

To illustrate, a happy family life means success and a bright future. It is systematically said that *the main enemy of this happiness is selfishness, which is poison against respect and love in the family. Emotional and religious attachments to the values make individually bearable against the difficulties and sacrifice herself / himself*. However, *pleasure-seeking on earth makes one selfish, and does not bear any difficulties and sacrifice* (Arslan, 2014: 32–33; Dönmez, 2014: 14–17; Sönmez, 2016: 26–27). Thus, *social motherhood is a dimension, an unprecedented feature, so motherhood does not require special training. The woman is a mother until death – no matter if she has a child or not* (Sönmez, 2016: 26–27).

Womanhood would be regarded as a kind of activity to implement new roles and responsibilities, which are determined according to needs because the woman is an artist of life (yaşam sanatçısı) (Yenen, 2009: 39). However, it is believed that *the woman cannot be a good mother, good wife, and good colleague at the same time, which is "superwoman syndrome". Only motherhood can make a woman feel stronger, but this does not mean that woman can succeed at both a career and motherhood. The working woman in the family brings about psychological and physical exhaustion. The woman's desire to achieve anything destroys the family as well as social life. Being a woman of the home and a mother of children provides unprecedented satisfaction. No other job or career can substitute this* (Yenen, 2009: 37–39).

In a similar vein, another article in Diyanet's journal states that a *working woman is torn between mothering and working. However, a non-working woman can invest her energy only in her family and children*. It is argued that *the woman is allowed to carve out a career unless she forgets her responsibilities based on her gender role. The insistence on having career and family life causes only burn out and guilt. Throughout her gendered socialisation the woman takes on different roles, but motherhood has the highest priority, whose vital influence cannot be replaced by kindergartens* (Özüdoğru-Erdoğan, 2016: 26–27). It seems that the woman's different socialisations and roles are implicitly underestimated and not found realistic. This has left woman socially alone. In a way, judgemental masculine discourse and pertinent discursive practices have been domineeringly overstretched, and these discourses make out the ways in which omnipresent knowledge-power crosses through minds. Knowledge-power about motherhood is produced through the proficiency and expertise of the likes of doctors, presidents, teachers, or even the elderly through their experiences (Rose and Miller, 1992: 188). The reason why all these elements of knowledge-power act in concert for the consent of the woman to "have it all" regarding family, children, happiness, and career is in discordance with new womanhood in post-2002 Turkey because conservative ideals need to restrict these wills and motives to "have-it-all" in line with its own political and economic interests (Rottenberg, 2014). That is to say, competition in Turkey is regulated according to the moral system embedded in the marketisation of values. Foucault observes in this context that "the great fantasy is the idea of a social body constituted by the universality of wills. Now the phenomenon of the social body is the effect not of a consensus but of the materiality of power operating on the very bodies of individuals" (Foucault, 1980b: 55).

Based on Diyanet's verdict on womanhood, a source of knowledge-power has been facilitated for biopolitics. For example, as a reflection of this religious knowledge on earth, pro-media, pro-leaders and pro-whatever pursue what Recep Tayyip Erdoğan characterises as the truth on religion, family, values and relevant sins. It should be clear that biopower is contradictory power (Bell, 2006: 393). It is a form of monitoring so insidious that one cannot notice whether it is conservative or progressive, or its religious traps (Bell, 2006: 393). The monitoring mechanisms on families, marriages, children, mothers, and wives govern and conduct individuals as ideal subjects around stimulating values and norms (Bayraktar, 2011). This monitoring, as well as everyday surveillance, has taken the form of moralisation and normalisation that begins from the moment of birth to school, the army and so on. Additionally, women and children are the focal points for monitoring the population and individuals' perceptions because under patriarchal authority and paternal heads, they are more exposed to change and transformation (Bell, 2006: 393). Therefore, with the *innate features of womanhood, the name of tolerance and forgiveness* is mother, which is the name of education kneaded with patience, and *the model of mother in the family is the future of society in microcosm* (Demirkan, 2007: 48–49).

Correspondingly, according to Diyanet, *the moral standpoint in life is related to emotions* (Koytak, 2004: 21). *Patience makes people cling to life. Moreover, it moves away, rebelling against living conditions and social duties. Patience against troubles is an exam measuring trust in God and joy for maintaining daily life*(Bayraktar-Karahan, 2016: 8–9). *The mother invests these emotions in the family; mothers impart self-confidence and morality in children. These emotions are a reminder of God by pointing to social belonging* (Kurt, 2016: 21). *Maternal affection is the way the individual learns the feelings and sense of belonging that are the source of happiness. However, individualism and personal success are aimed at the contemporary world* (Çekin, 2009: 14). *This individualistic seeking is what selfish mothers have done, who do not take a back seat in pleasure and satisfaction whilst raising the children and maintaining family life* (Koytak, 2004: 18–21).

Mehmet Müezzinoğlu, as the ex-Minister of Health, strengthened the political burden on the woman with these statements:

> Motherhood will never be abandoned; it is a career that will exist until the end of humanity's existence. Motherhood is an indisputable career. It's a career that men cannot have. It's never arguable. Motherhood is a career and a sacred career.
> HÜRRIYET, 02 January 2015

Indeed, I argue that motherhood should be taken into consideration as a category pertaining to the population. This category is determined by the female sex and her reproductive role. However, the crucial point is that motherhood belongs to the private sphere, and mothers are regarded as responsible for education in family school, which are actually the duty of public institutions. Motherhood acquires public meaning out of the private. Hence, it is worth questioning how the private sphere turns into the public through motherhood? How does motherhood come into the state's interest? In order to respond to these questions, I strongly suggest that motherhood should be realised as a population category.

My argument regarding motherhood as a population category may be reinforced by legal family regulations and family law, which manage the conflicts and violence that constitute basic threats to part of the woman. Family law and the relevant regulations aim to make the woman's conditions more secure;

this motivation ties the woman down to the family by means of population policies. According to Fatmagül Berktay, the regulations regarding marriage and family are the way in which power finds itself able to shape societal goals (2012: 102). In a similar vein, Sara Ahmed suggests reading these regulations by means of emotions to manage the crises in the population. She underlines fears and security in order to comprehend the focus of family regulations:

> It is through announcing a crisis in security that new forms of security, border policing and surveillance become justified. We only have to think about how narratives of crisis are used within politics to justify a 'return' to values and traditions that are perceived to be under threat. However, it is not simply that these crises exist, and that fears and anxieties come into being as a necessary effect of that existence. Rather, it is the very production of the crisis that is crucial. To declare a crisis is not 'to make something out of nothing': such declarations often work with real events, facts or figures (as we can see, for example, in how the rise in divorce rates is used to announce a crisis in marriage and the family)... To announce a crisis is to produce the moral and political justification for maintaining 'what is' (taken for granted or granted) in the name of future survival.
> AHMED, 2014: 76–77

Therefore, motherhood as a category of the population needs to carry specific features to help the family cope with crises. As Diyanet says, it is believed that *weak maternal feelings cause family ties to decay.* What causes *weak maternal feelings are the results of misunderstanding social movements based on sexual freedom and feminism.* To put it simply, *weak family ties are the result of the woman's freedom, as are other social problems like drug abuse, the degeneration of values, violence, single parenthood, divorce, alienation and identity crises* (Demirkan, 2007: 49). Despite Diyanet's comments on sexual freedom, there was never a struggle for sexual freedom in Turkey in the commonly understood sense of youth gravitating towards commune life in lieu of family life; instead, the 1960s youth of Turkey made demands for a more egalitarian family structure. That is to say, the youth in Turkey have always problematised the lack of public consciousness, which makes the social and political inclusion of the woman and the youth more likely.

The family was not underestimated with the social upheaval of the 1960s and 70s. Indeed, it was with the introduction of neoliberalism, which began via the authoritarian coup d'état in 1980 that this sense of loyalty first started to yield to individualism, which was then re-politicised as global liberty seeking (Aytaç, 2015: 13–17). As a result, the rise of identity politics, in general, gave

Islamists a new platform from which to oppose seculars. Islamists brought new anti-conduct demands instead of family planning, monogamy, and state marriage (in lieu of polygamy and religious marriage) (Aytaç, 2015; Göle, 2016). Looking at these demands, the reinforcement of Islamists within the neoliberal era inevitably needs to transform and convince the woman of the rights of the man and manhood based on religious knowledge. Nevertheless, what I am interested in is that with the rise of neoliberalism in the 1980s the empowerment of the woman and women's solidarity politically and economically gave a new impetus to family and social relations. Therefore, I argue that estrangement from family life has been never at stake in Turkey, although it is true that women have become less likely to remain in inegalitarian and oppressive family and marriage situations.

In addition, contraception is a discipline and biological surveillance through which sexual freedom is restricted by making her responsible for her reproductive control. Sexuality cannot be dependent on personal freedom because it must have rules and roles based on heterosexuality (Foucault, 2003a: 251–252). Likewise, neoliberal progression wants to govern all bodies in general and the female body in particular. In order to melt patriarchy and neoliberalism into the same pot, either punishment against the disobedient woman or rewards for the docile woman must be employed. I shall show some details about these brutal facts in chapter four, but now new contextual possibilities need to be highlighted here in order to explain the political and social focus on motherhood. Indeed, I would like to take it a step further and say that womanhood creates great tools to effectively reconstruct society. However, first of all, the woman should realise her social power not only within the limits of motherhood but as a free individual. For example, as Diyanet indicates, compassion is learned from mothers. Missing compassion and lacking humane sentiment bring about murder, corruption and robbery. Therefore,

> the family aiming to raise compassionate individuals should be reinforced by social policies based on basic social values because regarding the order of the compassionate individual, societal risk perception continuously increases and the management of these risks becomes challenging.
> ÇAPÇIOĞLU, 2015: 33

In this sense, I strongly suggest that the new state regulations and interventions generated from the woman's reproductive skills ought to be comprehended in tandem with neoliberal rationality in Turkey. Especially, the emphasis on natural births and the issue of abortion needs to be seen as a reminder of motherhood for the above-mentioned reasons.

2.2 Awakening the Sense of Motherhood

Relations among women, and relations between the woman and society intensify with motherhood. A woman after becoming a mother is *crowned* and exalted. Patriarchal control over the woman and political control over the female body tacitly borrow from the sublime and spiritual truth (Leite, 2013: 3–4). Womanhood becomes defunct without motherhood; therefore, contraceptive methods are, in a way, seen as anti-motherhood, and invokes imagery of sex only for personal pleasure, and therefore connoting selfishness in a woman (Leite, 2013: 8). In a way, it may be said that:

> Maternal mortality touches upon politically contentious issues that are often resisted by conservative networks supporting neoliberal control over public health sector reforms, principles, and practices. This debate deconstructs hegemonic feminists' rejection of motherhood while also acknowledging the importance of non-motherhood to motherhood debates. Non-motherhood as the other represents a move away from patriarchal values and creates a social reality that uses something else as a parameter.
> LEITE, 2013: 2

Womanhood is both bodily and intrinsically emphasised in the context of the sacred motherhood. These features in reference to motherhood provide new political forms to make out the loyalty and indulgence of the woman (Berktay, 2012: 119). In the Foucauldian literature, neoliberal subjectivity denotes self-governance, self-esteem, around social honour; and more importantly, neoliberal subjects must be self-sufficient against social and natural difficulties and catastrophe. Maternal subjectivity, too, is reconstructed when pursuing more self-sufficiency and endurance. In line with this, Emine Erdoğan, the wife of Mr. Erdoğan, says that:

> Birth, one of the greatest miracles in the world, is closely associated with civilization. However, women cannot live that special experience today in its more natural way. So much so that it has turned into a medical operation ... every unnecessary intervention affects the body's hormone release. A mother, who is not subjected to any medicine or intervention, will give birth under the influence of natural hormones and will be able to establish a strong bond with her baby as soon as she gives birth.
> Presidency of the Republic of Turkey, 27 September 2017

The rise of governmental demands on natural births – and in parallel, the increasing awareness of natural births – is a consequence of increasing political and social investments into natural mothering and birth practices. In a way, mothering and maternal subjectivity are reconstructed and reinforced through the felt pain of birth (Mack, 2016: 48). This is " 'masochistic motherhood', an ideology of mothering that naturalizes an idealized conception of motherhood on the female body and invites women to participate in self-renunciation through service as good mothers and citizens" (Mack, 2016: 49). That is to say, the discourse supported by knowledge-power is the very important way in which the woman's enlightenment, self-optimisation, and self-actualisation are ultimately tied up with her pain from the natural birthing process (Mack, 2016: 49).

Noel Ashley Mack somewhat apprehends this natural birthing and critiques of caesarian sections

> as a technology of self: a mechanism that invites the maternal subject to govern from within and ascend to a certain level of perfection and empowerment through the performance of a certain number of operations on her body, soul, thoughts, mind, and conduct. The assertion that the maternal subject must perform a kind of mental hygiene to access wisdom or empowerment is a key characteristic of several of the video narratives.
>
> MACK, 2016: 54

Maternal pain and patriarchy in a way naturalise the woman's self-victimisation. Likewise, the private sphere considers them woman-mothers, woman-wives, and so on. The woman is motivated by maternal feelings and family, childbearing, and care for the husband became the indicators of her endurance, capability, and self-sufficiency, which are awarded not only in micro- but also in macro-politics.

Beginning with the AKP's suggestions on increasing population growth rates and methods of giving birth, the discussion of caesarian sections should bring us to the state of being self-sufficient, which neoliberal subjectivity absolutely wants to achieve. Namely, birthpain seems to be a stimulation of self-realisation and self-enlightenment of the woman herself. It is noteworthy that state actors have weighed in on how to give birth. For example, regarding the widespread employment of caesarian sections, Mr. Erdoğan also said, "I am a prime minister who is against caesarean births". He also framed abortion as criminal in the same speech by drawing a comparison with the Uludere massacre – also known as the Roboski Airstrike – which was a military action that claimed 34 civilian lives. In other words, Mr. Erdoğan meant that he considers abortion to be murder. Additionally, he remarked, "you either kill a baby in the mother's womb or you kill it after birth. There's no difference"(Hürriyet Daily News, 26 May 2012).

In Turkey, abortion is legal during the first 10 weeks of pregnancy. The woman's consent is required but if the woman is married, the husband's consent is also required. I want to move this discussion beyond abortion and women's rights towards sexual freedom because I think that abortion is a right and women should decide if they want to have a baby or not, and in which way they give birth. In this context, what I am interested in is how the state's rationality is reluctant to support abortion even in the case of pregnancy by rape. The ex-mayor of Ankara Melih Gökçek's response to protests against a government proposal to ban abortion, which employed the slogan "my body, my decision", are clear:

> The body belongs to you, but life belongs to God. If you attempt to curate [life] by having an abortion, this is called murder ... [Regarding pregnancy by rape] find and punish those who rape her but what is the guilt of the child in her womb?! The state takes care of the child, brings it up, and even the child does not [need to] know this. How can you take the right to life from the child's hand?
>
> HABERTÜRK, 2 June 2012

Mr. Gökçek added, "if someone needs to die, why does the child die?! There may be [emotional] pain, but this pain does not legitimise abortion" (HaberTürk, 2 June 2012). The woman's initiative regarding her bodily rights and reproduction are insultingly excluded by Mr. Gökçek's words. This is problematic in itself, but even more problematic is the connection between this disregard for the physical emotional health of women and children and the previously discussed campaign to increase the birth rate. It is conservatively argued that pain is an indicator of responsibility, power, wisdom, and pleasure; therefore, bodily pain through birth brings about mental hygiene and an updating of the personality to find the woman's true role (Mack, 2016: 58–63). Nevertheless, it would be good to criticise the conservative expectation of bodily pain as a means to actualise what is 'natural', since if a woman is not ready, the consequences of medical intervention may be riskier.

That is to say, the priorities of ideal womanhood are firstly to be a mother and then a good mother. To be so, the woman first needs to gain awareness of her nature, and should know how to rationally use and promote her maternal skills with this stimulation of emotions. For this, the governmental rationality of daily life implicitly draws attention to the happiness of having children and the specialty of being a mother. For example, being a mother was framed as a "mystic journey of the individual actor" by depoliticising the woman's hardworking, self-sacrificing emotional exploitation and bodily pain in labour (Mack, 2016: 48). Ashley Noel Mack (2016) analyses this in terms of self-actualisation and self-empowerment through the feeling of bodily pain. For her, the endurance of bodily pain leads to psychological empowerment against the other difficulties related to the family and daily life, and this is about self-sufficiency, self-governance and self-making (Mack, 2016). What I find crucial in Mack's analysis is that she draws attention to "collective consciousness", which points to the "cultural rationalisation of self-governance" in neoliberal governmentality (Mack, 2016: 52).

In addition, the collective consciousness provides a vital bond between sacrificing motherhood through the common pains of womanhood and the function of political technologies and self-technologies through mothering norms. From this point on, neoliberal entrepreneurship joins the female body and the woman's agency in order to produce not only the new subjects of the population but also knowledge of homogeneous experiences about womanhood (Mack, 2016). It would be good to say that self-transformation through naturalising self-sufficiency paves the way for the transformation of society through motherhood (Mack, 2016: 52–53).

Overall, bodily pain is depicted as a way in which emotional pain is narrated as a must of good womanhood. The physical and psychological endurance of the woman is described in a competitive manner, which blinds one to the fact that being a mother is reduced to one's capacity for patience, and to endure the pain of childbirth. Indeed, daring to have a baby inevitably produces a productive domain to easily devalue or revalue womanhood through the maternity status of the woman. Moreover, natural birth and other medical knowledge regarding female nature aggravate 'the pain' of better integrating the woman into neoliberal expectations. However, caesarian sections are technically more profitable and quicker than natural birth, and may also benefit doctors, but I think if there is no stepback from capitalism, the emphasis on natural birth and abortion are still tactical interventions of neoliberalism that have strategic goals. And yet, while ideal womanhood is achieved through the 'sacred hormones of mothers', the other side of reality pushes some facts into *the periphery*.

2.3 Some Facts: Adultery, Homosexuality, Prostitution, Brothels and the Like

According to Penal Law No. 5237, prostitution is punished as an offence against public morality and family life. However, the reasons and conditions for prostitution are not seriously considered. Ultimately, prostitution is culturally seen as a masculinised mistake (Sancar, 2014: 239). In relation to this, according to social research (Konda, 2012a), two questions about homosexuality show that 10 % of society does not have any problem with freedom of sexual orientation. When asked whether homosexuality is crime or not, 11 % of the responses say that homosexuality should not be a crime; 32% demand the severest punishment for homosexuals; 22% believe they should be sentenced to prison; 29% suggest they should undergo an "extra societal cure". By comparison, 8% of respondents considered adultery not to be a crime at all, while others believed it should be a misdemeanour. Nevertheless, it is noteworthy that civil partnership is not accepted and seen as a shame by 90% of respondents (Konda, 2012a).

The value of honour is not only related to the purity of the female body and the woman's sexuality and her public behaviours, but honour belongs to the private sphere and intimate feelings as well. Love is a means by which to channel romantic desires towards heterosexual family life. Otherwise, 'forbidden love' points to 'deviancy of sexual relations', which are directly perceived as a threat against the family values of society (Cürül and Dönmez, 2013; Çitak and Tur, 2008; Parla, 2001). This being so, secret affairs and other forms of sexuality are outside the norm and are dangerous, so they need to be moved away from the family order. For this, there is a Misdemeanours Law (Law No. 5326) to protect the social order, public morality, public health, the environment, and economic order. Various acts of misconduct are roughly classified under specific articles, including gambling, drunkenness, noise violations, and inconvenience. However, the definitions of these misdemeanours are open-ended to signal a behaviour or case as inconvenient and a threat against public order and morality.

To illustrate, adultery was a criminal act between 1926 and 1998, and there was an attempt in 2005 to re-criminalise it in order to prevent marital infidelity and to enforce gender equality, but this did not come to pass (Çitak and Tur, 2008: 461; Bianet, 22 February 2018). It returned to the political agenda in 2017–2018, this time as a reminder of moral values with the aim of quelling sexual harassment and abuse, which were on the rise. Mr. Erdoğan gave a speech about adultery in which execution, terror crimes, and child abuse are all mentioned in an interconnected and interwoven context:

> The issue of execution is particularly important for us in terms of terror crimes. Working on the death sentence, terror crimes, and similar issues can come up with a constitutional arrangement. I think it would be appropriate to reconsider adultery in this context. This society has a different position on moral values. In the process of the European Union, this is a self-criticism; we made a mistake in this matter. Harassment, etc., perhaps we should consider within the same scope. It is important for Turkey to bring up different positions among the majority of Western countries. On the other hand, the issue of execution is important in relation to terrorism. Child abuse is never forgettable, ignorable. At the moment, six of our colleagues have begun looking into the subject, and we will quickly come to a conclusion about the issue and then move it to the parliament with a legal arrangement.
>
> BIANET, 22 February 2018

Values around adultery are a source of common morality. Furthermore, the discursive connection between adultery, terror crimes, and the death sentence are very important to see the state's point regarding public peace and its relation to sexuality. On the one hand, terror crimes awaken anger against those who brutally disrupt society and security; on the other hand, the same anger is directed to sexual relations outside of marriage. More importantly, the reasons for terror attacks, child abuse, and sexual harassment are evaluated and solved in the same moral package. Additionally, the ban on adultery enforced an anti-feminist approach because "some marginal women" were seen as guilty in adultery cases (Çitak and Tur, 2008: 461). That is to say, "extra-marital relations and sexual freedom" bring about moral degeneration because adultery is "something unacceptable". This affects the function and meaning of the family and also it is religiously forbidden (Çitak and Tur, 2008: 463).

Article No. 441 of Turkish Penal Law, which was abolished in 1996, stated that a husband who was involved with a woman would be sentenced to imprisonment for a period of six months to three years. The same punishment was given to a (single) woman who knew that the man was married. In 1998, Article No. 440 of the same law was abolished, which stated that a sentence of six months to three years of imprisonment would be imposed on a wife who cheated on her husband. The same punishment would be imposed on the man she was involved with her (Bianet, 22 February 2018). New bans and limits were proposed to replace the two abolished articles, but the problem is that as adultery is seen in the context of sexual freedom, it denotes the possibility of other lifestyles. Likewise, to include homosexual relations or civil partnerships in such regulations would be deemed as disobedience towards 'the order of things', which in turn becomes a security question.

In order to legitimise the necessity of values and traditions, disobedience against societal norms is presented as a threat in reference to motherhood and the family; additionally, the family itself as a private sphere is marked as a source of societal risk in order to highlight its *others* (Ahmed, 2014: 76; Nadesan, 2008: 66). In other words, "gay, sexually amoral, irresponsible, lazy, unpatriotic [citizens] are constituted as 'others' in need of surveillance and intervention in the neoconservative and religious imaginations" (Nadesan, 2008: 111). In this context, the family and womanhood become sources of social and mental hygiene by building moral conduct over "prostitution, homosexuality, obscenity, alcohol consumption, betting and gaming, censorship in the theatre, abortion and divorce" (Rose, 1999: 228). It is well known that cleaning is the responsibility of the woman, in private and public. Similarly, environmental and mental hygiene are asked of a woman as well.

Religious and traditional values need to be understood as a guideline to reorder, regulate, and manage the population by gathering all population segments – religious and ethnic minorities, women, men, and children – around common sense and sensitivities on the assumption that every standard subject will have the same priorities, i.e., everyone ought to want to have a family and children, stay together in safety and happiness. Taking for granted the loose and flirtatious man's sexuality as an undisciplined natural feature of manhood, the issue of happiness and security ascribes the woman a "key role". It is normally expected that woman easily and immediately adopt externally imposed moral values and intend to carry them forward to the next generation (Çitak and Tur, 2008: 464). This is a kind of gendered division of labour assigning who carries moral values. Therefore, while the woman acts according to accepted values, the masculine structure keeps it under surveillance.

However, there is a dilemma that requires highlighting, which is that of sex trafficking. The trafficking of women and prostitution are underrepresented in the missions of women's organisations. The position of the state in this area is limited to control health policy, which cares only preventing infectious diseases.

In line with conservative implementations, brothels in some provinces were closed for reasons of morality. Some women continued to work in other provinces, but those who remained in the affected provinces were pushed out of legal working conditions. According to Kemal Ördek, an advisor for Red Umbrella Sexual Health and Human Rights Association, illegal prostitution causes increasing violence and discrimination against sex workers, and in all respects, their exploitation increases. For Ördek, the long-term aim of closing brothels is the criminalisation of the sex industry. At least in recent years, for him, interventions confirm this (Bianet, 9 May 2017). Here, a moralistic view is more dominant than an evidence-based and need-based perspective. The rapid closure of the brothels and the growth of the informal sex market actually clarify the fact of that public safety and the safety of working women are being eroded at every level (Bianet, 9 May 2017). In this moralistic vein, sex workers provide services and to satisfy secret desires. Likewise, homosexuality exists, and nothing makes it disappear because if there are power relations, there must be a counter force to unfold the facts excluded by the reality that we see.

Overall, the family provides a space to make surveillance and correct sexual behaviours. Like schools, the family serves as a public institution to educate and discipline the individuals of the population by correction and redirecting abnormal tendencies to judge right and wrong through those norms (Foucault, 2003b: 57–58). Attempts to normalise subjects and behaviours take place through social practices in the context of framed rationality (Butler, 2004b; Foucault, 2003b). When the aim of normalisation meets Islamic norms, this paves the way for conservative measures and barriers in order to determine forbidden and permissible practices on sexual intimacy and pleasures. Family thereby becomes responsible for conducting and regulating all these normalisation processes, ranging from the determinant of the (gendered) authority to the sexual freedom of the woman.

3   The Last Sight on Family

3.1   *Consulting Services for the Betterisation of Family*

According to the 10th Development Plan (2014–2018), the family institution constitutes the core of society and holds individuals and society together. Individuals who grow up with love and mutual understanding are the foundation of a strong society. The 10th Development Plan states that with migration and urbanisation, an erosion of cultural values has increased. Moreover, communication between family members decreased, divorces increased, and the family institution began to weaken. Therefore, national action and development plans seek to arrive at basic objectives in the direction of the established problems of their program goal, which are:

i.   Protecting family welfare and strengthening the family institution
ii. Strengthening intergenerational solidarity
iii. Harmonising work and family life

iv. Increasing the total fertility rate above the regeneration rate (T.C. Kalkınma, 2015: 1).

The adjoining state institutions and civil society are encouraged to work together by pointing out the importance of the family according to their field of expertise. There are general suggestions for happy marriages. These suggestions are mostly for women. Islamic principles basically point that *the woman needs to know obedience and docility, while the man knows that the woman is entrusted of God* to him (Uysal, 1999). Otherwise, conflicts and violence inevitably cause the family unit to disintegrate. In order to prevent this, consulting services work under the control of Diyanet, the Ministry of Health, and the Ministry of Family and Social Policy. The other ministries indirectly support the family unit by encouraging the spouses to stay in family cooperation. Violence Prevention and Monitoring Centers were established by Law No.6284, and are important consulting services provided by the state. These centres are open full-time to provide empowerment and supportive counselling, guidance, and monitoring services with the assistance of highly trained staff. Preferably, female staff members work to effectively implement preventive and protective measures. In the implementation of services, public institutions and organisations, professional organisations such as universities, local governments, non-governmental organisations, the private sector may cooperate. Therefore, services for the victims of violence are carried out under the coordination of different units of these consulting centres.

Regarding people who will benefit from the services, they shall be benefitted by women, children, family members, and persons who have been subjected to unilateral and persistent follow-up. The rehabilitation services are carried out by the relevant institutions and organisations. Additionally, the Violence Prevention and Monitoring Centers prepare programmes and services for 'victims of violence' in order to resocialise women and to integrate them into social and economic development (Official Gazette, No. 29656).

There are also Family Consultancy and Guidance Offices aiming

i. To ensure that the society is properly informed about the family in terms of religion,
ii. To contribute to the protection of family structure,
iii. To provide moral support services to strengthen family members against the risks and new problem areas faced by social, economic and cultural changes,
iv. To provide religious guidance and moral support services in the institutions and organizations mentioned in the Ministry within the framework of the protocol signed with the Ministry of Family and Social Policies,

v. To contribute to the solution of the religious problems of our people especially family and family members,
vi. To work in cooperation with relevant public institutions, universities and non-governmental organizations (AIRB, 2013).

In addition to these two institutional consulting services, Family Courts seek suitable ways to promote mutual love, respect, and tolerance between family members with the aim of protecting family values. The problems that spouses and children face are determined and tackled by experts. The final decision is made on the basis of family values (AIRB 2013; Law No. 4787).

Nevertheless, it is clear that these institutions, without paying attention to the woman's problems in the family unit, insistently aim to keep members of the family in the same social cell in order to monitor micro-problems and to be able to solve these problems in a specific context. Diyanet also helps to show the spouses 'the key parts of a happy marriage' in order to develop and promote self-monitoring and self-control mechanisms in the pursuit of better problem-solving perspectives. It is important to keep in mind that Diyanet wants to reinforce the "traditional Turkish family" through Family Counseling and Guidance Offices along with the Ministry of Justice, Ministry of Family and Social Policies, and Ministry of Health (Mutluer, 2014: 11–12). Family Counseling and Guidance Offices respond to the questions and problems of family relations, parent-child relations, sexual problems, divorce, depression, abortion, and specific questions in line with Islamic motives and traditional sensitivities (Mutluer, 2014: 46).

Diyanet says that *love is not as important as we think because marriage should not be left to chance, so emotion should be tempered by reason. One should investigate prospective spouses and measure his or her values. Before marriage, dating causes degeneration and blinds reason quickly. By being patient, everyone should accept that the conflicts between spouses are normal. It is important to develop the ability to solve problems and reach consensus.* For Diyanet, *we need to know ourselves, we should know what we want, that is, self-awareness. Lack of self-confidence is a problem; we should trust our first impressions and have confidence in our values* (Akçay-Civriz, 2017: 17; Özbudun, 2014: 6–9;Demirkan, 2008: 35). *The family structure, which has changed with modernity, influenced the roles of personal culture and relations. It would be good to bear in mind that the family has a responsibility to society, and the individual to the family and society* (Beder-Şen, 2007: 39–40). Therefore, it is accepted that the family is a sacred unity in which especially children are institutionally and socially important, bridging the family members to society through the common values transmitted. Family is based on teamwork, not on a woman's choices or a man's arbitrary decisions as to whether or not to maintain family unity.

The child gains his or her personality and roles from mothers, who also organise and control the relations between children and their environment. Compassion, social and moral values are learned from mothers (Beder-Şen, 2007: 40). *Mothers are the carriers of norms. The father is the authority and with maternal love, this authority gains respect.* Thereby, *the father can govern the family in a peaceful manner* (Beder-Şen, 2007: 41; Kahraman, 2006: 21–22). *In order to struggle against violence, unfair competition, sexual display, the commoditisation of the human, and so on, children should be taught how to love and relent* (Toprak, 2006: 42).

Hence, all consulting services and suggestions repeat the same requirements and explanations for why family is important. Violence is reduced to daily life conflicts appeared between family members. Thus, I think it is questionable why violence cannot be eradicated, and women are confined to domestic home life under the family roof. With institutional booklets about 'the secrets to a healthy family life', we learn that one of the most important features of strong and healthy families is about spouses' ability to communicate in a healthy way. Healthy families are more open, clearer, and more frequently in direct contact with each other. Spouses, under ideal family relations, are not always looking for the others' flaws, and they listen to each other. Most importantly, they do not extend their resentment too much (Canel, 2012a; 2012b).

Taking all these points in the context of relations between the family and the woman, most of the burdens are undertaken by her. The family goes on the woman's emotional and physical investments.

3.2   *Divorce as an Impossible Practice*

When divorce is an issue, the relation between compassion and violence is highlighted in the name of rescuing the family. Diyanet agrees that *marriage and the family should not be a burden on woman and man, and family life should bring happiness* (Arslan, 2014: 15–16). Diyanet also is aware that *a battered woman loses the joy of living, the pressure on the ground of honour ignores that the woman has a personality and self-esteem* (Arslan, 2014: 19). Family is the *"life sphere"* (Çekin, 2006: 27), the sphere of responsibility. The Prophet Muhammed, in his last khutbah, appeals to a man that they have taken a woman as trustee of God. As much as man has a right over woman, woman has the same rights and duties over man (Yenen, 2009: 37-39). Nevertheless, whatever may come, women should not have their family honour violated. This is her fundamental duty (Yenen, 2009: 37-39). Diyanet warns that *a family is not property, but it is entrusted by God. Man and woman are mutually entrusted to each other* (Martı, 2014: 23).

According to the Turkish Civil Code (Law No. 4721), 17 is the legal age for marriage for both man and woman, but under extraordinary conditions, this could be 16. It is expected that the prospective bride[6] has the ability to distinguish between bad and good. Indeed, it is worth touching on the minimum marriage age before pointing out 'the reasons behind high-conflict divorce' because the young couples may not be ready to carry family responsibilities. Before attempting marriage, Diyanet warns about being ready for family life. Actually, I think that, taking account of the limited socialisation opportunities of young girls, marriage inevitably turns into a social and individual problem. Conservative and traditional values open up ways for violence as an archaic disciplinary method. Violence is widely seen as a common discipline method. Linking to a lack of family and especially mothering compassion, *divorce would be the main reason for the increasing rate of violence because the children cannot grow up under one family roof. The social wound, i.e., violence, is triggered by a lack of family education* (Beder-Şen, 2007: 43–45). Additionally, *divorce is a very serious social threat, opening up problems. So the collapse of the family unit is a difficult period and marriage must be correctly established* (Beder-Şen, 2005: 53–54). *The family should be approached only to solve the problems* (Beder-Şen, 2005: 54, Demirkan, 2008: 32–34). *New generations have found the meaning of life in the family* (Khutbah, 08 May 2015).

Diyanet addresses a question responded by itself: *"Why are there cameras in a Muslim society? Because cameras are a sign of being far away from religious life"* (Karslı, 2016: 8). Additionally, Diyanet claims a *"balance exam"*, which means not wanting too much. Reliance is the golden point, to find an optimum solution for both parties of the marriage. Both points of Diyanet highlight the importance of the family-based structure of society. Namely, *single life habits* cannot be *adapted to family life. Everybody should change their habits and realise their duties* (Koç, 2013: 44).

Thinking through Wendy Brown's understanding of neoliberalism and the push to have families in post-2002 Turkey together, Islam, which is an opportunity to decrease inequality and injustice due to globalisation, points to the woman as an exam-station (imtihan merkezi) (Martı, 2013: 23). Therefore, divorce is not suggested as a solution to the conflicts and violence under the family roof. Divorce is not always *salvation* because especially the woman has to cope with possible financial problems, social pressure, sexual harassment, and finding a home after divorce. *'Conscious marriage, conscious parenting'* should be encouraged in order to decrease rising divorce demands (Demirkan, 2006: 36–37; Akçay-Civriz, 2017: 17). Before making the choice to divorce, *it is suggested that couples should think twice: Are there unsolved problems? Are they*

---

6 This could be the groom as well, but in general the term connotes a girl.

really impossible to tackle? Is divorce the last resort? (Özkan, 2014). Implicitly, all courses of action remind the woman of her obligation to preserve the family. The Family Ombudsman was even approached to explain the results of the divorce and post-divorce problems on children's psychology in order not to erode the father's position in the family (HaberTürk, 12 November 2017).

Nevertheless, Diyanet states that *happiness is inside the family, not outside* (Martı, 2014: 31). If a woman does not have *fair enough reason to divorce,* she is deprived of *the blessings of paradise* (Özkan, 2014: 11). The spouses should accept their responsibilities as much as they try to advance their civil rights (Özkan, 2014: 10). There is a message for feminists as well. Feminists try to escape their responsibilities and deconstruct the social structure. The family has to have legal and moral roots. There must be consent between couples, and the promise of continuity for marriage. Maintaining the family order within marriage vows is a divine service. Otherwise, adultery increases, immorality pervades. The family needs to be started by legitimate cooperation.

Under these 'norm impositions', happiness has a definitive aim requiring an object such as family (Ahmed, 2010: 45). Therefore, a happy family life indicates success and effort. In a way, "family is a pressure point, as being necessary for a good and happy life, which in turn is how we achieve a certain orientation toward something and not others as good" (Ahmed, 2010: 46). It is important to realise the "pressure point" by observing the role of the mother in family life(Ahmed, 2010: 50–52).The gendered roles of the spouses and the definitive proximity of family life ask for a specific effort and energy in promising happiness and security. Within this happy frame, the docile homemaker assigns hard effort and labour for happiness by consenting to be good and loyal. Following consent, pride, passion, love, patience, and all motivative emotions becomes the image of a happy family (Ahmed, 2010: 50–52).

Since the family is the basic unit of society, rights and laws are shaped around the duties and rights of spouses. Family and sexual life are private issues. It is the duty of the spouses to protect the union of marriage. The state takes only measures to maintain the family itself for the formation of a healthy society (Canel, 2012a, 2012b). In this context, divorce is a case of a 'crisis' wherein the reasons for conflict between spouses should be clarified.

4   Concluding Remarks

Partha Chatterjee brings our attention to a novel and critical aspect of the "economy of power" (Chatterjee, 2004). He claims that collective identity with moral content and common values employs practical apparatuses of governmentality over a population (Chatterjee, 2004: 57). What is critical here is that the family as a basic unit of society allows manifold apparatuses to govern populations, in this case by producing the roles, generating the values and limiting the milieus of the woman. In order to set this out in full, it is important to understand why family and motherhood need to be re-understood in the context of neoliberal governmentalisation: i) family – I take it in totality, including community and national relations – is a cooperative in which emotional labour and physical endurance are regulated by imposing norms on the woman through her natural skills. To provide an "economy of power" (Chatterjee, 2004), especially subaltern classes are the target of biopolitical authority for the internal transformation of the self and its relations. ii) With the emphasis on family, individualism implicitly becomes the man's right while womanhood and the woman's rights are evaluated in terms of family and community relations. Womanhood is a norm, and her body is the main instrument to generate and protect the common values through traditional gendered knowledge and experiences. In this vein, individualism appears as a public right belonging to the man, while the woman is seen as responsible for the private sphere.

Along with this perspective, consulting services keep individuals informed about potential conflicts in the family and between spouses. Religious support for family unity perfectly provides *self-convincing mechanisms,* which are consent, faith, and destiny in order to prevent suicide, rebellion, and murder, and to reinforce endurance and patience against hardship (Subaşı, 2016: 37). Therefore, *Islam can solve and put barriers between individuals and problems with the help of traditional customs* (Subaşı, 2016: 40).

"Strong family, strong future" refers to a multi-layered reality. On the one hand, the woman should be awake to her national mission; on the other hand, the single-parent family or homosexual family cannot be at stake. Only a single form of family is endorsed, which is confirmed by religious and traditional knowledge. Equally, neoliberal modernity also wants to see this nuclear family form based on absolute gendered roles and having children. As a result, cultivating a child-centred family is the means of reaching ideal womanhood and healthy family relations. Therefore, drawing on a suffering and patient womanhood, problem-solving mechanisms being developed for couples and families take into account the possible risks of divorce, domestic violence, and abuse.

Consequently, the fact that violence affects one in three women does not provide an explanation as to whether violence is related to early marriage, but according to some field research, it is more common in such marriages (Bostan-Ünsal, 2014). Since violence eventually leads to termination of marriage, and since divorce in the conservative community is undesirable, the issue of child brides must be accepted as a categorical problem (Bostan-Ünsal, 2014: 22).

All in all, there is resistance to all norm impositions backed by religious references. Resistance is a reminder that there are other life forms apart from the heterosexual family order. For example, the Emergency Measures Groups against the Murder of Women read a manifesto in which the fact that "this life is ours" shows that:

> We have been struggling for many years so that another life is possible. We try to protect our lives every day and every moment in different forms. Now we have a couple of words to men, to the state, to government, to the president, to those who dictate how we should be living: this life is not yours, but ours! Into that life you draw your frame, there is no room for women, there is no breath. We refuse to give up our lives and ourselves!
> Sendika.org, 4 June 2016

Likewise, the 16th Feminist Night Walk on 8th March 2018 was themed again with capital letters reading, "We do not comply with your rules, we do not acquiesce, we are not silent, and we are not afraid" (Sputnik Türkiye, 8 March 2018).

CHAPTER 4

Reconsidering Violence as a Disciplinary and Regulatory Apparatus

I argue that violence is a kind of punishment, as if it were a 'result' of wrongdoing by the woman. Violence needs an object and reason to gain meaning, so to speak. The woman is the object of violence, and the reasons depend mostly on unequal gender relations. Yet, the reasons may still be changeable in line with moral values, political interests, and social order.

It has been reported that in the last decade violence against the woman has increased by 1400% (CNN Türk, 5 March 2015; HaberTürk, 6 November 2017). The rates and numbers are appallingly high, but the crucial point is that these high rates of violence have become quite normalised. Without discussing the high rates of brutal violence against women and children, its reasons and narrations focus on the woman's failures of the social and gender order. Media outlets and pictures of victims blatantly try to attract attention to why these women are raped, killed, and beaten. Bruised flesh, brutally attacked women, and bloody scenes are through a 'collective connivance' that legitimises masculine sovereignty and thus frames the issue as a private matter to be dealt with inside the family. From the point of masculine sovereignty, I argue that violence has always been an open-wound in Turkey (Sallan-Gül, 2013; Bora and Günal, 2014; Tekeli, 2011), but the rising visibility of gender-based crimes and violence should be studied as a social output deriving from political and economic inputs of manifold transformation. Violence is presented as an indispensable reality of womanhood if a woman fails to do her duty. Surely, this is still insufficient to be able to respond to the high rates of gender-based crimes, and to uphold their motivations in post-2002 Turkey.

Nevertheless, violence is related to the frustrated authority (Arendt, 1961) that surrounds womanhood in different ways and disciplines the female body and regulates her subjectivity with respect to identity formation. Therefore, it would be better to conceptualise authority as masculine sovereignty with the power of life and death over the woman. My observation of Foucauldian (masculine) sovereignty lies between the lines; that is, I intend to focus on "the process of normalising violence" with an emphasis on 'sovereignty' itself in order to decipher patriarchal impasses of gendered order (Lundgren, 2012) because sovereignty shapes everyday life through the constitutions of law and through the policing of populations. Sovereignty is demonstrated through delineation of exceptions to the rule of law and by the capacity to deny conditions necessary for life.

NADESAN, 2008: 35

Violence can be conceptually characterised as a disciplinary and regulatory *dispositif* of security. According to Giorgio Agamben, each dispositif of security desires to smoothly reconstruct subjectivities and direct them as apparatuses of the government. However, in case the functionality of these dispositifs decrease, violence as a blatant physical act emerges (Agamben, 2009: 19). He further points to

an apparatus in which a new I is constituted through the negation and, at the same time, the assumption of the old I. The split of the subject performed by the apparatus of penance resulted, therefore, in the production of a new subject, which found its real truth in the nontruth of the already repudiated sinning I. Analogous considerations can be made concerning the apparatus of the prison: here is an apparatus that produces, as a more or less unforeseen consequence, the constitution of a subject and of a milieu of delinquents, who then become the subject of new – and, this time, perfectly calculated – techniques of governance.

AGAMBEN, 2009: 20

There is a point that Agamben (2009: 21) wants us to see that dispositifs must de-subjectify and then re-subjectify the individual in order to gain their own security function. That is to say, there must be a changeable and dynamic continuity of processes of (de)subjectification. In this sense, I argue that violence as an apparatus of power reconstructs womanhood in order to render the woman as an obedient subject of public and private life. In other words, the risk of violence has a constructive impact on female subjectification. This obedience invokes authority and hierarchy through the control of freedom (Arendt, 1961). Authority or masculine sovereignty itself is not directly linked to violence because it refers to the order according to forms of authority. Therefore, I discuss masculine authority in conjunction with *the morality of power* in order to draw attention to the relationship between obedience and hierarchal structure (Khutbah, 20 February 2015a). The morality of power means that even if an authority has the power (kudret[1]) to act violently, it makes itself respected through consent and docility without resorting to violence. In other words, man has natural power (kudret) gifted by God, and if he wants, he can exert that power through violence, but his sense of morality should cause to not prefer to do so. On this point, one of the Friday Khutbahs states:

> My brothers! One of the manifestations of being a mature person and a perfect believer is being able to dominate anger ... It is not to carry more wood but water to the fire of anger. Because when one falls to his anger, his eyes become blind, the ears become deaf, reason and conscience grow out of control. The one who loses his temper is deprived of mercy and tolerance; he subverts and offends. He may even exhibit excessive behaviours that result in death. As a matter of fact, we are witnessing several negativities and examples of sorrowful images caused by anger almost every day. The devil plants the seeds of vengeance and hatred among us with its weapon of anger. Many kinships, friendships, and brotherhoods can be transformed into conflicts and fights for trivial reasons. A moment of anger takes away happiness and destroys dreams in families, business environments, and in many different areas of everyday life. The warm families are burning down with a momentary fire of anger. We are devastated by the fact that innocent wives, children, mothers and fathers, neighbours, and innocent bystanders pay the price for those defeated by anger, perhaps with their lives.
> KHUTBAH, 1 April 2016

A man should modestly recognise his power. Otherwise, the use of violence turns into an immoral choice. Equally important is that the woman should accept the man's power (kudret), and she should be afraid of her man (T.C. Başbakanlık, 2009: 130). As one of the authors says in Diyanet's journal, *the respect of the woman towards the man is the initial condition to develop healthy perceptions against the female body and womanhood.* Therefore, *perceptual transformation regarding womanhood and manhood in this respect is required, and by doing so, the man's protection may turn him virtuous* (Arslan, 2015: 39–41). Otherwise, *crimes result from failing morals and a lack of values* (Arslan, 2015: 48). Therefore, *in order to prevent crime, moral education takes precedence over the law* (Altıntaş, 2016: 101). This means that *while struggling against*

---

1 In Turkish, *Kudret* means power but this 'power' denotes ability to do specific things. Religiously, *Kudret* means God's eternal power. Güç is another word meaning power too, but it refers to physical energy and ability to resist and impact. (http://www.tdk.gov.tr).

violence and gender-based crimes, values and shame should not be forgotten. For this, *the family is the centre to solve social crises, including suicide, violence, and crimes* (Güner-Özduygu, 2016: 105–111; Altıntaş, 2016: 101–104). It is agreed that *there is no excuse for violence against women; however, it would be good to look at which women are exposed to violence alongside the reasons for it,* as Diyanet warns (Üresin, 2007: 17–18). Therefore, in the general context of Diyanet's publications, it is claimed that the rates and cases of violence should not be covered; on the contrary, it must be visible and debatable. This is because the transformation of daily life practices in the direction of Islamism becomes possible to talk about suitable dress, daily piousness and sexual politics with the help of social threats and violence against the woman (Cooper, 2008: 37).

Obedience towards authority – including the risk of violence in case of resistance – needs to be traced around the transition of power, that is, with respect to violence. This changing potentiality of power causes women to internalise violence as a component of womanhood within patriarchy, as a means to acquire the protection of a man. To illustrate, as mentioned in the second chapter, it is believed that the woman's sexuality is always active. Taking for granted the active sexuality of the woman shapes judicial decisions on rape issues. Rape, for example in marriage, was not regarded as a crime for a long time because the married woman was legally seen as ready to fulfil her sexual duty to her husband (Sen, 2005: 47). The risk of domestic violence is thought to decrease when the woman becomes more silent and sacrificing for her family in order to have a secure life. Therefore, "where consent ends and coercion begins can be an especially tricky task" in the analysis of exploitative authority and hierarchal relations (Siddiqi, 2005: 282). For example, 49% of women know that they should not argue with their husband, and 47% think that male members of the family are responsible for the woman's behaviour and attitudes (T.C. Başbakanlık, 2009: 187).

This perception towards the man's control over the woman's behaviours is used to justify violence, since it "is closely linked to the regulation of sexuality" (Coomaraswamy, 2005: xi). As noted earlier, the association between virginity and virtuousness is brought to the fore any time and the incident of violence against a woman receives public scrutiny, since her being deemed not virtuous would have potential implications against the social order and family-based relations (Özyeğin, 2009: 111; see also Sirman, 2004; Parla, 2001). As a result, the woman is responsible for the social order by taking 'responsibility' for her virginity – including from rapists and abusers. However, the traditional prevention method of encouraging the woman to depend on protection from the man within closed community relations creates problems of socialisation (Berktay, 2012: 127). Therefore, it is safe to argue that violence itself restricts the woman's behaviours. Furthermore, through the *sacred* family order, the woman and spousal relations are cast away because her life revolves around the children. (Berktay, 2012; Aytaç, 2015). In other respects, this provides an advantage such that the virtue of law and respect for traditions form a domain in which neoliberalism and right-wing values can produce and strengthen their governmental implementations (Rose and Miller, 1992: 199). In other words, "the demise of traditional forms" desire to rescue 'today' by stimulating fears and anxieties against some bodies and existences in reference to the loss of the past and the precariousness of the future (Ahmed, 2014: 78–79). This political strategy works to help rationalise violence, the erection of social barriers, and the woman's role in the family. This point supports my argument that violence is employed as a disciplinary and regulatory apparatus of security, i.e., violence in all forms and functions as an apparatus between the female body and the population.

In order to broaden these points, I begin this chapter with statistics about the rates and reasons for violence against the woman. By examining cases the received widespread media coverage, I will then explore how public life for a woman is reconstructed, and under which conditions the woman accepts public rules and cultivates self-protective mechanisms. In addition, the definitive shift from crimes of honour to crimes of passion displays the scope of masculine power and honour, and efforts to gain loyalty from the female body and the woman's behaviours. Along with these case studies, I occasionally elaborate multiple facets of the terms 'good conduct abatement' and 'grievous provocation'. Afterward, I re-problematise the reality of violence in its political context. I touch on current protective mechanisms and legal applications against the violence in Turkey. I pay particular attention to 'gendered mediation' and 'exalted masculinity'. I intend to clarify how these mechanisms gain the consent of the woman. As "consent mechanisms" increase, the reasons for violence and conflict solutions ask for an inner transformation towards the emotional achievement of good womanhood (Evrensel, 23 November 2017; Doğan, 2016). I consider that violence is not a private or personal problem and should instead be resolved interpersonally. States around the world need to create governmental milieus to eradicate violence. Therefore, this chapter generally aims to examine that despite conventions and protective mechanisms, violence is always seen as a risk to the woman and vulnerable groups. I particularise this paradox by questioning the depoliticisation of violence through neoliberal terms such as risk, danger, crimes, and immorality.

1 Statistical Facts and the Hard Truth

Statistics, surveys, and rates regarding the attacker and reasons provide grounds to grasp the fact of why and how violence is regarded as a risk for women, children, LGBTI+ people, migrants, and other disadvantaged groups/individuals. With the help of institutional risk analysis, it is also expected that women and other segments of society should make their own risk analyses by looking at the reasons and available data regarding gender-based and race-based violence and crimes. Reasons for violence, in a way, mirror the conflictual and disputed relations and unsettlement in society.

According to a research survey in 2007, the question of "why women are battered" is answered in percentage: 32% of women are exposed to violence because they failed to complete household chores; 21.6% because of personal problems; 9.8% because of a man's jealousy; 6.6% because of unfulfilled sexual relations; 3.3% because they went out without permission; 2.5% for expressing her thoughts and ideas. Finally, 19.7 % of women do not know why they are battered (T.C. Başbakanlık, 2008). All these reasons for violence are reformulated as daily life risks for women. These risks are tabloidised through sexual connotations related to their dress or behaviour (T.C. Başbakanlık, 2008). The silence of battered women about violence reflects its connotations with illicit sex or pornography. The battered woman is caricatured on TV shows, wherein a purported gentleman swoops in claiming to be the only one who can protect her and solve this problem of violence. In TV series, soap operas, topical programmes and news, violence is framed as an expected component of the experience of womanhood, and something ingrained in social and family relations. According to one of the Khutbahs (20 February 2015a), *those who have power but do not have 'morality of power' claim the lives of women*. It is stated that *rape, harassment, abuse, and humiliation are sins against God but that without fear of God, justice and administrative measures would be insufficient to prevent atrocities against women and children* (Khutbah, 20 February 2015a, 2015b). On the other hand, it is believed that *women are entrusted to men* (Khutbah, 07 March 2008; Khutbah, 25 November 2011).

One important survey that sheds light on the amount of violence in post-2002 Turkey was conducted by Ayşegül Altınay and Yeşim Arat in 2007. Some of the remarkable data addresses the question of why men are violent: 13% of the women respondents cited her disobedience, 14% cited men's economic difficulties, 6% reported marital conflict, and 9% identified men's psychological issues. Some women (13%) responded that men resort to violence because they were incapable and weak, others (10%) said that men use violence because they consider themselves superior. Additionally, an average of 50% of women reported that they ask permission from their husbands before going out to visit neighbours or family, or to go shopping or to the cinema or theatre. Only 3% of the women who were exposed to violence went to the gendarmerie or the police, or asked for other legal assistance. In addition, one out of every six men who had higher education resorted to violence against their spouse. One of the interesting results is that 44% of women said that they would not intervene if they witnessed someone using violence. The reason is the belief that it is a private interpersonal matter (Altınay and Arat, 2007).

Lale Karabıyık, of the CHP (The Republican's People Party), Deputy Chairman of Social Policy, prepared a report in 2017 titled Social Degeneracy Report. This research is unique in that it never references the woman's body and sexuality in order to underline "weakening common values" and "rotten values". For example, drug use has increased 11 times between 2011 and 2016, HIV increased by 426%, suicide increased by 1.3%, and antidepressant use increased by 25%. The number of children in prison was 1443 in 2010 and rose to 8993 by 2016, prostitution increased by 790%, divorce rates increased by 37%, homicide by 261%, child abuse by 434%, and sexual harassment by 449 % (HaberTürk, 6 November 2017).

Diyanet says that the woman and her body are not a commodity and sexual object. However, Diyanet itself forges a link between commodification and the intimacy of the female body. For religious principles, a woman must be aware of her womanhood in terms of her active sexuality. What religious principles say is that *the female body is inherently seductive so she should take preventive measures for better public morality by avoiding sexually provocative dress and behaviours* (Balaban, 2005: 22; Martı, 2013: 31–33; İlmihâl, Vol. 2). However, I consider it to be masculine perception that makes the woman a sexual object. A woman may want to seem beautiful and presentable, but not as an object; instead, it is the issue of her self-esteem and the perception that this may deemed problematic within the 'normalised' social order.

So why are women killed? It happens if they want a divorce or if they turn down someone who asks them out; that is, the relationship between man and woman in Turkey is such that the perpetrators of violence is usually perpetrated by the husband or boyfriend. This can be interpreted as a superior-subordinate relationship based on obedience and control that has been internalised by both man and woman (Sallan-Gül, 2013). In other words, the breadwinner man and the economically dependent woman reinforce the traditional division of labour within the family. Leaning on the emotional and physical exploitation of the woman, this structural relationship is covered by traditional codes (Sallan-Gül, 2013: 65).

The disadvantages of intersectional axes generating social hierarchies differentiate the man's social identity-ego (Shalhoub-Kevorkian, 2005: 162). The competitive relations of capitalism disturb the man's power by producing inequalities and insufficiencies. The man's efforts to reinforce his masculine authority may take the form of bullying or mansplaining (Berktay, 2012: 39; Shalhoub-Kevorkian, 2005: 162). Within capitalism, the man's ego may be bruised, which may in turn provide him an excuse to resort to patriarchal violence. The acceptance by women of the system also exalts male-based values (Sancar, 2014: 244). In other words, violence is normalised and accepted, and moreover is reinforced and legitimised by the stress associated with being the breadwinner (Sallan-Gül, 2013: 24). This has remained the essence of the gender reality in post-2002 Turkey. While the discursive suggestions and norms present good womanhood to the man's taste and testing, belittled manhood under neoliberal competitive relations powers his superiority of his role and his domination over the woman.

To illustrate, according to a research survey in 2007, 39% of women were exposed to gender-based violence. This corresponds to 4 out of 10 women, 15% of whom were exposed to sexual violence, and 42% of whom were exposed to sexual and physical violence. 44% of women think that they have been abused emotionally. Also, 29% of middle-class women experienced violence, which proves that poverty and other factors do not have to do with the high rates of violence at all (T.C. Başbakanlık, 2009). According to another study, the reasons for increasing violence are early/forced marriages, unemployment, and low income, as well as conflicts due to social and political differences (T.C. Başbakanlık, 2008).

According to the Human Rights Foundation's statistics, in the years between 2005 and 2011, 4190 women were murdered, and 3074 rape cases were brought to the courts. The rapists were police, civil officers, soldiers, school teachers, and someone encountered in daily life. The number of the reported cases of sexual harassment during those same years was 3330. Keeping in mind that an 40% of reported cases are never brought to court, whether due to fear or other reasons, the statistical data between 2005 and 2011 shows an increase of 38% (İnsan Hakları Derneği, 2011). According to the Ministry of Family and Social Policy's data (2014), an estimated 89% of those who encounter any kind of violence did not bring it to any institution or organisation. Police, as a common security mechanism, are asked for protection at most; indeed, 29% of cases are settled out of court through police mediation. Finally, 13% of the complaints are unresolved.

Regarding child marriages, child brides tend to be the second or third wife of older men. They are usually children or adolescents. They get pregnant and also have to take responsibility for their household. Since the brides are under the age of 18, the marriages are not officially recognised by the state; the practice is typically related to factors such as the force of family/community relations, sexual abuse, and poverty (Çakmak, 2009). According to Ministry of Family and Social Policy data, in 2010 45,738; in 2011 42,700, in 2012 40,428; in 2013 37,481; in 2014 34,629 and in 2015 31,337 child marriages were recorded. There is a social consensus regarding child marriages that produces norms and ethics legitimising it (İmdat.org,2016).

All in all, according to 2014 data from the Ministry of Justice, only an estimated 5% of rapists and abusers are identified, 1 in 1000 incest relationships is discovered, and a total of 650 cases of sexual abuse were reported to the Forensic Medicine Institute. The number of reports is increasing, with 2305 cases in 2012, 3002 cases in 2013, and 2449 cases in 2014 (İmdat.org, 2016). The numbers may differ depending on the source, but my aim is to underscore the high rates of violence and crimes.

2   Rape as a Justified Reaction against the Impropriety

"The boundaries of 'appropriate' sexual behavior" are built on the steep incline of positive and negative sanctions fostered by women's choices and behaviours towards codes of honour and sexual norms (Coomaraswamy, 2005: xi). "Women's transgressions of these codes", which actually form subtle moral boundaries, constitute "legitimate provocation", with the reasons for criminal acts attracting more attention than the criminal perpetrators (Sen. 2005: 49). Indeed, a demand of divorce, going out without permission, violating dress codes, adventurous and bold instincts, and perceived sexual immodesty may be well-recognised reasons for criminal acts (Coomaraswamy, 2005: xi; Sen, 2005: 47).

In relatively more traditional societies, rape is a transgression of communal norms, but it has begun to be seen as a violent act against individual rights. Feminists act as the voice of the oppressed and call for public solidarity against the rape and battery of women. Actually, the issue of rape and violence is discussed in different contexts, illustrating distinctive ways in which public debates determine parameters of sexuality and morality, as well as the remedies (Arat, 2000: 118). Likewise, the behaviours and styles of public visibilities are subjected to appropriateness based on religious and traditional parameters. Ultimately, these parameters are composed of norms and implement the progress of normalisation in order to establish the internal and external management of individuals nourished by technologies of the self and political technologies of power with the aim of constructing not only a realm of power relations between the other and the self but also of enabling and facilitating individuals to internalise the rationality and its inclusionary rules and norms (Foucault, 1997b, 2001b).

The sovereign and disciplinary powers are revealed in the biopolitical age as well, but this time their objectives are to nourish the apparatuses of security for the neoliberal art of government. To illustrate, disciplines in this context have a two-sided effect. On the one hand, they help individuals to adopt market rationality; on the other hand, they work as a mechanism (beyond different techniques and methods) enabling individuals to take control of their body, to realise its capacity and skills, and to enrich it with new skills and knowledge on the way to 'docility' (Foucault, 2008;Heyes, 2007). In fact, the breaking point for the transformation to biopolitics was the discovery of 'the body as object and target of power' (Foucault, 1995: 136). Therefore, docile bodies, which must be open to manipulation and analysis, and interferences for subjection and subjugation in order to characterise and cultivate personalities as useful, healthy bodies and normalised minds (Foucault, 1995; Nadesan, 2008). In addition, now that the human being had been furnished with reason and the capability to think, he should strengthen his autonomy, so to speak, or his self-government in parallel to self-care, self-estimation, and self-educating to create a better rapport with the truth of social practices (Heyes, 2007). Therefore, normalisation appears as the main principle in order to jointly govern the population and individuals by being able to verify what is true or false, normal or abnormal, successful or ineffective.

Therefore, according to Binnaz Toprak (2008), in post-2002 Turkey, sexual crimes are heavily punished but still, the common feeling and opinion drawing on narrations of these crimes and court process published in the media prefer to highlight the moral rules leading to behaviours and dress that make public life for woman comfortable. In addition, the time restrictions and place warnings for the woman ask special attention from her to prevent crimes. Furthermore, even if a woman complains about rape or harassment, the perpetrator – whether the husband or a stranger – may not be brought to justice due to insufficient mechanisms. Meanwhile, it is worth saying that women are more judgemental moral arbiters of appropriate behaviour. That is to say, the transformation through the mediator role of the woman and stories on gender-based crimes produce new norms and risky spheres that women learn to avoid. The definition of womanhood is girded by power by means of not only violence itself but also suggestions and mechanisms for how to avoid violence. Hence, women are in any case left alone with the question of 'how' to enact true and normal womanhood (Toprak, 2008: 86–91).

In this context, normalisation opens clearer and absolute ways of living in which security encounters us (Taylor, 2013: 96). The risk of sexual attack is defined by the scheme, which is normal for a certain reason. The expanding spectrum of these reasons advises women to be more cautious in choosing clothes and places. The details that come out of rape news, judicial processes and public reactions – especially fear and anger – do not address masculine sovereignty but call on women to produce solutions. Rather than resistance against rape and sexual crimes, women are advised to accept normalisation and order. Nevertheless, this returns us to what I advocated in the first place: the risk of violence is a regulatory and disciplining tool that imposes and also challenges normalisation itself in times of political and social transformation.

It seems that all types of sexual assault have accompanying justifications, its risks remind us of the normal order. Expanding the spectrum of such justifications offers the woman a stimulus field wherein seclusion is equated with security. As a result, the woman is encouraged to stay at home, or to be very careful about her choices outside the home. The sense of fear gets into a structural form with news on sexual violence and affects behaviours, perceptions of honour, and what others will say. In other words, fear of sexual violence is normalised by thinking that:

> Fear of 'the world' as the scene of a future injury works as a form of violence in the present, which shrinks bodies in a state of afraidness, a shrinkage which may involve a refusal to leave the enclosed spaces of home, or a refusal to inhabit what is outside in ways that anticipate injury (walking alone, walking at night and so on). Such feelings of vulnerability and fear hence shape women's bodies as well as how those bodies inhabit space. Vulnerability is not an inherent characteristic of women's bodies; rather, it is an effect that works to secure femininity as a delimitation of movement in the public, and over-inhabitance in the private.
> AHMED, 2014: 70

However, there is one remarkable point that sexual violence must be predicated on rape cases, where the possibility of resistance cannot exist and where the importance of saying 'no' is discounted. In rape cases, resistance and the existence of violation influence the definition and juridical step; however, sexual activity despite lack of the woman's consent is inconsistent with the definition of rape. Consent is problematic. It turns into a concept being applied by the law.

I would like to elaborate on the importance of this subject with two nested examples: In 2015, Özgecan Aslan was kidnapped, raped, beaten, and killed after boarding a public minibus by the driver, who then tried to get rid of her body by burning it. Since there is 'no traditional or moral justification' for rape, the case received a huge public reaction. Aslan was a 19-year-old university student on her way home from school at a 'reasonable' hour. She resisted the attack, as evidenced from the claw marks on her murderer's face. Therefore, public opinion presented her as an angel and a victim, since she did not give consent and, as is claimed, there was no penetration-as still claimed (HaberTürk, 14 February 2015). Although the rape itself could not be rationalised through 'tradition' or 'normality', one popular figure in Turkey, Nihat Doğan, used the crime as an opportunity to attack secularism, saying, "You will not cry and bawl if you're wearing a miniskirt and thus being harassed by the perverts of this secular system" (NTV, 2 April 2018). Indeed, the miniskirt has become a popular icon of the secular debate in Turkey, but Özgecan Aslan had not been wearing one.

Özgecan Aslan's case received the full glare of public attention and many women's organisations published notices in various places. The discursive detail on Aslan's resistance, and her characterisation as an angel (for having remained a virgin) in particular were criticised by these women's organisations. In one of these notices, a 16-year-old woman stated that she could not resist her rapist because he was too strong:

> I was trying to explain the situation to the judge and he was telling me just to sit ... He [the rapist] is free right now and wandering around freely. The lawsuit was held on 19 November at Kayseri First Criminal Court. I got worse when I saw him at the lawsuit. I attempted suicide many times. I went to a psychologist, took an antidepressant, and was taken to the intensive care unit, too. But he is still free. He stayed only one day in jail, nothing more, neither pre-trial detention nor punishment. I went to the state attorney in order to talk about this situation and he [the judge] told me that 'the other party claims you consented'... If there is consent, the punishment is about two years.
>
> BIANET, 16 February 2015

In order to clarify this, Catharina Mackinnon reckons these two different cases, by exactly overlapping each other:

> Whether the law calls this coerced consent or defense of mistaken belief in consent, the more the sexual violation of women is routine, the more pornography exists in the world the more legitimately, the more beliefs

equating sexuality with violation become reasonable, and the more honestly women can be defined in terms of their fuckability.
MACKINNON, 1991: 183

Severe class and sexual dominations obstruct the intervention of law. Domination and the pressure threshold become more severe while the law and medicine are counted. For example, it is a special situation when the mental health of a woman is impaired due to a sexual violation. While unimpaired mental health is seen as normal and does not affect punishment, a change of the woman's psychology before and after a rape does affect punishment (Özkazanç, 2013: 159–164). Two nested points need to be discerned, which depoliticise violence in terms of law and medicine: first, the impairment of mental health is taken as an indicator of whether or not there was consent, and therefore can be used to help mitigate punishment (Özkazanç, 2013: 160–162). Second, the problem or the crime itself is calculated based on the damaged caused, if we look at the issue with a neoliberal eye. The masculine motivation behind sexual violence is depoliticised from the damaged to the victim or compensation. Masculine violence to the woman is accepted as a normal and daily situation.

One of striking example of this is the legal struggle of a woman who was gang-raped by eight men, which has been ongoing for several years. The case is known as the Fethiye Lawsuit. The rapists were acquitted due to lack of evidence, and the woman was accused of lying since she was a daughter of divorced parents. The reason given for the result was that the woman had been given medication, so was eventually able to remember and recount the events thanks to psychological support. When the national law was unable to accommodate the victim's struggles, an application was made to the European Court of Human Rights (Evrensel, 22 April 2012).

An application was sent to the Ministry of Justice for 'reversal of the decision with written order' and a lawsuit was filed after four years (Evrensel, 22 April 2012). Even though there was one forensic report, two psychological reports, one psychiatric report and one gynaecological report that all supported the claim of rape, the Fethiye Criminal Court acquitted the accused on 22 April 2012. The reason was that the victim waited eight months after the rape before filing a criminal complaint. The forensic report proving the incorruption on mental health of the victim was not recognised. The Higher Court approved the decision, and the lawsuit was submitted to the Constitutional Court (Cumhuriyet, 8 March 2017). The process of the lawsuit in every sense was all about what a woman should be. The courts were sending a warning to society –which it also seeks to transform – about the psychological effect of being a child of 'divorced parents' when it failed to recognise and punish a rape reported by such a woman.

Sexual crimes are described through the victimhood of the woman and her wrongdoings, whose life is in general excluded from the social order. By these means, her misfit life is criminalised and marked as risky with brutal cases and symbolic representations (Sancar, 2014). In the norm system of disciplinary power, the question is whether the guilty party is going to steal or murder again despite heavy punishment, and the question is how this guilt can be transformed and normalised through obligatory works, moralisation, correction, and so forth. In the apparatus (*dispositif*) of security, the guilt, as well as guilty party's correction and punishment, are governed by calculated preventive measures. The average rate of criminality for murder or theft, and the prediction of a statistical number of thefts at a given moment, in a given society and in a given town are calculated. Then, questions on any decreasing or increasing effects of punishments for offences in order to calculate the cost of repression and delinquency to murder or theft, and the possible rehabilitation of the guilty around the disciplinary mechanisms arise. Obviously, any kind of criminality started to be taken into serious consideration within social and economic limits by calculating the optimal value of a given social function (Foucault, 2007: 4–6).

Therefore, technologies of security should be understood through the distinguished marks of biopolitics on the condition of reactivating juridical-legal and disciplinary techniques. Concordantly, Foucault points out the general features of apparatuses (*dispositifs*) of security by occasionally remarking on a concept of biopolitics but he intrinsically depicts the mechanisms in reference to causality. Specifically, disciplinary apparatuses hierarchise good and bad subjects in accordance with laws, moral rules, and their potentialities, their value and their level (Foucault, 1995: 181). In this vein of the ability of disciplinary institutions, the penalties and punishments develop a way of comparing, differentiating, hierarchising, and homogenising, while excluding the bad and the good in relation to one another. In the meantime, the penalties and punishments have employed normalisation as the significant instruments of power owing to the power of normalisation to render differences between individuals in order to qualify capabilities, classify their value, and punish (Foucault, 1995: 184). Discipline normalises and then divides the normal from the abnormal. This means that the normal has the capacity to identify and grasp the normal better than the abnormal (Foucault, 2007: 57). However, the main question for biopolitics in its modern form is the way the sets of apparatuses engage with normalisation if security is the most significant matter.

It would be good to draw attention to the influence of punitive policies and punitiveness in order to stimulate the emotions of fear and insecurity without making the power of law and order forget (Garland, 1996: 460). Punitive responses against offenders counterbalance the fear factor against potential crimes (Garland, 1996). This point is pivotal because the criticism that 'the punishments are not sufficient' broadens our perspective on sexual violence and makes us wonder why the existing punishments are insufficient. Two examples may be given here: Two men – identified as E.K. and D.S. – were condemned to 20 years for stabbing a woman in Istanbul whom they did not know, and for raping another woman whom they did not know (Bianet, 19 November 2018). A sentence of ten years was issued in another case on the grounds that the mental health of the woman is still good enough and there had been a provocation for the rape (Evrensel, 19 March 2015). In another case, a woman using public transportation at night was raped, and then blackmailed by the driver. It has been stated by the Higher Court that the rights of women are protected, and that a woman may pull out of the process at any time (Gazete Duvar, 13 December 2018). In another case, even though the victim – N.Ç., aged 12 – was systematically raped by 28 men, the convicted perpetrators received minimal sentences with the reasoning that she had consented (HaberTürk, 17 January 2013). Meanwhile, another man raped his girlfriend when she wanted to break up and was sentenced to 15 years (Bianet, 3 March 2016). Numerous examples point to the inconsistency of punishments for crimes such as rape with consent. In cases of rape and strong control over relations between men and women such as those cited here that involve legal and medical intervention, women also become victimised by society and the law.

In other words, severe punishments are important, but they can be evaded easily by pointing the finger back at the woman and accusing her of faults against proper womanhood. The heightened political climate has identified a semantic area of warnings within which risk factors relating to rape, abuse, and the female body more generally are expanded on by society itself. That is to say, besides normalised certain behaviours towards women, sexual violence itself becomes normal. Sexual violence becomes a masculine punishment enacted on a woman judged to be inappropriate. This normalisation causes fear for the woman living under masculine security, and pushes her to make decisions about her appearance and behaviour accordingly.

For this analysis, Claudia Aradau provides a remarkable framework:

> The subjects of security have been generally humans – be those more or less reified in particular communities, such as nations, states or regions.

> The referent objects of security have been particular social constructs: identities, cultural values, 'ways of life', and so on.
>
> ARADAU, 2010: 493

The relation between subjects and objects of security are regulated and legitimised by knowledge-power. While specialised knowledge regarding any issue is placed at their disposal, self-interests proceed on the way in which the motivating emotions and attachments cover unfair competitive relations. All of our relations and roles gain reasonable and hopeful meanings and functionalities without being alienated from market-society rationality. The discernment and prudence to grasp the norms of order and manage the self are the main corollary of subjectivations that engender the sense of transition in the process of producing truth. The concept of governmentality seeks that, subjects "conduct the conduct of other beings – that is, govern them" (Dardot and Laval, 2013: 5).

The notion of enterprise is at the core of social relations embedded in neoliberal governmental reason, and accordingly, the generalisation of enterprise in every sphere of life naturally carves out subjectivity itself (McNay, 2009: 55). Therefore, by Foucault's account, neoliberalism cannot define only economic relations and market interest; it implicitly encompasses social control among individuals (McNay, 2009: 55; Donzelot, 2008: 59). To grasp neoliberalism through this, the Foucauldian perspective is the crucial inception of critically approaching today's individualised and economised rationality of relations because freedom in (neo)liberal governmentality functions as a kind of apparatus to reinforce self-control and measure risks related to particular behaviours. Therefore, it is well argued that the principle of "equal inequality for all" renders daily life expectations to stimulate market rationality in the name of "personal responsibility" and "self-care" (Lemke, 2001: 195; Brown, 2003: 7; Donzelot, 2008: 123). Ultimately, regulatory and disciplinary techniques carve out the behaviours and normalise minds, on the one hand, and tame bodily needs and cultivate bodily skills on the other hand (Foucault, 1997b: 249; McNay, 2009: 57).

Regarding the analysis of criminality and delinquency, the offence in the framework of law (and social norms) applies equally to every subject, those who should have enough reason to identify things outside of laws and norms, also to cultivate their consciousness not to kill someone, and even not to break rules that might cause detriment to oneself or someone else (Lemke, 2001: 199). Taking all these expectations together, it can finally be said that the neoliberal subject should grasp the grafted neoliberal rationality in order to increase its sense of belonging to society and to have a place in the normalised order. All of the subject's roles and identities in life should intrinsically gain competitive meanings by being objects of security, such as to be the best mother, the best wife, the best man or woman, the most successful, or even the most misfit character.

To illustrate, in 2018, Şule Çet, a 23-year-old university student, was thrown from the 20th floor of the residence where she was working. She was slipped a drug and then raped before being killed, but the perpetrators made it look like a suicide. The lawsuit is ongoing, and the severity of the perpetrators' sentence seems that it will rest on the question of suicide or murder. The first forensic report included statements such as, "If a woman agrees to have a drink with a man in an isolated place, this means that she consents to sexual intercourse" (HaberTürk, 13 February 2019). The other party's lawyer has stated that, "The virginal membrane of the murdered woman was already ruined, and the rape did not cause a loss" (Deutsche Welle, 7 February 2019). As mentioned, the case should end with a conviction and the severest punishment, but it is still hard to predict how successfully notions of tradition might be used to construct an argument that Şule Çet killed herself. Nevertheless, the two highlighted statements about agreeing to a drink and the condition of the hymen characterise Çet as a 'free woman' with respect to lifestyle. In what follows, the expectation is that Turkey is understood as a risky society for women, since the risk of violence is presented as a reality taken from countable and predictable real data; the uncountable part is kept in mind in daily life decisions and cautious behaviours (Dean, 1998).

Relying on the definition of Ericson and Haggerty (O'Malley 1999: 144), the risk society denotes a surveillance system, which suggests more privacy and intimacy in order to promote safest relations by abandoning public participation. This is why family relations are falsely presented as a salvation from the risk society. In parallel with this, as the spectrum of risk-profiled people expands, the feeling of disenfranchisement among those from "not so identified groups" increases as they become understood as abnormal. As a result, inequality between population segments cause social divisions that map out the structure of the risk society (O'Malley, 1999: 144). Therefore, sexual violence is a fact of the risk society in that groups of women are categorised in line with their lifestyles, choices and sexual preferences.

According to Foucault, power over life leans on two forms: one of these forms is centred on the body as a machine, which necessitates "disciplining, optimization of its capabilities, the extortion of its forces, the parallel increase of usefulness and docility, its integration into systems of efficient and economic controls" in the name of *discipline: the anatomo-politics of the human body*. The second form is strictly connected to the "species body". The species body, or the new form of the body – i.e., the population – is permeated with the mechanics of life and biological processes such as propagation, mortality, health condition, life expectancy, and longevity, which were interchangeable. Therefore, the species body needs to be supervised in the name of *regulatory controls: a biopolitics of population* (Foucault, 1998: 139, 2003a: 249). Overall, this awakening of life brought about the development of numerous and diverse techniques aimed at shaping docile and subjugated bodies towards the control of sustainable populations. Foucault identifies this eighteenth-century rupture as one of biopower/biopolitics (Foucault, 1998: 140, 2003a:243; O'Malley, 1992: 255).

Thinking about this in the context of masculine sovereignty, sexual violence against impropriety may be seen as a social punishment that takes its legitimation from social honour and constituting a hub of disciplinary mechanisms entwined in regulatory mechanisms. Rape and all other forms of sexual violence do not have to do with sexuality and satisfaction; they are forms of violence (Mackinnon, 1991; Bell, 1993b). Through this form of violence, with the help of these interwoven mechanisms, the process of making individuals responsible for both the self and the population as a new form of social warning enables the production of new behaviours by deconstructing old habits and thoughts (Garland, 1996: 452).

3 From Crimes of Honour to Crimes of Passion

There is a simple distinction between crimes of honour and crimes of passion. The former are based on collective social processes, while the latter are considered individualistic and unplanned (Shier and Shor, 2016). With crimes of honour, direct sexual transgressions are necessary in order to murder the woman, but crimes of passion are due to provocative behaviour of woman or lack of loyalty to the husband or boyfriend (Shier and Shor, 2016). Honour is the value of man or woman according to social virtues, so it is about proximity to the values and pride (Pitt-Rivers, 1965: 21). Social honour is the essence of a prestigious life through which community-based family relations are governed and valued (Baroja, 1965: 87; Abou-Zeid, 1965: 258; see also Sirman, 2004). In Turkey, what dishonours the man, and the community, has gradually been subtle in the definition of ideal womanhood. The excuses and reasons to kill a woman are widespread, from burned cooking to infidelity. Furthermore, the honour of a definitive norm of ideal womanhood provides an active semantic field to control and legitimise violence on account of various spheres of social honour, including neighbourhood honour, workplace honour, and family honour. Honour is both individual and social: It is social because it is a component of an individual's identity in the social context. It is individual because it is a (self-)control mechanism and is related to underdevelopment because it is prised within an exaggerated masculinity, so it already contains the crime. This is why the cultural motivation for crimes of honour is very high, because a man's emotions and motivations are always justified (Doğan, 2016; Koğacıoğlu, 2007).

Dicle Koğacıoğlu elaborates this well:

> In Turkey as women, we face many questions in terms of the fiction of honour about what we will do with our bodies. Some of us are killed for the sake of honour; some of us are beaten for wearing miniskirts; some are warned over the way they sit at work by their bosses; if they are considered to be dishonourable, they are targeted; some of us cannot get custody of our children, and others of us live with the fear that custody will be taken away for some reason; some of us are looked at with the evil eye, and others of us are not not hireable because we may attract the evil eye. These kinds of examples multiply so easily. We all know that something will happen if we do not behave properly. Even though we give less importance to honour in our lives, we in a way live our lives according to it. Despite big differences and inequalities among us, honour plays a big role in our lives and on our bodies, such as how to sit down and stand up/ our physical behaviours, where to go, which part of the cities are safe and how to go there safely, when is it appropriate to have sex, etc. We live in Turkey where women's bodies are disciplined over honour, and where women discipline themselves over this fiction.
> KOĞACIOĞLU, 2007: 1

Honour is a disciplinary norm that must reconstruct itself in order to sustain its influence (Koğacıoğlu, 2007: 7). In 2004, an amendment in criminal law invalidated the defence of 'honour' in murder cases. Despite this amendment, the matter of honour persists, instead taking on new forms (Koğacıoğlu, 2007: 7). In other words:

> There is little doubt that 'honour' is now an overdetermined concept – the preferred term, in many regions, for practices linked to reputation, pride, masculinity or respectability. Honour enables sexual, economic and political control, through gendered violence and governmentality, and through the protection of women.
> GREWAL, 2013: 15

In this context, honour is a motivation to resort to violence or crime (Welchmann and Hossain, 2005: 4; Sen, 2005: 45; Hoyek and Sidawi, 2005: 128). Defining these crimes against women in terms of motivations – which are typically passion, honour, or pride – aids acquittals and helps perpetrators to minimise the criminal dimension of their actions. The driving force behind such crimes may be "washing away shame" and the "bad conduct of the victim", both of which are about the removal of the woman-object dishonouring the family and polluting moral values (Hoyek and Sidawi, 2005: 128; Parla, 2001: 77).

Crimes of passion are differentiated from crimes of honour with respect to collective punishment as well as motivation (Sen, 2005: 55). The distinction between the two is relevant because the framing of the crime affects the style of defence mounted. For example, crimes motivated by emotions such as pangs of love, provocation, and pride are adjudicated as "fits of fury", "sudden bursts of anger", and "manslaughter" (Welchman and Hossain, 2005: 10; Sen, 2005: 50). The judicial system considers crimes of passion to be unpremeditated violations of public morality, as reactions to the woman's behaviours and degree of conformity to visibility conventions. Legitimate behaviours form the honour backed by the law.

To illustrate, in October 2017, Elvan D. was stabbed to death by her husband after she refused to make tea for him; he also suspected her of cheating on him. Fulya O. was killed by a perpetrator identified as A.M. due to severe provocation and was imprisoned for life. A woman was killed by her husband because she wanted to divorce; he was sentenced to 54 years in prison (Bianet, 19 November 2018). A woman was killed by her brother after flying into a range upon learning that she had become pregnant out of wedlock (Kadın Cinayetlerini Durduracağız Platformu, 2014). Nevertheless, it is still not completely accurate to claim that there is a relationship between harsh judicial penalties and the dramatic upsurge of gender-based crimes. It seems that honour, as well as the anger of the man, is regarded as a comfortable reason to rationalise violence.

A combination of shame and respect make honour, which is the essence of social order. This logic of social order leads to murders. The law is surely a universal intervention into such crimes, but when we look at the reasons for crimes and violence, these attacks are legitimised in the hands of the justice system (Abu-Odeh, 2014: 243; Coomaraswamy, 2005: XI). According to religious principles, *Islam does not see punishment as a deterrent. Instead of punishments and confinements, emotions, the social environment, and all other means should be employed to ameliorate and regenerate such situations. A seductive gaze or word should be prevented, and veiling and intimacy should be preferred* (İlmihâl, Vol. 2: 130). *Religious and moral education needs to be taught. Intemperance should be avoided. Virtuous individuals should be brought up. The social environment is considered to be the key factor to prevent these kinds of crimes. Too much freedom, intemperance, and imbalance destroy society. A sense of responsibility is valid for spouses provided that they keep their eyes averted from sins that may lead to fornication* (İlmihâl, Vol. 2: 130–132).

Therefore, *in order to prevent crimes of passion, since man and woman are excitatory to each other, they should take precautions to protect their chastity, as it is something that cannot be regained once it has been lost* (İlmihâl, Vol. 2: 132–133). Social losses due to sexual freedom cause crimes of honour because honour is a sign of social quality (Abu-Odeh, 2014: 258). Crimes of passion are a substitute for honour killings.

Crimes of passion stem from an excessive emotional reaction, while honour crimes are premeditated. With the former, the perpetrator is portrayed as a man who is passionately in love, and who kills a woman who fails to return that passion satisfactorily (Abu-Odeh, 2014: 263–264). Crimes of passion are situated in love relations, which create suspicion of the role of emotion in marriage. Love causes chaos in family life, so regulative strategies are initiated to manage this chaos and reveal the dangers of passion and love. If family and marriage are at issue, love should be kept apart (Sancar, 2014: 266–267). In line with Islamic principles, *chastity and honour are related to social morality; therefore, it cannot be set free. A strong order needs to be established, which is strengthened by justice as well as moral and religious rules. Family, justice, and religion should be intertwined* (İlmihâl, Vol. 2:184–185). Honour carries basic constructive codes of ideal manhood too, which establishes a moral linkage to family and community, while the woman's sexuality requires, for practicability of honour, belonging to the body of the ideal woman. Therefore, the notion of honour provides a causal link between collective regulation of women's behaviours and violence against her (Coomaraswamy, 2005: xi; Sen, 2005: 45–48).

According to Foucault, the government is equipped with techniques to form, transform, and direct the conduct of individuals. These techniques roughly constitute technologies, including "techniques for producing objects; techniques of communication, through which individuals communicate between themselves; and techniques of government, through which individuals act on each other's conducts in order to attain certain ends or objectives" (Foucault, 2014: 24). These techniques and technologies converge on *the sense of responsibility to God, yourself and society* (İlmihâl, Vol. 2: 197), which is also expected from neoliberal governmentality. Neoliberal governmentality suggests that criminals are not socially or psychologically problematic; on the contrary, they have reasons for risk management and losses at the expense of their criminal acts, although they may have pathological tendencies (Lemke, 2001: 199). Against the rising rates of gender-based crime, the public service ads of the Ministry of Family and Social Policy have a clip wherein a voice over warns, "Do not wait for death to wake up" as a way of blaming for women for their own victimisation, with particular reference to their individual responsibility (Günaydın and Özdoğan, 2014: 75). As the Khutbah (23 August 2013) states, *freedom and responsibility are two interwoven concepts, although they have opposite meanings and connotations. Individuals are free as long as they fulfil their duties towards God and society.* Otherwise,

> femicide is a major fear for girls and young women. They are willing to forfeit their liberty, the right to education, and choice of husband in order to escape it. Furthermore, if raped, women are obliged by cultural and legal codes to marry their rapist as a means to avoid being killed and prevent the shame that would stain the family if they refused to do so.
> SHALHOUB-KERVORKIAN, 2005: 168

As already pointed out, this can be elucidated in the context of the relation between law and norms because the biopolitics of Islam reflects deeply on the juridical system as well. In the case of womanhood, norms have always had a dominant place in law. This is observable in several juridical decisions regarding violence against women in the name of honour. It should be noted that some changes in the law against honour and in favour of women's rights have taken place since 2004. And yet, the strong patriarchal structure in the Turkish judicial system impedes the proper implementation of the law. From recent lawsuits, I can see that honour as a norm often supersedes the law. Therefore, honour proves to have a superior position over the law in the hands of judges. We observe this clearly from cases of violence against women in the name of social honour, wherein judges continue to be influenced by such norms in the implementation of sentences despite the favourable 2004 changes (Koğacıoğlu, 2007;Sirman, 2004).

In order to stop gender-based murders in the name of honour or passion, "the development of the concept of state responsibility" tries to be plausible through strict penalties and sanctions against violence by seeking strategies and reasons for its eradication within the scope of an international problem (Coomaraswamy, 2005: xii; Welchmann and Hossain, 2005: 2). The specific definition of these crimes, such as honour or passion, provides not only an ultimate excuse but also paves the way towards recognition of some religious and ethnic differences within tradition and cultural forgiveness. For example, crimes of honour have been globally studied because of Islam and Islamic treatment against a woman in an implicit reference to backwardness, which in a way makes impossible prevention and punishment at an international level (Connors, 2005: 35; Sen, 2005: 42). As for Turkey, honour or custom killings are weighed again upon the east of Turkey by particularising it within the Kurdish question and ethnic conflicts again[2] (Altınay and Arat, 2007: 71; Sirman, 2004: 40; see also Koğacıoğlu, 2007; Grewal, 2013). In both cases, crimes of honour are deemed as a barbaric expression of power, "which have no place in contemporary societies and for those seeking to join the club of enlightened, secular and rational societies" (Sen, 2005: 45). In Turkey, these crimes in line with customs and traditions had been somehow legitimised by reducing it to the common fate and destiny of the woman (Hoyek and Sidawi, 2005: 120; Günaydın and Özdoğan, 2014: 75; Koğacıoğlu, 2007: 19).

Thereby, sovereign rationality legitimises honour-related practices that reproduce power; furthermore, calling a woman a victim of tradition and custom, power blurs possible political cooperation between women by repositioning the issue of violence as a question of womanhood (Koğacıoğlu, 2007: 20). In post-2002 Turkey, when power touches on the female body and gender norms in order to stimulate the traditional sensitivities relating to the honour of the family and even the honour of the nation, crimes are increasingly legitimised, pointing to the unsatisfied desires of men. Therefore, the ethnic explanation of gender discrimination against women does not speak to the fact that women throughout Turkey have always lived with the fear of honour killings embedded in passionate love, passions, and desires.

Grewal puts it well:

> Though feminist debates on the subject of 'honour killings' have yet to engage with popular culture and media as a source of meaning of the term, ... the term 'honour killing' has circulated because it has the power to diagnose the nature of a crime and its solution as being linked and confined to some particular societies following a racial logic.
> GREWAL, 2013: 2–3

---

2   In a nutshell, crimes of honour and crimes of passion are different faces of patriarchy embedded in modernity and backwardness, which we understand through the lens of Turkish-Kurdish cultural conflict (Altınay and Arat, 2007; Grewal, 2013; Sirman, 2004). In a way, crimes of honour are presented as criminal habits of Kurdish culture in which crimes and violence are seen as normal (Grewal, 2013; Sirman, 2004).

There is always an explanation and avowal for such crimes. Criminal subjects accept their crimes and explain their reasons, which are about the inappropriateness of the object. The avowals or explanations constitute the "material confirmation of a truth that was otherwise established, it should have sufficed and satisfied the judges" (Foucault, 2014: 215). According to Foucault, judges need to hear something about why this crime is committed (Foucault, 2014: 216). Instead, it should be focused on criminal subjects. Thereby, the avowal itself reconstructs criminal subjects through their regrets, reasons, and so on (Foucault, 2014: 227–228).

In this context, crimes of passion because of divorce or rejection are downgraded to civil law. This has consequents. The cost of a criminal penalty, for example, is regulated by taking the crime in the context of public peace as opposed to personal safety and rights. Discussions over these sorts of crimes are reduced to the scope of daily life questions through symbolic representations related to "disgusting" news, "incomprehensible" murders, "heartless" fathers, "unconscientious" husbands, "godforsaken" lovers (Sancar, 2014: 239).

From crimes of honour to crimes of passion, emotions are described as triggering murder and brutal violence. The crucial point is that emotions are learned and experienced (Hoyek and Sidawi, 2005: 132). Anger, fear, or love seek objects to be projected onto in order to gain meaning. Therefore, justifications and motivations based on feelings prompted by the object are learnable expressions through the social process (Hoyek and Sidawi, 2005: 132). In Turkey, the media juxtaposes the reasons for criminal acts with the pictures of murdered women and the crime scene. Presented in this way, violence and crimes constitute the third-page news, exploiting feelings of fear and concerns about the woman's life and body. Problems that should be placed on the political agenda are depoliticised by means of marriage, protective masculinity, and religio-cultural sensitivities.

As one of the Khutbahs states (25 November 2011), *violation of women rights and the lack of moral values are in a causal relation. Violence against women and children is the result of a perspective that has degraded life to hedonism. In Western societies, women are rendered as objects of sex and violence owing to the lack of moral values.* There is no way to refuse the commodification of the female body. The Khutbah is right to emphasise violence, sexual objectification, and consumption culture together, but it is still problematic to frame this as a West-led problem. In order to uncover the faces and forms of patriarchy, the major reason the female body, sexuality, and violence are objectified may be explored by facing the power regime's political and social interest in post-2002 Turkey.

Nevertheless, religious responses fail to answer questions relating to patriarchal hierarchy. This kind of an approach towards problems of gender-based violence, on the one hand, sheds light on how Islamism can produce its own political and cultural power by positioning the woman against Western or global values. On the other hand, the rejection of gender-based violence works in favour of neoliberalism. To illustrate, Diyanet generally argues that there is no gender question, but the questions of disciplining and educating women are exactly what neoliberal rationality seeks for the management of womanhood. Certainly, women are not granted their own means of preventing violence, due to social and economic restrictions that inhibit many of them. There are mechanisms surrounding women's existential experience. To illustrate, faith, destiny, sense of guilt, and wrong spouse selection intrinsically point to the control mechanisms that the woman herself rationalises violence and its reasons.

In line with this, the visibility of violence comes with narratives about the battered woman. The reasons for violence are asked to the woman, not to the man who applies it. It is expected that the woman explains, so to speak, why she does or does not deserve violence. Hearing the reasons for violence from a woman is the key disciplinary and educative means to teach violence within its social and political functionality. Hence, I put forward that the fact of violence is depoliticised by defining it as an existential and indispensable element of womanhood. This is a dilemma taken into consideration in order to sincerely respond to why violence against women cannot be eradicated in spite of widespread protective mechanisms.

These risks, because of the political line of conduct, are presented in an apolitical way wherein, for example, violence against women is reformulated as a lack of self-care with respect to their risk reality because of the sexual potential of the female body. Additionally, women need to raise their consciousness of sexual connotations and possible attacks. Under specific social and political conditions, these vulnerabilities regarding women, children or sexual minorities are consciously highlighted through the impossibilities of the female body against violence and the limits of self-defence (Butler, 2004b: 29). Therefore, hate crimes, honour crimes, and crimes of passion are narrated through happenings to female bodies, migrants, refugees, trans-bodies, thereby ignoring the reasons why and how these bodies are exposed to violence, and which mechanisms determine the risks to fragile lives. For this, it is clear that public attention to the rising rates of violence and crime is manipulated and sidetracked by creating artificial agendas and problematisations revolving around migrant questions, war, economic crises, morality, the youth's and woman's lifestyles (Agathangelou, 2004: 10).

4 Political Reality and the Depoliticisation of Violence

Today the changing face of authoritarianism is acknowledged, as is the new authoritarian way of thinking and rationality, which *speaks softly but carries a big stick* (Case, 2017). Holly Case (2017) describes it well that the new authoritarians no longer declare naked mass violence against the subject as long as the consent of silenced individuals can be governed by authoritarian actors. As she said, these new authoritarians want individuals to keep up with the times, gain self-discipline, and be self-sacrificing, but not to make individuals better but to make them feel better about not wanting to change. In line with this, I want to take a further step in developing an alternative analysis of the masculine character of the authoritarian governments through the problem of violence and relevant preventive mechanisms. I expect to arrive in the major form of knowledge-power in "the rationalization of governmental practice in the exercise of political sovereignty" (Foucault, 2008: 2). In my opinion, economics and social transformation with political anger and authority negatively influence everyday life and social psychology, but still, there is a point requiring specific care in order to understand gender-based violence and crimes within neoliberal governmentality, which cannot find a solution in either liberal or authoritarian rationalities.

The neoliberal rationality of modern government is intrinsically based on violence, which essentially aims to gain consent through the promise of safety, comfort, and actually foolproof happiness. According to Sara Ahmed (2010), this happiness looks like "the face of privilege", which is associated with "relative proximity to social norms and the ideals". This new norm actually manages and regulates the choices and practices of subjects in the name of liberty and freedom, and in the name of "risk analysis and assessment". Therefore, governmentality has to do not only with the government of others but also it has to do with self-government. Employing Dardot and Laval's analysis of "the way of the world", subjects are expected to be their own manager for their risks. The subject is responsible for the results of his choices. According to Dardot and Laval, risk as the new norm of neoliberal rationality refers to the "individualization of fate", which runs parallel to the above-mentioned vulnerability and loneliness of the subject (2013: 307). What is at stake here is the naturalisation of events, dangers, violence, and exclusion, which are always stimulated by means of emotions – especially fear – regarding governmental expectations. Particularly, the threat of gender-based violence becomes a "corrective action" by which a woman learns where she should walk, what she needs to wear, or how she needs to behave (Hier, 2008: 183). Moreover, this gendered fear makes women correct each other in order to prevent violence in the name of wrongly represented womanhood (Hier, 2008).

According to Johanna Oksala (2010, 2011), neoliberalism depoliticises violence by taking account of it in the context of economic rationality regardless of its political and moral reasons or results because "its cost and profit can also be calculated, analyzed and managed" (Oksala, 2011: 480–481). This rationality has to manage these profit-cost calculations associated with different types of crimes and different forms of violence. The reason why domestic violence or violence against women or hate crimes is tolerated is simply that these certain forms of violence are too disproportionately costly to be fully eradicated (Oksala, 2011). On the other hand, neoliberalism by its very nature does not want to eradicate such crimes. It asks subjects to take responsibility for their own acts, which is at the heart of the "moral economy of everyday living" (Hier, 2008: 182).

In addition to the defined crimes of society, there are "potential victims" such as teenagers and women (Hier, 2008: 182). In post-2002 Turkey, Islamic 'norm impositions' have focused on the woman and her bodily discipline by reinforcing the idea that the female body is the property of society. On the one hand, the female body is controlled and monitored according to Islamic moral rules and religious prohibitions. On the other hand, authoritarian neoliberal interventions have tried to regulate reproduction, the family structure, and the woman's sexuality by pointing out demographic issues and the need to generate new subjects. In a way, Islamic neoliberal rationality makes possible the simultaneous control of both the external and internal worlds of the woman. Religious and traditional values provide opportunistic interventions for neoliberal necessities. That is why particular interest groups such as parent organisations, families and police are called to handle societal issues such as increasing moral degeneration and deviancy (Hier, 2008: 176; Arat, 1998: 118). That is to say, the state itself calls on families and mothers to protect their children.

Political and religious discourse in post-2002 Turkey has an important influence on the people. It is said that gender equality cannot be achieved when natural differences between the sexes are emphasised (Milliyet, 24 November 2014) or motherhood as a career for women is emphasised (Hürriyet, 2 January 2015). What follows is that the same food is cooked every day (Milliyet,2012), undesired clothes and lifestyles (Hürriyet, 23 August 2013), the desire to divorce (Sabah, 12 May 2011), or the rejection of a relation (Gazete Yolculuk, 25 May2016), and being alone on a public bus at 7 pm when it is dark (CNN Türk, 17 March 2015); all of these become reasons for men to kill or rape their wives, their beloveds, their customers, their passengers, their friends. When we think of all this brutality and hate against women in parallel in the context of high political ambitions, we can see how the operationalisation of violence pushes women to be more docile and submissive. Concisely, violence is about expectations and fears, which rationalises the devaluation of real women and current models of womanhood in favour of an idealised image (İnceoğlu and Kar, 2010).

For instance, Mr. Erdoğan commented on the case of 18-year-old Münevver Karabulut, who was brutally murdered by her boyfriend:

> As mothers and fathers [of the current generation of young people], we need to question ourselves these days if we hear of undesired murders, killings, massacres. We should ask ourselves, 'Where did we make mistakes?'. We are really getting worried about this social order of unlimited and uncontrolled moral degeneration. That is why we shall protect the family! We can't let our family, our children go with the flow. Girls who are left on their own fall for musicians.[3]
> MILLIYET, 20 July 2009

Traditional forces are rationalised by the courts and laws that tend towards decreasing sentences for crimes for good behaviour. The courts seek unjust provocation by the woman against the man. The issue of consent during rape or sexual harassment also considers factors such as the woman's clothes or accessories, whether she provoked him, whether she broke his heart. Sexual crimes against the woman are at the heart of gendered relations because the threat of sexual crimes builds a male-dominant culture (Butler, 2004b: 54–55; Brown, 1995: 22; Connell, 2009: 69). Therefore, male dominance is a double-edged sword for women, wherein consent actually means "incitement" (Brown, 1995: 155). This is manipulative because the sexual connotations of the female body, as discussed in the second chapter, can be generated so that the thing inciting the man is unrecognisable. Therefore, if a man enjoys absolute freedom, the risks of womanhood entrap her somewhere between consent and incitement (Brown, 1995: 155).

Obviously, the regulations and judicial rules about especially sexual violence show us a two-faced problem: The first is liberal law theory, which seeks individual profits and privacy in a more conservative context. This gains institutional and disciplinary impacts and functionality on judicial decisions (Özkazanç, 2013: 194). In other words, these institutional decisions through the

---

3   This is a translation of a Turkish-language proverb: "Kızını boş bırakırsan ya davulcuya ya zurnacıya varır".

lens of the liberal-individualistic empower normative definitions for gendered relations and have no potential to unsettle and reconstruct sexed relations in more equal ways (Özkazanç, 2013: 194). The second is that sexual harassment is a part of the culture, which generates fears and crime narrations. As a result, security questions negatively affect socialisation processes, which paves the way for more conservative and intimate relations (Özkazanç 2013: 195). Therefore, tensions, transitions, and interwoven decisions exist at the crossroads of neoliberalism and neoconservatism, and this is reshaping manhood and moral discourses. In a way, there has been a demise of "patriarchal bargaining" (Özkazanç, 2013;Kandiyoti, 1987). Political reality empowers moralistic judgements, and it thus aims to strengthen the family (Özkazanç, 2013: 234–235). Forms of violence hide sovereign and authoritarian practices, which are the result of unequal state approach (Özkazanç, 2013: 243).

I claim that there are two basic dimensions of womanhood in Turkey. On the one hand, as previously mentioned, women have always been the subject of politics and modernisation throughout Turkish history. On the other hand, women have constantly been excluded from the realm of politics. This reminds us of the concept of "inclusionary exclusion" as proposed by Giorgio Agamben (1998). These two basic paradoxical dimensions of womanhood could be put as follows: As seen in recent political debates about female fertility, the proper number of children for the benefit of society, abortion, the clothing of female deputies, and the headscarf in the political and public spheres, have a central place in political discussions. Recently, these issues have become the constitutive elements of the political agenda in post-2002 Turkey. What is more, the closer examination suggests that in the field of politics these issues are disputed in accordance with neoliberal governmentality and norms. In order to grasp this point as a political reality of violence and its depoliticised methods, I would like to briefly touch on important protective mechanisms and legal applications to clarify the liberal legal order. Protective manhood and gendered mediation also provide insights from the expectations of high politics and the reality of politics in two ways, by which I can observe depoliticised boundaries of violence between freedom, conservatism, and authority (Arendt, 1961).

4.1 Protective Mechanisms and Legal Applications[4]

The National Action Plans prepared within the framework of *zero-tolerance* against gender-based violence covers three implementation periods: short

---

4 For more details see:
  T.C. Türkiye Büyük Millet Meclisi İnsan Haklarını İnceleme Komisyonu.2011. Kadına ve Aile Bireylerine Yönelik Şiddet İnceleme Raporu. 24. Dönem 2. Yasama Yılı.

(2012–2013), medium (2012–2014) and long term (2012–2015 and later). The aim of these plans is to gradually implement the necessary measures for the elimination of all forms of violence against woman in Turkey. The updated aims are:

i. Making legal arrangements and eliminating problems in the implementation of gender equality, violence against women and domestic violence,
ii. In order to eliminate the negative attitudes and behaviours that give rise to violence against women, to create social awareness and *mental transformation* in terms of gender equality and violence against women,
iii. Arrangement and implementation of health services for women/children who have been subjected to violence, and those who are violent and likely to apply,
iv. Empowering institutional/organisational and relevant inter-sectoral cooperation mechanism for the provision of services for the child and, if applicable, for the victim (T.C. Aile, 2012).

Behind these implementations there is a long-term woman's struggle. The worldwide liberal left atmosphere of the 1980s created critical political vacuums that led to problems directly relating to the rise of the new right. This period corresponds to the rise of the feminist movement, during which identities and differences came under criticism in Turkey. The fields of women's and gender studies in particular highlighted violence as an urgent problem. Thanks to consciousness-raising groups, women were informed about their collective experience and ways they could unite in action against violence and the masculine mindset, and were able to bring the fight to an institutional level. Since the implementation of Convention on the Elimination of All Forms of Discrimination Against Women (CEDAW) in 1986, the Solidarity March against Physical Violence has been the most comprehensive campaign and series of

---

T.C. Başbakanlık, Kadın Statüsü Genel Müdürlüğü.2008. Kadına Yönelik Aile İçi Şiddete İlişkin Hukuksal Durum ve Uygulama Örnekleri.

T.C. Başbakanlık, Kadın Statüsü Genel Müdürlüğü.2009. Türkiye'de Kadına Yönelik Aile İçi Şiddet. Ankara.

T.C. Türkiye Büyük Millet Meclisi.2015, May 08. Kadına Yönelik Şiddetin Sebeplerinin Araştırılarak Alınması Gereken Önlemlerin Belirlenmesi Amacıyla Kurulan Meclis Araştırması Komisyon Raporu. Vol: 1. No:717.

T.C. Türkiye Büyük Millet Meclisi.2015, May 08. Kadına Yönelik Şiddetin Sebeplerinin Araştırılarak Alınması Gereken Önlemlerin Belirlenmesi Amacıyla Kurulan Meclis Araştırması Komisyon Raporu, Vol: 2, No:717.

T.C. Aile ve sosyal Politikalar Bakanlığı. (n.d.). Kadına Yönelik Şiddetle Mücadele Ulusal Eylem Planı (2007–2010). Ankara.

marches against violence in the family. In 1989, Our Body is Ours – No to Sexual Abuse organised another series of marches and street demonstrations, and also prepared and published short articles. As a result, in 1990, Article 438 of the Turkish Law of Penalty – which provided remissions in case of the rape of a prostitute – was abolished. However, the masculine field – either semantic or discursive – discriminates against women according to sexual norms. Within that masculine field, being a virgin or not expands its discursive impact both on the remissions and in sending the message that there are "acceptable reasons to attack women" (Tekeli, 2011; Bora and Günal, 2014; Altınay and Arat, 2007; Arat, 2005).

Nonetheless, thanks to the struggle of the women's movement against domestic violence and sexual harassment, 64 institutions were opened, and the power of women's organisations was institutionalised. Moreover, this number rose to 350 by 2004 and has continued to increase. The most important achievement of the rising women's voice was that in 2001, sexist and discriminatory language written into the Turkish Law of Penalty and Civil Code was broadly discussed together with 40 commissions, and with the support of the bar association (Tekeli, 2011; Bora and Günal, 2014; Atınay and Arat, 2007). According to the Report of Impunity Problem (2015), punishments for violence began to change with respect to considerations about the age, physical appearance, education, sexual orientation, and sexual identity of victims. In 2005, sexist statements were removed from the Turkish Criminal Code. The legal statute on Crimes with Regards to Public Morality and Family Order, which included honour killings, was amended to become Crimes against Individual Rights and Freedoms. Legal language that recalled traditional sensibilities such as murder for honour was targeted for removal in favour of framing murder as a violation of one's right to live. Moreover, the contents and definitions of sexual crimes were expanded. The remission in case of rape within marriage was removed and marital rape was made a crime. Domestic violence was recognised as well. According to the Turkish Criminal Code, impairment of physical and/or mental health is also a factor which makes the punishment heavier.

Government Notice 2006 aimed to prevent violence and honour killings. In order to specify the reasons and measures to be taken against honour killings and violence against women and children, a big inter-institutional mechanism was developed and applied to government policy. Bearing in mind that the reality of violence is not rejected but disregarded as an open-wound question regarding women, quick-fix remedies to decrease violence against women without implicating masculine power have also been applied. With memorandums from the Prime Ministry (2006/17) and the Ministry of Interior (2010/10), local action plans are regulated with the aim of protecting and empowering women. Likewise, universities and NGOs are encouraged to coordinate to work on women's questions. In the Grand National Assembly of Turkey and city councils, commissions for equality have been founded. There was also an increase in the number of easily accessible official resources for women. These include Family Consultancy and Guidance Centers, and Violence Prevention and Monitoring Centers that specifically work to the benefit of women who are victims of violence.

The most radical change in law was in 1998, when Article 4320 – Protection of the Family and Prevention of Violence against Women – was enacted. Since this article protected married women against violence, in 2012 Article 6284 – Prevention of Violence against Women – was enacted. The most crucial part of this article is that when a person demands protection, he or she would be protected on the basis of his or her statement without asking for additional evidence; this article protects not only women but also men. This is a groundbreaking change in Turkish law, but it is not an article supported by those who identify as traditional or conservative, as it was claimed that such protection of women might change marital dynamics. For example, domestic violence and forced marriage became grounds for divorce. This article is the foundation for the prevention of violence or potential violence against women and children. It is based on protection and problem-solving. For this, police and administrative chief issue decisions for protection, and both victims and perpetrators receive guidance.

Nevertheless, liberal law with the thought of freedom obviously manipulates the required interventions against domestic violence since it is seen as a private question. In other words, ignoring the fact that violence is a violation of human rights in public and private, (domestic) violence is depoliticised in the hands of private and public actors (Berktay, 2012: 50). With debates ranging from child brides to the regulation of protective mechanisms, the institutional plans and precautions show that different forms of violence have been taken account for a long time in order to tackle the problem. For example, in 1985 CEDAW was signed to empower gender equality in Turkey. With the signature under CEDAW, statistical and informative reports were prepared, in many meetings, and the issues of violence and women's empowerment were discussed. The Istanbul Convention, namely the Council of Europe Convention on Preventing and Combating Violence against Women and Domestic Violence was executed in 2012 to finalise the regulations. It was executed in order to cleanse any remaining elements of sexist language that might be an obstacle to ending violence and discrimination against women. Personal rights for women such as employment, education and decision-making autonomy have been internationally protected. Laws and conventions have been harmonised according to the Convention, which aimed to block regulations (impunity, credit for good behaviour, and provocation) that favour perpetrators. The Istanbul Convention is based on 4P principles: prevention, protection, prosecution, and policy. It aims to prevent rather than simply punish violence, provide protection, maintain consistent contact with victims, and remove obstacles preventing victims from moving forward.

Violence is never acceptable, not only in terms of community health but also individual health. Provincial social services, the Republic of Turkey Ministry of Labour, Social Services and Family hotline – Alo 183 – health institutions, law enforcement officers, public prosecution offices, women's solidarity centres governed by local authorities, bar association-sponsored law and solidarity centres, associations, foundations, and NGOs are the known official institutions and organisations working to support women and prevent violence against women.

4.2   Manhood and Violence

Widespread internet access and the extensive scope of public spaces influence the self-construction of subjectivities. Islamic social integration into neoliberal individualism has given new romantic tastes to man-woman relations. For example, 'half-witted femininity' and 'protective masculinity' have become the normative scenario of heteronormative relations as a result of conservatism, which characteristically venerates the 'parental generation's gender ideals' (Özyeğin, 2009: 108). The self-reflexivity of traditions and religious restrictions constitute the modern components of conservative subjectivities measured in neoliberal values (Özyeğin, 2009: 109–110). The modern woman is a source of paradox for the man, whose ego seeks to protect his traditional social status and role (Sallan-Gül, 2013: 68–69).

In a broader sense, by means of codes of honour and the virtue of shame, the female body is defined as a 'belonging'. When she is single, her body belongs to the family and community. After marriage, the husband becomes the new owner of her body. This ownership and belonging emotionally reconstruct the reality of protection of the female body, which is religiously confirmed as well (Hoyek and Sidawi, 2005: 113; Shalhoub-Kervorkian, 2005: 169; Ismail, 2011: 859). The man's authority is naturalised while the woman internalises the protection of the female body. These reciprocal internalisations set the stage for gender-based crimes and violence on the grounds of the woman's transgression or perceived transgression against such codes. The woman is examined as an object of these crimes in narrated criminal acts, while the man who commits these crimes stays out of focus. Violence is a progression; that is, the deep inequalities between the sexes lead to violence over time because submissive relations are relationships of hierarchy and discipline (Lundgren, 2012). As Mackinnon elaborates:

> Gender is a social system that divides power. It is, therefore, a political system. That is, over time, women have been economically exploited, relegated to domestic slavery, forced into motherhood, sexually objectified, physically abused, used in denigrating entertainment, deprived of a voice and authentic culture, and disenfranchised and excluded from public life. Women, by contrast with comparable men, have systematically been subjected to physical insecurity; targeted for sexual denigration and violation; depersonalized and denigrated; deprived of respect, credibility, and resources; and silenced – and denied public presence, voice, and representation of their interests.
> MACKINNON, 1991: 160

Manhood is reconstructed in a collectivity with collective practices and aims, these being the military, fatherhood, and being a husband according to social norms (Connell, 2005: 77; see also Altınay, 2004). Seeing that gender is all of the social practices, authority belongs to men so this privilege is proved by violence and the subordination of women under gendered relations of domination (Connell, 2005: 77). These relations meet conservative neoliberal expectations because the reasons for violence and the definition of manhood and womanhood change according to family and market values (Connell, 2005: 255). Honour as a fixed value can thus attach easily to market or family values in different ways. Honour is regarded as man's possession, and this blinds us to the fact that honour enforces masculinity in society. Ideal masculinity is protected and preserved through violence and norms.

Vikki Bell questions this well in reference to feminist work by indicating "how the 'well-founded fear' of sexual assault on the street means women enter into a relationship with a 'protective male'. This notion that men will protect women works, in turn, to make women reliant upon men (and to make women in domestic violence situations feel trapped, isolated and like a failure") (Bell, 1993b: 23–24). In a Foucauldian vein, power is everywhere, and it is not individually possessed. If power does not belong to anyone, though, masculine power does not actually belong to the man. Instead, masculine power regulates and practices behaviours and morality by producing norms through the female body. There is no repression. This masculine power is thus constitutive since it can gain willingness and volunteer participation (Bordo, 2004: 310; Hartsock, 1996: 28). Bodily and facial expression is the signifier for whom is subordinated (Bordo, 2004: 312). Subjectivity is formed by power. In other words, power relations are also gender relations, and these gender relations may lead to submission, violence, domination, and obedience (Hartsock, 1989/1990).

The sharp sword of sovereign power cedes its place to non-sovereign or disciplinary power, which is enacted through death and fear (Foucault, 1995: 197), and whose maximum efficiency and minimum expenditure can be calculated (Foucault, 2003a: 36). Discipline produces subjected and practiced bodies, docile bodies (Foucault, 1995, 1984b). It is important to stress that Foucault dwells on the 'docility' of bodies and pertinent techniques and mechanisms in order to emphasise the importance of disciplinary mechanisms in terms of increasing 'the forces of the body (in economic terms of utility)', and of diminishing 'these same forces (in terms of political obedience)' (Foucault, 1995: 138, 1984c: 173). Disciplinary apparatuses hierarchise good and bad subjects in accordance with laws, moral rules and their potentialities, their value, and their level (Foucault, 1995: 181). Discipline forms firstly the norm, then it classifies, divides, hierarchises, collaborates, and finally normalises. As with discipline, security normalises but it firstly separates the normal from the abnormal. Through different curves of normality and basic calculations, the norm is crystallised (Foucault, 2007: 63). All these general features of the *dispositifs* connect with the population in order to recognise the abnormal to be corrected (Foucault, 2003b, 1997d).

Linking to this theoretical framework, protective manhood reinforces the male gaze on a woman and thereby a reminder of the self-government of a woman on her own. As a result, the male gaze turns into an "automatic functioning of power" (Bell, 1993b: 34). Masculinity becomes the governmental order of the public in which the homosocialisation of men increases the dynamics of violence, and this is why, for example, rape is seen as the result of a woman's failures of behaviour (Bell, 1993b; Wood, 2009, Lundgren, 2012; Nadesan, 2008). Therefore, it would be argued that while violence reproduces manhood within systematic facts and practices, womanhood is devalued and changed in line with the rationales of criminal men. This is a normalising process of violence (Lundgren, 2012: 17). Violence, power, and normalisation meet each other at the hub of control relations in which the man has jurisdiction over the life and death of the woman (Lundgren, 2012: 20–21, 36). The woman's distance from life is managed by the man, and deadly protection of a man becomes the love by which the woman's life is restricted and her submission to power is reinforced. In a way, her participation in this system and emotional attachments to the man are subdued by the violence that blurs the difference between death and love, caressing and beating (Lundgren, 2012: 39, 47).

In other words, "safety became gendered" through violence, rapes, wars, drugs (Grewal, 2006: 36). The home is protected against patriarchal violence by ignoring domestic violence. So the "gender of security" finds its meaning within family values that are patiently and sufferingly protected by a woman (Grewal, 2006: 32). The limits of the state in the eradication of violence strategically produce mothers to protect the family and actively join the surveillance of children and family members (Grewal, 2006: 38). On the other side of the coin, obedience and dependence on masculine protection are enforced at home and in the private sphere. This masculine protection at home is exalted as courageous, responsible, and virtuous, with the man replacing aggressive and selfish manhood outside the home (Young, 2003: 4). Because of the dangers and risks of the public, good manhood finds its place within neoliberal logics and safe family relations. The man becomes another watcher of the family in the public gaze (Young, 2003). Thereby, the difference between a bad man and a good man is determined according to the quality of protective manhood (Young, 2003: 4). Concomitantly, protective manhood generates some values suggesting that good manhood is seen as a kind of ability to foresee the risks of life better than the woman. It is like a pastoral power: to protect and care for the family and women benevolently and gently, which leads to the legal codification of some restrictions in the name of security like state authority (Young, 2003). Fears and hierarchical respect are therefore seen necessary to produce the security discourses and mechanisms. The woman entrusts herself to the man in order not to be left to fend for herself.

In other words:

> A "good" woman stands under the male protection of a father or husband, submits to his judgment about what is necessary for her protection, and remains loyal to him. A "bad" woman is one who is unlucky enough not to have a man willing to protect her, or who refuses such protection by claiming the right to run her life. In either case, the woman without a male protector is fair game for any man to dominate. There is a bargain implicit in the masculinity protector role: either submit to my governance or all the bad men out there are liable to approach you, and I will not try to stop them.
>
> YOUNG, 2003: 13–14

State security is the reflection of masculine authority. Therefore, if the relationship between gender-based violence and masculine authority fails to be recognised, this causes a depoliticisation of violence and loses its political essence (Acar-Savran, 1994: 45). This is why rates of domestic violence increase. Those men see their wives as their possession and reinforce their sense of authoritative manhood by making women serve them. Therefore, the basic excuse of men as to why they resorted to violence against the women in their lives is that those women did not accommodate their basic needs. This excuse finds its response in traditional and religious values, so violence is thus legitimised and normalised (Acar-Savran, 1994: 52). By the same token, the division of private and public orders is a basic consequence of liberal rationality. If it is private, state attention is not necessary because it is argued that the state does not have the right to intervene in private. The crucial point is that even if state intervention is required in the case of gender-based crimes and violence, in reality it is taken as a private issue rather than an apolitical reality. This is because of the omnipresent gaze of masculine power.

That is to say, police, courts, and other security mechanisms tackle private problems by trying to mediate compromise. The dilemma about the liberal definition of the private and public appears in its most rigid form when the privacy of various societal subsections becomes a security question, in which exercise of power can legitimise itself (Ackelsberg and Lyndon-Shanley, 1996: 223–224). For example, homosexual relations are publicised because sexual orientation is seen as a security problem on the level of population and public life. Likewise, gender-based crimes and violence in lower-class families are scrutinised by making the private lives of the poor public, while the issue is consciously ignored among the middle class (Ackelsberg and Lyndon-Shanley, 1996: 224–227). By looking through the lens of governmentality, these relativistic exercises of power point out that violence is an obvious political reality, and its depoliticisation enables power to reach well-regulated transition between the public and private or vice versa. Violence can, therefore, restrict the woman's participation and rights both in public and private (Ackelsberg and Lyndon-Shanley, 1996: 227). Additionally, the heterosexual public order stays the same and lower-class people are positioned as a security question and risk factor in society. However, there is still a need to discuss the high rates of father or husband violence against women. As Grewal put it:

> While the main messages of the battered-women's movement was that women were more at risk of physical assault at home than outside it, and more from relatives, lovers, and acquaintances than from strangers, the war on the terror, curiously, has inverted this belief as well as relied on it to create a gendered form of widespread anxiety about safety that takes shape in ideas of motherhood and family. At the same time, however, the continued reporting of this violence suggests that neither the state nor private and feminist agencies can completely eradicate this violence, however much they may try.
>
> GREWAL, 2006: 35

Violence occurs when the balance between force and consent is broken. This consent is reproduced by law, language, culture, education, media, and social forces. The behaviour pattern is generated and specified as normal. The superiority of men comes from here; this is not only about physical power at all. He is superior. Faith and culture accept his supremacy (Doğan, 2016: 22). And also, modern emotions such as love help to reconstruct manhood and womanhood by aggrandising impossible relations, difficult togetherness, tears, and drama because

> the heterosexual couples whose love is prohibited are often the agents of social transformation. Heterosexuality becomes the basis for narratives of reconciliation as if such love can heal the wounds of the past.
> AHMED, 2010: 190

4.3 Gendered Mediation

With the rise of violence, the new political culture points to reconciliation mechanisms, which help solve 'conflictual' cases to generate pathways to 'consent' from the woman. I problematise gendered mediation in terms of conflict management between the parties, who consist of dyads such as rapist-victim, husband-wife, parent-child, etc. The crucial point is that the main argument based on absolute reunification is reinforced by the core status of the family in society. The family values of a society push individuals to find their own 'peaceful' solutions that generally make violence subtle and even invisible. This is only possible with gendered mediation that asks a woman to become reconciliatory.

This gendered mediation is the new face of power, demanding reconciliation from the victim, who needs to forgive and forget. In order not to resist, victims are expected to erase their memories of the violence. And through such events of violence, the political culture of conflict management and meditation serve as an indicator of a strong masculine society, one which needs maternal forgiveness and compassion. Therefore, as Berrin Sönmez (2018) suggests, the new resistance domain for women is not to compromise through gendered mediation that rely on mechanisms of "deterrence" and "consent" (Evrensel, 23 November 2017). Women can resist by refusing reconciliation. There are of course solvable and unsolvable problems. In marriages, the imposition of absolute solutions are legal efforts to reunite the woman with her abuser. Mediation stirs fake justice (Dumrul-Karabacak and Danacı, 2015). In this way, the woman forgives the man for resorting to violence; meanwhile, brutal violence and crime themselves are reduced to personal conflict.

Nevertheless, this process of obtaining the woman's consent needs to be interrogated. According to the Purple Roof Foundation's report (Mor Çatı Derneği,2018), the woman is seen as responsible for the violence to which she is exposed. She is pressured over her complaint by law enforcement personnel in order not to prolong the process. By applying pressure, making accusatory and sexist suggestions, and using dissuasive tactics, the woman is compelled to withdraw her complaint. Examples of dissuasive information include pointing out the conditions of shelters, warning of economic and social difficulties and the future of the children in the case of divorce or a lack of compromise. One way or another, the woman is convinced to stand by her violent husband, marry her rapist, or ignore her harasser on the grounds that this is safer than complaining or resisting. I argue that the reasons women are pushed towards compromise should be viewed as a consequence of depoliticised violence. Violence and rape are reduced to interpersonal conflict, and the solutions are reinforced by social honour and sexuality codes in order to legitimise regulative interventions in the name of risk management.

In this context, I would like to specifically emphasize three issues: i) the rising numbers of forced/early marriages; ii) rising violence in the domestic sphere; iii) rising demands for compromise solutions to violent conflicts in daily life.

The first is known as "shame motion", which mediates the relation between a rapist and an underaged girl through marriage. In 2016, in order to reinforce the political and social consensus, the Minister of Justice proposed to the parliament the issue of "the consent of the minor" to sexual relations and marriage (İleri Haber, 18 November 2016). Even though he stressed that the proposed regulation on early marriages was not motivated by the issue marriage between rapist and victim, it would clear the way for many such marriages using a logic of legitimising the sexual desires of and incidents of reproduction among young people. In order to achieve public consensus for this, different arguments and necessities were juxtaposed by political actors, but the proposed "shame motion" did not find enough support in society and was withdrawn. Nevertheless, its discursive impacts stimulated abusive intentions against the child body. In other words, child marriages are gradually normalised with this kind of discursive practice:

> A rapist escapes liability when and only if he agrees to marry the woman he has "deflowered". While the nation-state does not undertake revenge killings to punish the offenders of sexual honour, it rebukes, disciplines, penalizes the "transgressors", irrespective of distinctions of victim/

aggressor, through regulations that ensure the continuation of the family at all costs.

PARLA, 2001: 78

Similarly, the authority of Muftis to solemnise is given as an official right that opens pathways to early/forced marriage because state marriage has a minimum legal age (Evrensel, 23 November 2017; BirGün, 28 July 2017). In this way, child marriages that are recognised by the state can still protect women's civil rights and control parental decisions over girls' marriages. Therefore, the 700% increase in child abuse cases is no coincidence according to a report by the Organisation for Economic Co-operation and Development (OECD) (Evrensel, 23 November 2017). Forced marriages push child brides to the intersection of violence and community-based family relations, and inhibit their personal, social, and economic development. In other words, as the woman is seen as responsible for her rape, she experiences pressure to repair the social order and honour for the sake of the family by meeting her rapist under the family roof (Çağlar-Gürgey, 2015: 62–69; Sallan-Gül, 2013: 21–22).

Regarding domestic violence, in 2016, the Divorce Investigation Commission at the Grand National Assembly (TBMM) was established in order to understand the reasons for divorce to develop new consent mechanisms to rescue a family from collapse through *true* mediation in the case of violence. The Ministry of Family and Social Policy reports that 38% of 7500 married couples were dissuaded from divorce, which were taken as signs of successful mediation. With successful mediation, married couples should be assisted to find a solution to maintain their life rather going to court. There is an ambivalent function of mediation, which should draw our attention to its twofold expectation: First is that domestic violence is reduced to a simple issue of family life so the man's violence against the woman under family cooperation is normalised. Second is that mediation serves as a shield by pragmatically leaning on family intimacy and privacy (Evrensel, 23 November 2017; Uygur, 2015; Sallan-Gül, 2013). Either way, the foci of mediation helps gendered society build upon the woman's gendered silence, docility and compromise. Mediation is in a way a gendered consensus backed by social roles and family relations.

The gender experts and professional mediators depoliticise patriarchal problems because they are presented as normal happenings of everyday life. Through the development of problem-solving skills, a woman's problems are actually individualised by rendering her as a victim of the male-dominant order (Fraser, 1989: 174–176). As repeatedly stated in this chapter, there has been a dramatic rise in gender-based crimes and violence but more crucially these murders and violence have been getting wilder and more brutal: Burning the woman who wanted to break up, throwing the woman who filed for divorce into a water tunnel, stabbing the wife and burning down the house to kill their children as well, removing her teeth; stabbing the wife 30–40 times in front of their children (Evrensel, 23 November 2017).

"Public warnings" about clothes and behaviours have drastically increased as well (Evrensel, 23 November 2017). In the public sphere, verbal harassment, attacks, and taunts seem to construct the 'normal' and 'appropriate' visibility of public life for woman and man. In a way, this spreading bullying and 'toxic masculinity' becomes the main element of the life of the woman in the family, in the workplace, or anywhere. Mediation between 'conflictual parties' turns into the woman's consent to recover and change her behaviours. In other words, each solution to prevent violence creates another cleavage between gendered relations and the social hierarchy.

Nevertheless, it would be good to say that "the law of mediation" for legal disputes is rejected for cases of domestic violence by virtue of the equality principle; but this is only in principle. Despite all, this proves that mediation between married couples is gendered and operates inequality in favour of the man. The Ministry of Justice defines that "the purpose of the consensus is, as a rule, direct communication between the perpetrator and the victim of the offense, in order for the perpetrators to understand the consequences of their own actions".[5] This may be a sound but not completely convincing strategy to eradicate gender-based violence, whose motivative rationality leaks into each sphere of life with the help of exalted masculine dominance. In other words, consensus is not possible where the woman's death due to gender-based crime is seen as an aspect of ordinary life.

It seems that consensus and mediation should not be a necessity of a well-ordered society if the woman is responsible for solving conflicts through patience and enduring hardships. It shows that the truth of the regime is shaped through justice. If justice points to the law of equality or the law of mediation, judges' decisions are more or less based on basic norms and values (Duva, 2015: 39). Therefore, it is always argued that "law is unjust" (Uygur, 2015). Discriminatory practices and prejudices are legitimised under the promise of legal justice (Uygur, 2015). Therefore, jurisdiction and justice are not the same concepts because justice is exercised by judges, who despite oaths of impartiality have the same implicit biases of anyone else. In this way, bias colours legal decisions, and in the case of domestic and family cases this is clearly observed as gendered discrimination. Liberal law separates the private and

---

5 http://www.uzlasma.adalet.gov.tr/.

public spheres, and the inequalities and injustices of the private sphere are left there (Çağlar-Gürgey, 2015: 59; 62–69).

The security mechanisms against domestic violence and the issue of child marriages in Turkey help to clarify the point that the preventive interventions against violence somehow or another depoliticise the reality of violence and crime. This process of normalising discrimination and the subordination of women turns into a question of lack of conscience and moral degeneration by insistently reminding the wrongdoings of the woman. It is crucial to note that family values and Islamic public peace are the main dynamics counterbalancing the rate of violence but not eradicating it. Mediation and reconciliation turn women into apolitical subjects with respect to their civil rights (Brown, 1995; Fraser, 1989). Women cannot socialise as they are excluded from public life due to the exalted masculinity. In a perverse circle, the women are deemed as half-witted and in need of protection. All in all, community responsibilities and public morality make it impossible for the woman to individualise herself.

5   Concluding Remarks

According to a research survey by a leading centre of investigation in Turkey (Konda, 2012a), there is great parallelism between cases that society labels crime and those it labels shame. 55% of society thinks it is acceptable to use religion as a reference point for both law and morality. The crucial point is that this percentage is not drawn from a single demographic segment; on the contrary, the results show that different societal groups may meet each other at the point where legal justice meets moral judgement.

In line with this, I have argued that the increasing upsurge in violence highlights a required apparatus in order to establish discipline and order between woman and man, and other hierarchical relations. This required apparatus is a *dispositif* of security, through which "rational and autonomous subjects of neoliberal government, illustrating both pastoral power and technologies of the self" realise social rules for and public perceptions of ways of living specific moral conditions and risks (Nadesan, 2008: 150). More specifically, the exclusionary and disciplinary impact of violence draws parallelism with social problems and moral questions, which are defined based on the woman's behaviours, dress, and locations. Therefore, violence aspires to correct and change all abnormalities and differences in the eyes of masculine authority. In the second and third chapters, idealised womanhood and society are scrutinised in order to uphold the fact of violence as an indispensable element of womanhood. Namely, lifestyles, choices, and decisions, dressing or behaving out of the drawn context, may be the reasons for violence. Talking about the reasons, trying to find the *best* solutions, initiating public discussion, and deciphering images generate new mechanisms to keep womanhood under control whilst powering manhood up. Thinking in this critical vein compels us to realise the nexus of analytics between the consent of the woman and the provoked man because the woman's life is precarious, with justice, norms, and legal regulations reinforcing each other, and where moral and social values are produced.

Therefore, gender-based crimes and violence must be regarded as political problems by looking at perpetrators and motivations through a gender-free lens. For this, statistics must carefully be collected to be able to clearly explain why brutal violence against women and children is increasing as strong society, strong family, and strong individual are touted. Religious references are everywhere in daily life, but yet the social and legal mechanisms to protect women remain insufficient. It seems to me that instead of external protection, internal and relational mechanisms in the name of reconciliation or public consensus target correcting the behaviours of womanhood. Therefore, instead of questioning violence itself, the truth is produced through the logic of violence and victimhood. Likewise consent, shyness, shame, enculturation, and acquiescence become virtues generated by violence and masculine surveillance. Political culture wants to reconstruct an uncontentious society by redrawing the justice of hierarchical relations with respect to differences in gender, class, and ethnicity.

Before concluding this chapter, it would be good to emphasise the nexus between public consensus and established consent, both of which need docile womanhood. The docility of womanhood refers to the normalisation of unequal relations and acceptance of masculine authority and power. Authority is related to discipline and order. From this angle, violence is a disciplinary and regulatory apparatus of power. It is disciplinary because violence is an efficient means of control to keep the individual away from moral failures and mistakes.

The neoliberal rationality of governmental desires strong and self-confident individuals. However, neoliberalism met with the new right in the 1980s; new values and statuses were produced in order to unsettle elite bourgeoisie culture in which working hard, and business skills are more important. However, neoconservative counterculture pushed the boundaries of freedom by emphasising the importance of self-control instead of self-government (Cruikshank, 1998: 145). Counterculture proceeded on hierarchy, traditional and discipline between groups of the population; thereby, personal responsibility comes to occupy definitive gaps between the boundaries of these intra- and interrelations in order to elicit governmental action (Cruikshank, 1998: 163). Realising these gaps through a sense of personal responsibility does not allow exclusion and violence against its social and political fellows (Cruikshank, 1998).

Therefore, it is claimed that family, after all, is a unique social institution to stop violence and spread compassion in society.[6] That is to say, violence is a regulatory apparatus because the risk of violence obliges women and children to turn to the family and protective manhood, which properly regulates order and gendered roles. Thereby, gendered subjectivities and technologies of self are internalised and developed through the reality of violence and death. In other words, masculine sovereignty requires the silence of the woman in order to protect its own authority. In this sense, the intimacy of the family also belongs to masculine sovereignty. That is why marriage once again constructs itself as the most proper and secure form of unity between woman and man. In parallel, different lifestyles and sexual orientations are criminalised. This makes conditions more insecure for the women.

As a final word for this chapter, not everyone is exposed to physical or sexual violence, but violence is everywhere as a disciplinary and regulatory instrument of masculine sovereignty (with the constructive help of military and other protective institutions), while the woman forms the culture of violence (Selek, 2002: 17;; Altınay, 2004).

---

6 As Diyanet confirms (Beder-Şen, 2007: 43–45), *traditional discipline in families is provided by violence*. It is actually a disciplinary technique.

CHAPTER 5

Islamic Neoliberal Female Subjectivity in Post-2002 Turkey

This book has proceeded on an argument that 'there is an interplay between security and freedom'. Arguing this point in a general context, the tenets and merits of Islamic neoliberal governmentality brought moral and religious practices to the attention of 'how' the social order of the population would be at large and 'how' ideal womanhood in particular would be. This argument is insistently reiterated: On the one hand, political interest in the woman's sexuality and bodily functions increases. On the other hand, the upsurge of violence against the woman is discussed around the 'wrong behaviours and failed image' of a woman and the moral degeneration of society. That is to say, the problematisation of government insistently points to the corruption of societal values, and political and economic impasses by zooming in on solely the *right and wrong* choices of the woman. From violence to being a good mother, a woman's choices are dichotomised according to religious and moral doctrines. These choices differentiate one woman from another by assigning values to her decision-making abilities and legitimise particular personal choices (Foucault, 1984a: 195). As such, the manifold transformation compels me to define Islamic neoliberal female subjectivity, whose interests and perceptions have been reconstructed by the interplay between rational values and moral values.

In other words, if I take 'the Islamic neoliberal way of thinking' to understand the ingrained Islamic values in the subjectivities, I should seek to essentially find out what neoliberalism destructed in Turkey and then how neoliberalism found a way to maintain itself. Neoliberalism itself is based on a destructive creation (Brown, 2003, 2018; Harvey, 2006) but still, I should make clear it has become most destructive for today's subjectivities at large and female subjectivity in particular. Thinking on neoliberalism and Islamism in tandem, the perspective of governmentality draws attention to the reconstructive elements of female subjectivity. If the woman in Turkey has always been under patriarchal control from the early periods of the Republic to the present, this fact emphasises the 'governed woman', which points to 'masculine sovereignty', 'bodily discipline based on religious principles and social norms, and the individualization of the woman's choices in biopolitics'. To put it more clearly, for the governmentalisation of womanhood there must be a new truth in which the subjectivities realise the norms in order to be subjected, transformed, and improved (Foucault, 1984b;1984c). Docility and the obedience of the woman grow into her individuality, but what convinces her to obey the rules is the main question of this chapter to be explored.

Violence against the woman and political suggestions on the female body, and social rewards for sanctioned behaviours ultimately remind a woman of her life goals and existential reasons to arrive at the salvation from the 'punishment of sovereign power', and to render her obedient through 'norm imposition'. Truth, obedience, and salvation comprise a set through which subjectivities find themselves free. Religions and other social doctrines create the truth in different ways, but I explore Islamic neoliberal governmentality, which recalls Islamic principles for truth, punishment, and rewards for obedience, as well as individualised goals for salvation. Eventually, the reconstruction and reproduction of subjectivities are about "life regimen" and "to take greatest advantage of one's life" through biopolitical authority and expertise (Foucault, 2014: 131). Regulating behaviours and teaching the permanent codes for a permanent state of obedience require three virtues: humility, patience (*patientia*), and submission (Foucault, 2014: 138). Hence, the governed woman is subjected to multiplying *corrective mechanisms of governmentalisation* in which power benefits from social honour. It is actually a milieu of values ranging from politics to economics.

To comprehend this milieu of values and power mechanisms shaping womanhood, in this chapter, I explore the rise of political Islam in order to pinpoint the main components of the traditional and nationalistic political culture in Turkey, since it has transformed into moderate Islam or conservative democracy (Yavuz, 2003; Akdoğan, 2004; Kaya, 2004). Yet, it is actually "to a large extent the neoliberalisation of Islamism" (Öncü, 2014). I then move on to discuss the current Islamic bourgeoisie and the altruistic individuals of Islamic neoliberalism. In order to analyse the Islamisation of politics and the great transformation of post-2002 Turkey, it should be noted that political turning points have ultimately paved the way for the development of the neoliberal economy in Turkey, which went hand in hand with conflicts ensuing from class, classes, political, ethnic, and religious conflict. These conflicts have legitimised the explicit reasons for authoritarian military interventions, which finally became the essence of political culture in Turkey in order to forcefully employ economic and social regulations corresponding to political and social problems.

As a consequence of authoritarian regulations especially with the coup d'etat in 1980, identity politics and individual demands gained the momentum to direct political and social agendas in line with the development of problem-solving mechanisms. Nevertheless, military interventions within democracies lead to a neoliberal order according to "technocratic and authoritarian modes of governing" (Gürkan, 2016: 85). Paraphrasing Wolfgang Streeck, the authoritarian governing of the political, economic, and social order in contemporary neoliberal government is actually related to concerns about sovereignty situated in economic crises, which leads to political and social crises, along with other articulated problems (Gürkan, 2016: 85).

In order to realise and solve these articulated problems, Foucault helps to identify how and why the mechanisms of power have been transformed in the historical flow. However, he especially highlights the structure and aim of mechanisms characterised by different forms of power, i.e. disciplinary and sovereign power, and the government. This means the mechanisms of disciplinary power that existed in the legal system of sovereign power, or the mechanisms of security in biopolitics, were also old mechanisms in the normal order of disciplinary power. That is to say, one mechanism does not necessarily abolish another mechanism of power. Therefore, the society we live in should be analysed in its own rational and logical un/-changed mechanisms if we want to recognise the mechanisms of sovereign and disciplinary government.

In Foucault's words,

> There is not the legal age, the disciplinary age, and then the age of security. Mechanisms of security [in biopolitics] do not replace disciplinary mechanisms, which would have replaced juridico-legal mechanisms ... what above all changes is the dominant characteristic, or more exactly, the system of correlation between juridico-legal mechanisms [sovereign power], disciplinary mechanisms [disciplinary power], and mechanisms of security [biopolitics].
> FOUCAULT, 2007: 8

In this context, the authoritarian character of the Turkish political structure has been showing its face as paternalistic disciplinary regulations and/or militaristic sovereign pressure limits on freedom. Therefore, it is worth considering the governmental rationality of the AKP in the context of a 'challenging unity of sovereign power, disciplinary power, and biopower' in order to carefully develop an analytical framework to grasp the demanding and imperative *language* of power through social practices, particularly referring to the female body, family life, gender justice, faith, and 'successful' womanhood. This perspective allows me to deepen the concept of 'equal inequality for all' by locating it in Islamic conservatism and neoliberalism. In this way, gender justice takes on new meaning through which I can address

Islamic consent towards gendered duties and the morally entrepreneurial subjectivity of neoliberalism. In other words, the gender justice of Islamic neoliberalism perfectly fills the gaps due to differences and the unjust distribution of the rights. In a way, Islamic and neoliberal values 'complement' each other, yet it is still worth questioning and even speculating in which aspects they legitimise each other. This point is crucial to uphold the *creative destruction* of neoliberalism negotiating Islamism and its demands by posing governmental problematics regarding the human fabric and social fabric of Turkey.

The Islamic bourgeoisie has been developed by Muslim businessmen coming together with principles based on the Islamic work ethic at MÜSIAD (the Independent Industrialists' and Businessmen's Association). This organisation differentiated itself from TÜSIAD (Turkish Industry and Business Association), which is comprised of business and industry men of the secular values of Republican Turkey (Yankaya, 2014). MÜSIAD became a mirror of the will to change society through capital transactions according to cultural expectations. Therefore, the construction of the Islamic bourgeoisie denotes a "public manifestation" through which discursive practices and identical behaviours and lifestyles form new social subjectivities (Yankaya, 2014). Dilek Yankaya (2014) describes it well: Subjectivities are generally publicised and objectified, then the identical axes of the different parties are coordinated through these objectified subjectivities. Thereby, a struggle for existence emerges (2014: 21–22). Yankaya, therefore, says that the Islamisation does not have to do with the religion of Islam because it is about Islamic belonging to make collective mobility easier during the transformation of social and symbolic values in line with an Islamic framework (2014: 22). That is to say, public manifestation through Islamic values and symbols points to a politics of Islamisation embracing Islamic lifestyles and traditions, because Islamic transformation should bring a specific morality to mind around which collective consciousness and virtues can move together (Yankaya, 2014: 25–26).

In this vein, the relation with Islam is commodified and new Islamic marketing methods are developed (Yankaya, 2014: 67). "Social life culture" connects the past and present in order to carry power into the future by presenting religious and cultural symbols within the production of market-society relations (Yankaya, 2014: 67–69). However, there is still a missed point in the analysis of contemporary Turkey's daily life subject formation and standpoints of subjectivities because whilst the Islamic bourgeoisie politically increases as a counter-hegemony to the Kemalist bourgeoisie, it draws an image by which "classlessness", "balance", and "harmony" are shown as the cultural and political elements of society (Karahanoğulları, 2018). However, there is no classless society, and the balance regarding the distribution of the sources in post-2002 Turkey. This being the case, (gender) justice, belief, and strong-will, which are the main conditions of a *successful life*, help the Islamic bourgeoisie to gather individuals around the same neoliberal values with different motives, i.e., conservatism instead of secularism; stay-at-home mothers instead of careerist women; docile and silent women and workers instead of assertive ones.

In Turkey, there are always dichotomised conflicts between parties: the periphery against the centre; civil society against the state; the people against Kemalist elites; Democrats against authoritarians (Karahanoğulları, 2018). However, today there are some basic dichotomies between 'you and me', 'she and he', and between 'they and us', 'spiritual and material', 'public and private', all of which are governed by the inclusionary and exclusionary values of daily life, gaining functionality according to the individual choices and their proximity to Islamic norms (Koğacıoğlu, 2004; Yuval Davis, 2009; Ahmed, 2014). However, it is still noteworthy that the Islamic bourgeoisie's values based on the image of a "big family" reflects the same symbolic relations in daily life based on the image of strong hierarchical relations provided in harmony (Karahanoğulları, 2018).

This chapter, therefore, concludes by stressing the impetus of moral values leading to social prestige and gains, by redrawing new boundaries and exclusionary details dealing with behaviours, choices, and everything basically related to consumption and belongings. In a different but critical vein, Islamic high marketing values prevail into each sphere of life regardless of any economic profit. In other words, besides pure economic profit and interest, the economisation of social relations and life spheres is at stake in reconstructing new Islamic neoliberal subjects through the "conduct of conduct" in order to transform lifestyles, norms, and regulations of the social environment, conditions, and law (Gürkan, 2018a;Dean, 1995; Brown, 2018). This is because power does not only have to do with the absolute amount of economic capital but also power; it also relates to human capital, reforming and transforming the social fabric. Overall, the woman becomes a 'reconstructed collective subject' (Braidotti, 1994: 188), so it is appropriate to think that the woman is always the main element of the Islamist Project (Toprak, 2005: 169). The woman and the female body are thus at the centre of the reproductivity and productivity of this Islamic project, which is at the heart of this power regime transformation under AKP rule in post-2002 Turkey.

1 Reading Political Islamism in Its Own Governmental Nature in Turkey

The Republic of Turkey, founded in 1923, adopted authoritarian ways in its early days, in which the idea of a "single party, a single nation and a single leader" was promoted by the party leader İsmet İnönü after Mustafa Kemal Atatürk's death in 1938 (Ahmad, 1999: 88). Subsequently, the Second World War broke out and this apparently legitimised the intervention of the "single party-CHP" permeating every sphere of life. More importantly, the war years brought about economic change and difficulties, such that new laws and regulations were arbitrarily and severely employed in the name of economic progress (Ahmad, 1999: 88–90; Zürcher, 2009: 274–275).

To clarify, secularisation was the backbone of this cultural transformation, which centralised only in bureaucracy while failing to trickle down to the periphery. Combining cultural transformation with economic difficulties, the gap between the rulers and the ruled widened, resulting in two polarised cultures at that time: a westernised secular minority deployed into the bureaucracy; and a religious populous entrenched in localism and characterised as backward (Ahmad, 1999: 114; Zürcher, 2009: 284). As a result, the alienation of people against their rulers became a central question. Among the religious populous, secularist state interventions did not make sense.

The imposed secular modern order inevitably found a counter-narrative. Different interest groups ranging from the landed gentry, bureaucrats, and tradesmen sought to establish a new party. Thereby, the single party regime gave way to a multi-party system after the war, and these interest groups quickly assembled with the establishment of the Democrat Party in 1946 (Ahmad, 1999: 113; Zürcher, 2009: 306). These groups were motivated by Islamic sensitivities that the Democrat Party deftly capitalised on to produce discourses that gained it mass support (Ahmad, 1999: 114; Zürcher, 2009: 338–339). These discourses and tactics revolving around Islam and tradition formed the foundation of 'Islamic revivalism', which has grown more conspicuous under the AKP's rule. Hence, democracy with the commencement of the multi-party system noticed the transformative power of religion on individuals. Between 1946 and 1961, the influence of Islam over the masses could be felt at the polls, as the Democrat Party consistently won general elections, and purported to express the single 'national will' by overtaking the leftist, secular and liberal opponents (Ahmad, 1999: 133, Zürcher, 2009: 336). Eventually, the increasing pressure of this monadic democracy on political freedom sparked the counteraction of the 27 May 1960 coup d'état.

The army's interference in the political process had started as early as the mid-1950s. The army had been troubled by the arbitrary rules and practices aiming to reinforce the power of the capital and the interest of specific groups. While the new Republic had expected to tackle problems inherited from the earlier Republican period, the discourses of the Democrat Party were targeting economic growth while ignoring the civilisational project of adopting secularity. Under these conditions, not only the corruption of the secular project but also runaway inflation prompted increasing complaints from the middle and lower classes, which in turn caused political conflicts. As a result, the 27 May coup d'état was understood by liberals and intellectuals as an attempt to rescue the Republic of Turkey from Islamic political control. Meanwhile, the industrial developments of the time had affected the political orientation of the people positively, resulting in a growing sense of class consciousness among the workers; more importantly, the establishment of TÜSIAD invigorated the bourgeoisie as the new secular, political elites. It is important to take into consideration here that liberal-secular proceedings and economic relief led to new consumer habits, such as alcohol consumption and a new dress style, both of which were viewed as being in conflict with the Islamic lifestyle.

More to the point, the majority was politicised for a better and more secular, liberal, equal life. Accordingly, the CHP's discourses on the 'nation' shifted from one of nationalism to one of patriotism by referring to 'the people' (Zürcher, 2009: 366). As a result, the rightist groups were bound to appeal to Islam and Islamic discourses in order to win the hearts and minds of those disenfranchised by leftist-liberal thoughts (Ahmad, 1999: 170). This means Islam as a transformative instrument had been gradually moving onto the political and social stage in the face of secularism. To put it more clearly, the manipulative power of political Islam was discovered in order to give "free reign to all sorts of obstructionism under the guise of restoring the freedom of religion and in the name of democracy" (Berkes, 1998: 503).

The fact that the rightist discourses were leaning on political Islam inevitably produced two different ideological formations that were institutionalised under two right-wing parties, the MNP (National Order Party) and MHP (National Movement Party). Both were against the open market status of Turkey towards Europe and the USA. The secular culture was troublesome for both in terms of different aspects of moral degeneration. While the MNP espoused Islamic (economic) life by coming together with the entire Muslim world, the MHP localised Turkishness as an ultranationalist party (Rabasa and Larrabee, 2008: 40). Meanwhile, increasing demands by workers and trade unions and rising inflation, plus severe economic crises at the end of the 1960s and the beginning of the 1970s, made ultranationalist and Islamic movements a lot more aggressive; that is, political violence in across all population segments was on the rise (Ahmad, 1999: 181; Zürcher, 2009: 380). The high political tensions and the capital crisis of the promised welfare, so to speak, called for the army to step in once again. The 12 September 1980 coup d'état was the last heavy-handed intervention in political and social life in order to impose the neoliberal transformation of Turkey with a promise to ensure law and order (Özçetin, 2011: 213;Toprak, 1996: 93).

Ultimately, in order to mend all these breaking points as well as the 12 September 1980 coup d'état, with the rise of the AKP, the political actors need to be reiterated and the cultural atmosphere should be depicted as well by pointing out the identity crises and the personalised political demands of excluded groups. In other words, Turgut Özal[1] and his reforms are politically and economically significant for noting the neoliberal transition in Turkey and the increasing visibility of political Islam in the name of an empowered civil society. Just before the 12 September 1980 coup d'état, he was already the leading actor for the 24 January Decisions in 1980, which enabled the development of economic liberalism in Turkey. In order to clear the way for the free-market economy and a strong civil society, the 12 September coup d'état lent a hand to promoting economic liberalism without leftist voices. The coup zeroed in on two things: first, silencing all opponents as much as possible in order to shape the required political and social conditions for a transition to neoliberalisation. The second was to depoliticise 'politics' and the next generation's worldview in order to continue neoliberalisation, and for the new political and cultural reconstruction (Rabasa and Larrabee, 2008: 38; Toprak, 1996: 94; see also Kaya, 2004; Buğra and Savaşkan, 2014).

From the development of economic liberalism, neoliberal political and cultural construction shifted its axes from the state to the individual. Daily life was thereby repoliticised by daily life problems. Revolutionary thoughts about the future gradually gave way to today's personalised concerns across the board, and in a way, the consensus wanted to live in the present and urgently tackle actual problems (Göle, 2011: 7;Toprak, 1996). Under this dark *enlightenment* of the coup d'état, an attempt was made to promote two related themes, albeit paradoxically: "the consolidation of democracy and the strengthening of civil society" (Toprak, 1996: 92–93; Zürcher, 2009: 408). In a way, dramatic changes between state-economic relations surely affected state-society relations, too. At this point, the hinge connecting Islam with

---

1 Özal was 8th President of Republic of Turkey (1989–1993). Previously, he had been General President of ANAP (the Motherland Party) (1983–1989).

politics was tempered and reinforced by the neoliberal expectations of the individual and society. After this, as clearly stated by Feroz Ahmad, this historical overview should ultimately bring us to the juncture where neoliberalism, the manipulative power of political Islam, and the new potential of the right meet (1999: 240). Broadly, individuals had to internalise the competitive nature of neoliberalism; therefore, in order to maximise their chances in a market society, civil liberties and freedom were supposed to be guaranteed (Toprak, 1996: 101). For this, the participatory civil society was concerned with daily life questions and restrictions across the board.

However, an interesting point is concealed in the fact of the 12 September coup that actually brought the end of all coups as an ambitious intervention: on the one hand, it destroyed and repressed all institutions of civil society such as trade unions, universities, and the leftist intelligentsia; on the other hand, it stimulated civil society into reinforcing a commitment to civilian politics, consensus-building, civil rights, and issue-oriented associational activity. In line with this, a string of international agreements on human and social rights had been signed not long before (Toprak, 1996: 95, 97,104; Zürcher, 2009: 410). As the Turkish government was aligning itself with civil liberties and human rights, Islam entered the stage as *the other* of secularism, attempting to gain a voice in the name of participatory society. This unprecedented harmonisation of interest groups came to the fore under ANAP's rule that rose to power in the 1983 election with the coup's control. With the aim of consolidating democracy, Turgut Özal, as the general president of ANAP, became virtually the most impressive and influential political actor until the 1991 election. His government was specifically significant for observing the three components of the Turkish right at the same time, these being Islam, nationalism, and capitalism (Ahmad, 1999: 227; Zürcher, 2009: 407).

In light of neoliberal transformation and its driving forces in Turkey, the social structure changed, too. On the one hand, the regulations in accordance with privatisation forced the reconstruction of the class structure. The welleducated urban middle class gradually disappeared and were replaced with the extremely rich and the terribly poor. Likewise, internal rural-to-urban migration reshaped the general flow of life. The rising rate of unemployment, external debt, political favouritism in bureaucracy, and bribery as a means of cutting through red tape created confusion over power relations (Ahmad, 1999; Toprak, 1996). The market was looking for competitive and powerful individuals, but the distinctive factors were not based on ideal neoliberal competitive values. In other words, new politics brought about new actors and political figures, which had been educated in a secular atmosphere but did not hesitate to hide their religious side, either. However, the only thing that matters is that these new political actors coming from the rural bourgeoisie were relatively traditional but also highly educated professionals.

The technical knowledge of the new bourgeoisie did not suffice to respond to the cultural developments in social life and the demands of competitive neoliberal subjects. In order to compensate for the lack of intellectual expertise regarding the people's needs and to depoliticise the social and economic results of neoliberalism, political Islam became a corrective and instructive means of discourse through which political actors and government favours were allowed enough time to amplify their social, political and economic influence (Göle, 2011; Türkmen, 2014) because in one way or another neoliberal rationality needed to permeate every sphere of life. Hereby, political Islam became a useful means of infiltrating each sphere of life by reshaping the meaning of life and reminding people of the morality of togetherness.

Indeed, in response to the 1968's progressive movement, the army also preferred to foster a religious culture as of 1980, characterising the generation before as idle. To do this, obligatory lessons on religion were added to the primary school curriculum, with the support of the army, to supplement what is taught in the home. The idea behind these religious regulations was to prevent social division and to introduce a focus into their lives despite the secular semantics of bureaucracy (Ahmad, 1999; Göle, 2011; Toprak, 1996; Zürcher, 2009). More importantly, any thoughts regarding resistance or uprisings were to be minimised in everyday life. Hence, as Niyazi Berkes reminds us, "the transformation is needed in political, social, cultural, and religious structures and values before such economic changes can be effective" (Berkes, 1998: 507). Therefore, the imposition of religious culture and education with the support of the army was no coincidence in the move to bring about neoliberal rationality before Turgut Özal and his government came to power in 1983.

Subsequently, political Islam was publicised by Islamic actors. Incorporating these new actors required the reconstruction of subjectivities for the proliferation of the neoliberal culture in Turkey. This does not mean that modernity needed to be redefined, rather that Islamic filters for the internalisation of modernity were used to produce new subjects in neoliberal Turkey (Göle, 2011: 14–15). In order to grasp how to use (political) Islamism to govern and conduct a society, it is necessary to recognise that the political usage of Islam has critically shifted from the DP to the AKP. The DP used it in a populist context to motivate people along specific societal lines by excluding the Kemalist elitism grounded on secular values. With the rise of neoliberalism in the 1980s, the military took advantage of Islamic principles first as a disciplinary power to depoliticise individuals and then to regulate them (Kaya, 2004: 101–102; Buğra and Savaşkan, 2014: 58; Çarkoğlu and Kalaycıoğlu, 2009: 4). For this, education and schools became important domains in which to discipline and 'normalise' people. Under the military regime between 1980 and 1983, the number of religious personnel schools (imam-hatip okulları) and Koranic schools increased (Kaya, 2004: 101–102; Buğra and Savaşkan, 2014: 58).

As a result, Islamic movements seriously accelerated in society. Moreover, the polarisation between seculars and Islamists became more profound. Apart from the Islamic parties, illegal radical Islam groups such as Hezbollah or IBDA-C[2] were at their zenith (Zürcher, 2009: 417). In parallel with these developments on the part of Islamic movements, the RP (Welfare Party), the original of Islamic party as it were, started to take important steps to gain parliamentary sovereignty. Indeed, the RP was able to win the majority of the municipalities at the 1994 local elections. Likewise, it managed to oust even ANAP in the 1995 general elections by getting the majority of votes.

Those Islamic values undeniably controlled the lives of women in the first instance. It caused imperative social assertiveness about male-female relations and the social necessity of self-control. For example, different vehicles for women or early marriages and a lack of educational chances for young girls were rationalised with religious knowledge, especially in rural areas (Ahmad, 1999; Göle, 2011). However, on the other side, the status of women could be discussed in the context of economic liberation. Business and career were on women's agendas as well. In the cities, women could have their own lives or could easily consider a divorce. More importantly, issue-oriented politics enabled women to explicitly talk about backdoor problems such as domestic violence, sexual harassment at work, the education of women and so on (Ahmad, 1999; Göle, 2011;Toprak, 1996).

Nevertheless, Islamism or religious conservatism is a cultural politics with an aim to change society (Buğra and Savaşkan, 2014: 62) but the multidimensional 'liberation' of the free-market economy laid issues bare that had even been ignored by the left. Considering both sides of this fact, the ensuing dilemma forces us to think about the driving forces behind neoliberalism in Turkey. In other words, neoliberalism proceeds along two parallel lines in the country: On the one hand, there are regulations on health, education, national security, and other institutional implementations; on the other hand, the new subclasses are conducted and managed under the control of the state in order to maintain neoliberal continuity (Bedirhanoğlu, 2013: 56–57). Namely, "political stability" is bound to neoliberal development, but this stability is provided

---

2 The Great Eastern Islamic Raiders' Front, İslami Büyükdoğu Akıncılar Cephesi in Turkish, IBDA-C abreviated.

by pressure and authoritarian measures to keep opponents and marginalised groups under control (Bedirhanoğlu, 2013: 56–57). This is why Turkey has unprecedented neoliberal components, which must be read within the context of its own political culture and cultural politics.

Before setting out this point, it is necessary to touch on the RP,[3] which came to power in the 1995 general elections, and which explicitly pointed to the Islamic lifestyle and the intimacy of the female body. In 1998, the RP was closed down on the grounds that it was as a serious threat against secularism as a fundamental Islamist Party. The RP renamed itself as the FP (Virtue Party), and subsequently was banned from politics in 2001, too. All in all, the political instability in Islamist politics resulted in a rift, with one faction remaining fundamental Islamists, while another faction, led by Abdullah Gül and Recep Tayyip Erdoğan splintered to form the AK[4] Party as a reformist wing following the National Outlook (Milli Görüş) movement established by Necmettin Erbakan.

The AK Party quickly gained support and won the most votes (34%) in the 2002 general election. Its popularity continued to increase, and the party won 47% of the 2007 vote and 49% of the 2011 vote. Despite losing some support in the contentious 2015 general election, where it won 41% of the vote, it remained clear that the people's will was to see AKP at the centre of political power. Its strong popular support opened up a critical path by which the AKP could transform political culture, and the party took serious steps towards the Islamisation of politics in parallel with neoliberalisation. Other avenues of power also followed this same transformative course, these being sovereign, disciplinary and biopower.

2   Islamic Neoliberal Governmentality: Challenging the Unity of Sovereign Power, Disciplinary Power and Biopower

The AKP, by winning the vast majority of votes from all general and local elections consecutively, is a distinctive political party to draw a bold line between pre- and post-2002 Turkey in a transition of power in the direction of the

---

3   Necmettin Erbakan was the founder leader of MNP (1970–1971) and MSP (1972–1980), like the RP.
4   The party's acronym stands for Adalet ve Kalkınma Partisi, meaning Justice and Development Party, but the party chose to pronounce the first two initials as "Ak", which is a Turkish adjective meaning 'white' or 'bright', and may connote 'clean' or 'unsullied', depending on the interpretation.

Islamisation of society. The transition of the power from the Kemalists to neoliberal Islamists has brought new social groups to the fore. These new social groups are actually the consequence of the shifting capital among power relations, so when this capital gains parliamentarian power, political power finds its way into society to produce its own identities and also Islamic neoliberal subjectivities. As mentioned above, Islam and capitalism find meaning in each other and are developing together, such that both of them form a new interwoven reality in which democracy, responsibility, unity, rationality, and morality, outliers, and similarities disclose the Islamic public representations in different ways and styles (Yankaya, 2014: 36).

The religion of Islam is based on spiritual doctrine, but this is seen as an obstacle to economic development; in other words, guidance on sense of responsibility, asceticism, and patience is framed through morality rather than mysticism or destiny (Yankaya, 2014: 28–29). The spirit of work becomes translated into management skills, performance, success, profit, power, and social status in pursuit of specific values, in which the principles of prestige can be gained through proximity to Islamic bourgeoisie values and the power to influence the social order (Yankaya, 2014: 167). In order to possess such Islamic prestige, the spirit of the Islamic bourgeoisie rests on three basic pillars, these being religion, family, and work (Yankaya, 2014: 181). This composition of high Islamic culture imposes its values as new norms by highlighting that the internalisation of Islamic morality is the core element of social order and public peace (Yankaya, 2014: 188). In the same context, the public reason is a kind of intervention of authority, through which some groups of people are brought to the fore while others remain outside the real domain of power relations (Çınar, 2008).

The new Islamic order[5] and economic rationality place Islamic traditions and conservative values in themselves by defining what is successful or unsuccessful (Yankaya, 2014: 33). In a way, the new Islamic bourgeoisie paves the way for new experiences and interpretations with capitalism and Islam together, because both are so real that new values such as entrepreneurship and sense

---

5 'New' characterises post-2002 Turkey by differentiating the 'new political Islam' from its ideological traditions based on the *National Outlook Movement*. It would be good to note that the MSP, which was the active Islamist political party in 1972–1980 after the MNP was outlawed in 1971, began to form *counter-elite* groups by legitimising the traiditonal roles and values that Kemalism had moved away from. In accordance with these roles, the MSP led a new fashion and consumption culture (Toprak, 1982: 371). This is why it is suggested that 'the new' Islamic order should denote pure neoliberalism and Islamism in post-2002 Turkey.

of responsibility can be situated at the intersection of capitalism and Islamism (Yankaya, 2014: 34).

Approaching this intersection, the 'submissive entrepreneur' in the Islamic and neoliberal context needs to be deciphered with the harmony of these components to constituting Islamic neoliberal subjectivities. It is important to understand Fatima Mernissi, who claims that "traditional society produced Muslims who were literally "submissive" to the will of the group. Individuality in such a system is discouraged" (1991: 22). Following this statement, I deepen my argument in line with the fact that the entrepreneur individual is convinced by religious necessities to gain consent to obey the truth. Islamic values are however employed via this truth to constitute the basic features of neoliberal subjectivities, which need to *successfully* be good, patient, and also conscious about one's life goals like a real entrepreneur.

Narrowing the point of Islamic neoliberal subjectivity to female subjectivity, I would like to reiterate that religion initially offers submission and consent to focus on youth and women. Women and youth are strategically suitable groups of the population for change and reconstruction because the woman especially produces the truth itself when she legitimises control and codifications regarding her body and social identity (Braidotti, 1994). Therefore, the disobedience of the woman can be explained if Islamic neoliberal female subjectivity fails, as order proceeds on the dichotomy of the obedient and the disobedient. To illustrate, the unchaste *wrong* woman and the suffering *true* woman are affirmed under the guidance of Islamic principles (Toprak, 1982: 362–364). However, the matter is to apprehend the internal Islamic logic with a holistic and integrated approach by highlighting the neoliberal art of government. The woman's gender question, social crises, and violence turn into the consequence of *unsuccessful life management* and *the lack of faith of the female subjectivity*, which falls on the normative margins. In other words, entrepreneurship is related to life management and adaptability skills towards life's challenges. As a result, happiness becomes the output of well-managed challenges.

According to a survey in 2012, as piety gets stronger in Turkey, the reasons for happiness become further away from the concrete achievements of neoliberal life goals. Happiness is seen as a mood that is detached from 'ambitious' entrepreneurship and limitless career plans (Konda, 2012b: 29). However, Islamic neoliberal governmentality unsettles this oblivious piety under AKP rule. The AKP insists on "the change", which differentiates it from other Islamist parties (Çitak and Tur, 2008: 455). The reforms and political packages in the name of adaptation to EU and human rights standards indicate this well. Surely, there is no reformist or evolutionary understanding of change, but what the AKP understands from the change is social engineering and political engineering

(Çitak and Tur, 2008: 463). Its motivation comes from religious values related to tradition and morality although radical change cannot be at stake because radicalism brings about a rupture from the past as well.

The political turmoils in post-2002 Turkey paved the way for increased spiritual values among some population subgroups, in conflict with the Kemalist status quo. At the same time, these conflicts brought the AKP, which is a conservative-democratic party based on an open market economy, in which everybody has equally limited opportunities. Thereby, blind piety is integrated into the market society as "the multiplying powers of ... engineers of the human's soul" by reconstituting the relation between the self and authority through beliefs, wishes, aspiration, and desires (Rose, 1999: 3). Thereby, happiness and peace themselves become success by shaping relations between employer and employee, mother and child, wife and husband, as well as friends, lovers, and coworkers (Rose, 1999: 3). Under the social engineering of the AKP, religious values as norms of measured happiness and adaptation generate governmental techniques and mechanisms by turning the mystical salvation of religious obedience into the real salvation of market values in terms of idealised lifestyle and faithful performances.

Therefore, the AKP has its own specificity in modern Turkish history, and this should definitely be understood as a break from Kemalism and a resurgence of Islamism. However, these breaks and continuities from the past to the present have come together and were embedded in the new neoliberal political rhetoric of political actors and institutional language. This means, on the one hand, there is a new understanding of Islamisation breaking with its fundamental Islamist roots, i.e., the National Outlook movement under Necmettin Erbakan, as mentioned, which opposes the free market. On the other hand, this new Islamisation wanted to settle an account against Kemalists' pressure on Islamists with the intention of protecting secularism as well. Either way, in the modern history of Turkey the AKP cannot be defined by a specific causality because its rise indeed signifies a rupture. I believe that this should be grasped with respect to the interwoven relation between 'violent transformation' and 'transformative violence' in order to maintain itself. This ambiguity actually fits neoliberalism well, making it politically manoeuvrable. Mitchell Dean (2002) questions this "dirty secret" between the globalisation of marketing values and localisation of moral values by discussing, for example, freedom of propaganda and the threat of police violence in the same context (Dean, 2002).

According to Pınar Bedirhanoğlu (2013), the AKP represents a "power practice" in that oppressive and authoritarian state structure is reproduced upon an Islamic conservative model. This is why she does not see these developments in Turkey as a rupture from the past but continuity and transformation.

As said, neoliberalism has transformed the society from above through authoritarian demands and interventions, but with support from below through mechanisms of democracy (Bedirhanoğlu, 2013; Gürkan, 2016; Buğra and Savaşkan, 2014). According to Bedirhanoğlu, the AKP's success is its ability to conduct the conflicts and disagreements through Islamic conservative politics. Therefore, Bedirhanoğlu suggests, realising that the AKP's government is not a structural transformation but it is the discursive transformation of Turkish Politics (Bedirhanoğlu, 2013). As mentioned above, "political stability" is the most important condition for reinforcing the integration of neoliberalism into life itself; this explains the connection between political stability and security, and thereby the AKP's strategy of strengthening state power by reminding the public of the insecurity and instability under coalition governments in pre-2002. As such, discourses around the insecurity of living conditions and precariousness become a political mechanism to hold sway over various population segments on issues ranging from gender relations to opposing political parties.

Security mechanisms such as police services, gated communities, and the military have been endowed with special authorities in the name of protecting society. In line with this transformation of society and politics, differences and inequalities due to neoliberal regulations have been covered up by strong Islamic conservative promises. Neoliberal regulations and religious conservatism have been producing and reinforcing each other through inequalities and differences (Bedirhanoğlu, 2013; Gambetti, 2009). This gives an authoritarian character to the state government, and this would also be a reason to think about neoliberalism with authoritarian conservative measures (Gambetti, 2009; Arendt, 1961). As Arendt (1961) states, the character of authority has been always changing, so crises of authority direct childrearing and education in order to put across its authoritarian will. For her, authority makes everyone feel "equally powerless" in accordance with the same oppression and insecurity (Arendt, 1961: 99). Therefore, *equally powerless* subjects by the authority gravitate to regulating their private domains according to personal relations and roles. This is why the protection of the family and home is related to the "security of the life process", which brings the question of security to the public realm from the private as well (Arendt, 1961: 156).

Before this, the AKP had primarily secured its electoral base under the guise of democracy. It has successfully transformed the society with the help of regulations and reforms on health, education, communication, welfare, human rights, democracy, the Kurdish question, and minority rights. Namely, issues that had been an obstacle ahead of this development were regulated, transformed, and conducted by legislative implementations (Zürcher, 2009; Bedirhanoğlu, 2013; Türkmen, 2014;Arat, 2010; Buğra and Savaşkan, 2014). One way or another, the AKP was able to gain internal and external trust as regards its liberal stance beyond its Islamic identity. It declared itself a "conservative democracy" (AK Party, 2012: 4; Akdoğan, 2004). The emphasis on conservatism, according to the party program, is a "key promise" in order to stake a claim on traditional values and historical gains (AK Party, 2012: 6; Akdoğan, 2004). Actually, this emphasis on conservatism and traditional values in place of Islamism paved the way to use Islamism in principle. In order to transform society by the virtue of social solidarity, conservatism based on Islamist moral principles becomes a strategy favouring new human capital by which the rupture from Kemalist tradition was supposed to be managed as well (Atasoy, 2007: 123; Türkmen, 2014: 118).

That is to say, nobody is principally against Islam in Turkey, even under Kemalist rule. This strategic usage of Islam diversifies the regulative mechanisms of government, and more importantly, it shifts it into the new role of the manipulator to make government mechanisms and interventions more plausible. Therefore, we need to bear in mind that the manipulative power of Islamism in post-2002 Turkey is well used in conjunction with neoliberal necessities. To put it differently, the strategies of Islamists are built on a political imagination, which is not so far away from global political imagination (Iqtidar, 2011: 537). However, the political imagination of Islamists are evaluated separately from its global reality so the discursive practices, albeit globally seeking their legitimations, are recognized within a very limited scope, which is actually insufficient to identify the references to democracy and freedom (Iqtidar, 2011: 537–552)

Therefore, I suggest that Islamic neoliberal governmentality should be understood in the context of its local conditions with its global aims. The manifold transfer of the power regime in post-2002 Turkey acquires a new face coloured by Islamic motivations, neoliberal freedoms, and risks. In addition, I argue that neoliberal governmentality in post-2002 Turkey meets Islamisation in terms of moral risks by legitimizing the restriction of freedoms in reference to Islamic values. Therefore, Islamic neoliberal governmentality has been transforming political and economic values by increasing imperative suggestions against different lifestyles for security purposes.

As noted in the Foucauldian account, neoliberalism is governmental rationality of life. Taking all forms of powers together – these being sovereign power, disciplinary power, and security (government) from ancient Greeks to the neoliberalism of today – governmentality is not reducible to a set of mechanisms and technologies, but encompasses the art of our thoughts and practices associated with political rationality that precisely needs specific knowledge in order to govern us internally and externally (Foucault, 2008).

Foucault puts it more clearly:

> We need to see things not in terms of the replacement of a society of sovereignty by a disciplinary society and subsequent replacement of disciplinary society by a society of government. In reality one has a triangle: Sovereignty discipline government ... which has as its primary target the population and as its essential mechanism the apparatuses of security. The deep historical link between the movement that overturns the constants of sovereignty in consequence of the problem of choices of government; the movement that brings about the emergence of population as a field of intervention and objective of governmental techniques, the process that isolates the economy as a specific sector of reality; and the political economy as the science and the technique of intervention of the government in that field of reality. Three movements –government, population, political economy – that constitute from the eighteenth century onward a solid series, one that even today has assuredly not been dissolved.
>
> FOUCAULT, 2001e: 219

However, there is still a remarkable point that Foucault expects us to realise: Biopower is an extension of sovereign power, which has an ability to proliferate destructive elements and monsters in order to manage life for life itself (Foucault, 2003a: 254; Rabinow and Rose, 2016: 197, 200). Ferda Keskin (2016) locates Foucault's power forms in the governmental art of Turkish politics by highlighting the mechanisms of disciplinary and sovereign power in biopolitics. For him, the early Republican period after the collapse of the Ottoman Empire was the sharpest time for disciplinary power to increase the capacity of human capital whilst imposing new behavioural and visibility codes which were expected to be smoothly internalised by the new Republican subject (Keskin, 2016). Inspired by his argument, I further put forward that disciplinary power becomes stronger during times of transformation, which ensures docility and guides the process of reconstructing new subjectivities in the direction of the problematics of the new government.

In the Turkish case, Ferda Keskin (2016) provides us a map to follow sovereign and disciplinary power upon military interventions, and regulative implementations on the human capital of a population as well as certain individual freedoms. According to him, the transition to a multiparty system in Turkey, as mentioned above, forced the open-market economy by battling anti-imperialist early Republican doctrines. Problems with secularism were therefore highlighted by political Islam, which proceeded on the (new) right, interchangeably reinforced by nationalism, paternalism, political Islamism, and finally neoliberalism with the 24 January initiation of the authoritarian military coup d'état.

On the one hand, the military tried to discipline individuals and pressure opponents. On the other hand, the governmental art of neoliberalism was urged to produce ambitious, free-minded individuals (Keskin, 2016: 78). Among these conflicts between the governmentalisation of the authoritarian state and individualism, its control mechanisms suggest a manageable freedom whose limits should be understandable for individuals if its restriction required. In other words, in contrast to disciplinary power, sovereign power remains ready to employ its mechanisms and technologies of control. Therefore, it may be said that sovereignty conceals itself in definitive and authoritarian practices of power (Nadesan, 2008: 11; see also Dean, 1994).

Turkey under AKP rule becomes an Islamic neoliberal governmentalisation of the state, with disciplinary power and security meeting at the intersection of authoritarian suggestions of religious conservatism. To illustrate, as argued in Chapter 3, there is no consumption ban for alcohol, but its marketing is regulated. Regulating its consumption pointed to 'how' alcohol consumption should be done. Likewise, womanhood and maternal skills are regulated and defined in special reference to motherhood and marriage by suggesting it as the best career option for population development (Keskin, 2016: 78). However, these suggestions and problem-solving mechanisms insistently remind individuals of moral development. To put it more clearly, there are no particular bans and prohibitions related to lifestyles, sexual freedom, or the visibility of woman. There is instead a systematic practice to create a model-subject to secure the Islamic life itself in reference to religious restrictions and prohibitions, as well as legal regulations (Gambetti, 2009).

Against the possible threat of a new coup d'état, the governmentalisation of the state under AKP rule undermined pro-coup cliques in the Turkish army in pursuit of a stronger democratic order without fear. However, the authoritarian character of Turkish politics has always sought to serve itself as the guardian not only of the political and economic structure but also of the moral order. During the 1980s, leftist ideas were described as degenerated and deviant. At that point, military power was always the safeguard of social order and morality. A consequence of declining military power in post-2002 Turkey passed on this guardianship role to the governmentalisation of the state under AKP rule.

As a result, the enemies of its sovereign power changed, and security questions of biopolitics became derived from public morality (Dönmez, 2013; Keskin, 2016; Gambetti, 2009, Dean, 2002).

The decline of military power shows that secularity does not need external protection. Islamism gained a political and economic place to produce its discursive practices by problematising the social and political habits left by secular Kemalist era. As noted, Islamist transformation naturally targets youth and women to put its principles into practice. Public morality and problem-solving mechanisms directly signal new mechanisms and technologies for the reconstruction of youth and womanhood, which had degenerated under secular-western direction. Therefore, there is instability from the liberal government to the authoritarian government in post-2002 Turkey, which determines and leads the mechanisms of disciplinary power or sovereignty from individual to population (Dean, 2002). As a result, in post-2002 Turkey, there is a state-effect to provide security by removing the militarist order. *State governmentalisation* is the new guardian of social security by producing moral measures to differentiate true and false behaviours (Foucault, 2001c: 225, 230).

It seems again that if public morality is at stake, the woman and the female body inevitably become the target of disciplinary power, sovereign power, and biopower to govern womanhood as a category of the population. The population as the multiplicity of the human species became a fundamental component of the state's power in terms of the workforce in the context of the state and wages. The population is the source of wealth, productivity, and disciplinary supervision. It is tied to the regulatory apparatuses of a political project, which are engaged with the birth rate, production processes, labour, the distribution of products, and so forth (Foucault, 2007: 69). Before anything else, the "population will be considered as a set of processes to be managed at the level and on the basis of what is natural in these processes" (Foucault, 2007: 70). The naturalness of the population was problematised firstly in the eighteenth century, and does not, in fact, refer to individuals inhabiting a particular territory; neither is it solely a reproduction of itself. It is based on many variables such as climate, the surroundings, the laws of subjectivation, morale and religious values, etc. (Foucault, 2007: 71). In fact, the population is more than its first meaning in terms of the object and subject of itself. Hence, the population brings with it the question of how it should be governed. To put it roughly, the answer to this should be accompanied by the logic of biopolitics.

As Gilles Deleuze (1992: 4) asserts, different control mechanisms, which are as equally strict and harsh as the previous models of confinement surrounded by disciplinary techniques, have appeared in parallel with the development of neoliberalism. However, currently, subjects can be kept employed in spite of more pressure, control, surveillance, and liabilities through the discourse of the spirit of cooperation used to suggest a familial environment and codes. Emotions that are stimulated through summoning familial bonds retrain conflicts and intolerance towards (professional) public spheres (Deleuze, 1992: 5). It is worth emphasising that the idea of a corporation plays a key role as a neoliberal technology in return for destructively competitive relations. As Deleuze ironically characterises "the soul of cooperation":

> Marketing has become the center or the 'soul' of corporation. We are taught that corporations have a soul, which is the most terrifying news in the world. The operation of markets is now the instrument of social control and forms the impudent breed of our masters. Control is short-term and of rapid rates of turnover, but also continuous and without limit, while discipline was long duration, infinite and discontinuous (1992: 6)

Contemporary biopolitics, especially after the 1980s, has taken on a new form focus on traditional, religious values and norms accompanying neoliberal aims. American neoconservatism, for example, is based on moral-political rationality and neoliberalism; both are intertwined and at the intersection point, where democracy appears as a balanced element (Brown, 2006: 691–692). Without questioning whether or not democracy addresses social and political needs, the question of how neoconservatist rationality enters the fray along with neoliberal rationality is more significant. The first has a regulatory and moral role, while the second is based on a completely immoral, exploitative and exclusionary logic (Brown, 2006).

Nevertheless, constitutional and human rights are restricted by these political rationalities as well. In addition to neoliberal subjectivity, neoconservativist rationality with the help of religious and traditional references aims to strengthen loosening ties with increasingly isolated individuals. In spite of the upswing in working hours for better living standards and the breadth of 'free rights', these processes actually create more depressed individuals but more fundamentally a decline in the birth rate, a weak population, a lack of sense of belonging to society, and a rise in criminality and conflicts because due to a lack of family cohesion and love relations. At this point, neoconservativist rationality of the government steps in to fill the gaps posed by neoliberalism. With the help of the notion of citizenship, individuals are subjected to control and surveillance as required by security dispositifs through licenses, codes and insurance numbers or bank account numbers. The matter of control emerges from neoliberal subjects as citizens of the state. Therefore, a good citizenry should take responsibility for a stronger welfare society and secured relations in families, firms, and communities (Rose, 2000: 325–327).

There are marginalised spaces associated with anti-citizens, non-citizens, and failed citizens, those who cannot or do not enterprise their lives or manage their own risk, not additionally become attached to any moral and traditional communities (Rose, 2000: 331). Failed citizens are bad subjects who somehow do not want to participate in an 'active life'. Therefore, an ideal citizenry that is endowed with self-governable subjectivity becomes the most important indication of liberal democracies. In a way, idealised liberal democracies are described as welfare societies. Neoliberal rationality can occupy land by promising 'modest-power sharing' through free elections and individual liberties for the sake of democracy (Brown, 2003: 9). Nonetheless, it would be good to keep in mind that as Foucault pointed out, the technologies and strategies of power in line with its problematisations can be shifted with respect to "the sovereignty-discipline-government triad" (Nadesan, 2008:7).

To illustrate, according to Diyanet, values – i.e., shame, honour – manage us, and we should freely and voluntarily go along with these social values. According to Binnaz Toprak's research, if it is said that fasting is a religious obligation, one is convinced to fast; individuals freely prefer to fast without any political force. However, there is a felt control on the dress and consumption, as well as pressure regarding ethnic, sexual orientation, and lifestyle differences. The crucial point is that there is no state mechanism forcing individuals to change their lifestyles and to narrow their secular choices, but there is increasing interest in knowing the habits of different lifestyles and increasing control and transformative mechanisms for these habits (Toprak, 2008: 14–19). Therefore, the problematisations interested in disciplinary and security power demand more transparency and relevant solutions. In order to achieve this, power seeks to be more authoritarian (Razavi and Jeniche, 2010: 843). The AKP does not force anybody to perform religious rituals, but it must be understood that there are new religious and traditional norms that conduct relations among individuals, and to regulate gender and public relations. This is another reason why post-2002 Turkey needs to be observed in interchangeable forms of power.

In democracy and divorce relations, there is an additional nexus between the authoritarian regime and control of the woman (Scott, 2010: 131). If the family is a reflection of the state, then the egalitarian or patriarchal authoritarian family structure displays the rationality of the state and so the gender regime. Especially during times of transformation, authoritarian power determines the division of labour and distributes duties to the woman and man according to private and public considerations. Linked to the above-mentioned remarks of Arendt, the family is an indispensable domain of good government. This is why marriage is promoted, because family is related to the security of authority itself. All of these, in the end, are linked to population (Foucault, 2001e: 216, 219).

Normative definitions of gender help to carry power relations through the sexes and particularly womanhood. According to Joan Scott, high politics itself is a gendered concept because its authority and activities need to be explained reasonably regarding why power relations are regulated by specific actors and insist on excluding women from the political stage (2010: 132). It is interesting that although womanhood and gendered duties are debated in an idealised way, regulative and transformative power leave control to the man. Overall, this is related to the paternal understanding of security.

Similarly, authority fears the loss of influence and control. This is why security and order ultimately grow into normality, where difference is seen as a threat that needs to be corrected, avoided, and punished. This is the reason authority makes its way upon normative dichotomies and differences, excluding social, sexual, and ethnic minorities in order to keep solidarity among "us" (Çarkoğlu and Kalaycıoğlu, 2009: 37; Buğra and Savaşkan, 2014: 17).

That is why targeting being *good* or *ideal* rather than obeying the rules does not keep security politics and the need for police in the background because there is still the power that wants to protect its authority to control and oppress the social body, population, and individuals (Dean, 2002). Surveillance and monitoring are still the vital ways of power to pursue and to govern daily life activities because "the marketisation of social" is actually important, no matter if obeying rules or being good for the self (Ismail, 2011: 846). "The emotional power over the masses" expands a subtle domain to speak to the good woman and man in a complementary way. Religion rationalises the 'complementarity of differences' by means of God's justice. The duties of women and men are, thus, taken for granted.

According to Hartmann (1981), patriarchal postulation also seeks a complementary balance on gender roles, by which the woman is expected to care for domestic affairs while the man is the breadwinner working outside the home (Hartmann, 1981). Indeed, man and woman complement each other, but this does not change the fact that there are hierarchal relations reinforced by religious traditions as well, which consist of "men of power" and "men of good (and of God)" in order to increase the influence of Islamic practices and the mediation of Islamist actors (Ismail, 2011: 859).

All points considered, there is a "benevolent patriarch" as "the selfless and wise protector whose actions aim to foster and maintain security" (Young, 2003: 7). The state promises to secure its citizens by using its wise authority.

Therefore, the interventions on lifestyles and the female body must always be plausible because it mainly refers to the necessities of the population and nation. In a way, the 'depoliticisation of social problems' call on the subject to self-care with respect to moral development, which leads to authoritarian government through religious references to political discourses and plans. There is a concomitant result of Islamic neoliberal governmentality, which comes to function in line with "truth-authority-submission" (Brown, 2006: 706–707). Power relations flow from above to below in post-2002 Turkey by using the same authoritarian voice as a reminder of common values and threats in order to *defend society*.

3 Rethinking Gender Justice in the Context of Islamism and Neoliberalism

Knowledge-power produces new values and control mechanisms, by which self-technologies and political technologies of power need new instrumental concepts such as, gender justice instead of gender equality. In order to achieve the "dewesternisation of knowledge" regarding social virtues based on (gender) equality and human rights (Tibi, 1995: 4), local knowledge based on traditions and religion is applied to neoliberal measures, asking for patience and obedience towards working and living conditions. Inspired by the ideal of gender equality as a biopolitical technology of population and productivity (Repo, 2016), I would suggest that gender justice is a new apparatus of the biopolitics of Islamisation to transform society according to gendered roles, and in order to increase the woman's reproductivity and docility as a biopolitical means of cultivating a religiously conservative population.

According to Jemima Repo (2016: 137–138), gender equality policy enables women to participate in economic development by transforming into and actualising the aim of becoming an entrepreneur and job seeker. Gender equality policy aims to regulate gendered sexual behaviours in order to increase fertility rates and the woman's role in reproduction by enhancing her "life function" through "management of the powers of production and reproduction" (Repo, 2016: 141). Her seminal argument says that gender roles "as a key variable" prompt individuals calculate and manage their own lives and choices according to their sexes; therefore, gender equality policy becomes a governmental means by which the "rational-economic" subject is able to perform self-governance and self-examining by regulating the life expectations of women and men through sexed norms (Repo, 2016: 146, 155–156).

In line with Repo's argument, I say that while gender equality policy points to self-entrepreneurship surrounded by pure market-society values, gender justice as a biopolitical technology of Islamism relies on the moral development of particularly women in order to integrate them into the governance of population through only her reproductive nature and mothering role. In gender justice, there is a twofold functionality: i) it aims to safeguard womanhood against neoliberal feminism, wherein free career steps and motherhood are described in the same 'happy' frame of life. Through self-promotion, for neoliberal feminist women to "have-it-all" is presented as possible for every woman regardless of class, race, age, and other differences which already undermine the plausibility of gender equality policy (Pollack and Rossiter, 2010; Rottenberg, 2013; Lavee, 2015; Walby, 1997; Walby, 2004). ii) Related to the first argument, it intends to regulate 'mothers' of the population as a responsible subject to the self and others by emphasising moral values in pursuit of better transforming the population in the direction of Islamic neoliberalism.

Islamic sociologist Abdurrahman Arslan is an important intellectual from which to gain insights as to how the morality of Islam defines relations between woman and man. He says that Islam cannot define any other gender role independent of the sexes. Gender roles are directly sexed and this is based on the naturally unequal distribution of labour by gender. This is why, for him, the demand for gender equality is a rejection of the sexed status of woman and man, and a demand for another's role. Therefore, Islam does not accept gender equality in that the woman is encouraged to enter a professional career instead of performing her fundamental duty to be a wife and mother. Motherhood is an indispensable duty of the woman in Islamic understanding (T24, 30 September 2008).

Arslan claims that insistence on gender equality unsettles the moral norms of Islam by which gendered relations are regulated and managed. He emphasises that there are clear restrictions between the sexual behaviours of woman and man. To ignore these biological differences and skills is actually unfair and unjust against the woman (T24, 30 September 2008). Islamic principles support the fact that *man and woman are human, and the woman's rights are protected under the human rights of Islam. The woman is temperamentally weaker than the man, so his duty is to protect her. Besides this, the ability to give birth is granted to the woman* (Ilmihâl, Vol. 2: 315). This duty-based definition of rights leads justice to find responsible subjects of God. One of the Khutbahs points to the same biological differences between woman and man, saying that *these differences do not denote any deficiency or supremacy in the presence of God. Supremacy is ensured by devotion and godliness* (taqwa), *so both woman and man for the sake of God should recognise their responsibilities towards each other* (Khutbah, 05 March 2010; Khutbah, 02 March 2012).

Likewise, Diyanet describes *life as a stage for our responsibilities, roles, and duties* (Çekin, 2006: 27). That is why we learn from another Khutbah that *life is based on community relations; based on conscientiousness and responsibility towards family. Also, national and spiritual values also need to be taught* (Khutbah, 08 June 2012). Therefore, *girls and boys should not be brought up to discriminate, and parents must be just and fair regardless of the sexes of their children* (Khutbah, 08 June 2012). Ultimately, *the human is possessed of reason and responsibility, which makes him or her fair and just* (Khutbah, 31 July 2015). *Islam gifts the status of motherhood to the woman so that those who educate their girls well are heralded by heaven* (Khutbah, 02 March 2012). However, as Yeşim Arat remarks, gender justice is reduced to the mutual conditions of woman and man; in this way, sexist values are circulated by religious references (Arat, 2010).

In post-2002 Turkey, the most important changes are about women's rights in terms of equality at face value. According to the Turkish Constitution, Article 10, "everyone is equal before the law without distinction as to language, race, color, sex, political opinion, philosophical belief, religion, and sect, or any such grounds". In Turkey, equalities are under state guarantee (Çitak and Tur, 2008: 456). In order to promote the sense of equality, international and national regulations and treaties were prepared and signed.

Just as Turkey signed CEDAW (the Convention on the Elimination of all Forms of Discrimination against Women) in 2011, it also accepted the conditions of the Istanbul Convention. At the national level, family courts were established to specifically care for family issues and women's rights according to the Family Law. The Law of Penalty was amended, and honour killings are charged as criminal cases rather than matters of tradition.

In addition, new legal regulations deem municipalities responsible for providing shelters for women and children (Çitak and Tur, 2008: 456). This closed a legal loophole, so was deemed a success of the woman's movement and civil society. As such, in 2001, the "head of household" article was changed to give equal status and responsibility to both parents to manage family cooperation and to fulfil the necessities of family life. However, there is still no clear gendered division of labour, which implies that the woman's commitment to family relations is ensured by gender justice.

Linking to the governmental rationality of Islamic neoliberalism, Mr. Erdoğan stressed the "delicate nature of the woman" (*fitrat*) at a summit on justice for women (The Guardian, 24 November 2014). He reveals his ideas:

> Our religion has defined a position for women: motherhood ... Some people can understand this, while others can't. You cannot explain this to feminists because they don't accept the concept of motherhood ... You cannot make women work in the same jobs as men do, as in communist regimes. You cannot give them a shovel and tell them to do their work. This is against their delicate nature ... What women need is to be able to be equivalent, rather than equal. Because equality turns the victim into an oppressor and vice versa.
>
> THE GUARDIAN, 24 November 2014

Furthermore, he emphasises gender justice in another speech critically referring to Western values:

> It is not surprising to us that the [Western] mentality that used women as a commodity yesterday is using women as a commodity in the packaging of equality today ... The future of a society where the family institution is not strong is equally dark for men and women ... As human beings, we have responsibilities independent of our gender. We have responsibilities as women and men; women have additional responsibilities ... We cannot discriminate women against men. Because it is necessary to look at the same as all creatures. When I got your attention, I started with 'Ladies [*hanımefendiler*] and gentlemen [*beyefendiler*]'. It is very important for men and women to be called *efendi*[6].
>
> BIANET, 14 July 2018

Westernised rights of equality and Easternised judgement against Western knowledge, in my view, need to be understood in their own context. There is a clear conceptualisation of "honor nomos-driven justice perspectives" in the Islamic context in order to differentiate between "opinion-independent reality" and "the opinion of a *hakk* (true or virtuous) witness as the legitimate basis of the just ruling" (Öncü, 2018: 2). Opinion –independent reality – is related to human rights and written law, which are based on documents and rules in that there is no decision-making mechanism, i.e. a witness to do justice to acts and rights (Öncü, 2018: 2). Nevertheless, both perspectives on justice are based on local values and knowledge to ensure moral order as agency. However, there is still a critical nuance between natural human rights and God's justice. As

---

6 *Efendi*, originally Greek word, may be used as either a title or adjective. As a title it denotes authority. As an adjective, it refers to a well-educated, polite, and kind person. Either way, it has a masculinised meaning even when it is used for women. (http://www.tdk.gov.tr).

justice is "a reality" and "established fact", the truth reflects the facts in the Westernised context of the rights (Öncü, 2018: 1–3). As for the justice of Islamic sensibility, the truth becomes a unique reality, which is God and its "ultimate authority governing the lives of all people" through absolute fear of God's judgement.

When these woven justice perspectives are thought about alongside the current political agenda in Turkey, the discussions around headscarf would be relevant to highlight the injustice of the headscarf ban in the context of human rights. Islamic foundations and organisations found this ban to be an unjust implementation of equal rights. The same Islamic movement and foundations cannot take this same decisive standpoint against other gender inequalities for the sake of justice (Aslan-Akman, 2008: 76–79; Arat, 1998: 126). Therefore, in line with Sevinç Doğan's remarkable argument, the power of the AKP's government stems from the claim that the AKP is the judge and distributer. As evidence of this, the freedom to wear the headscarf is a sign that the party brought justice to Turkey. This means there is an atmosphere of fear of injustice on the part of Kemalists in case the AKP falls (Evrensel, 26 February 2017). Razavi and Jenichen put forward a similar argument, saying that:

> There is unmistakably a recent narrowing of agendas of various (though by no means all) religious actors and movements, not only Islamist, around an exclusive moral, ideological and identity-based politics. Many such movements capitalise on gender issues to demand a greater public role for themselves as moral guardians of the nation promising justice and redress.
>
> RAZAVI AND JENICHEN, 2010: 837

In a similar critical vein, Richard Sennett puts it well that:

> Renunciation is the task of religion. Religion generates the belief that the laws of survival and justice in society come from a superhuman source, and therefore are beyond human reason and human questioning. The terrors of the state of nature are replaced by terror of the gods' wrath. But the presence of the gods must be directly felt in the world; they are believable only if they show themselves through extraordinary persons, through leaders. The "Grace" of the leader gives him emotional power over the masses; only leaders who appear to have Grace can demand that men renounce their worst passions, can ask them to be good rather than just to obey.
>
> SENNETT, 1978: 273

Therefore, as Doğan (Evrensel, 26 February 2017) suggests, there must be an integrative women's movement and solidarity to find absolute justice and equality instead of having faith in the masculine promise of justice. As Najmabadi warns:

> Thinking of Islam as the antithesis of modernity and secularism forecloses the possibilities of recognizing these emergences and working for these reconfigurations; it blocks off formation of alliances; it continues to reproduce Islam as exclusive of secularism, democracy, and feminism, as a pollutant of these projects; and it continues the work of constituting each as the edge at which meaning would collapse for the other.
> NAJMABADI, 2000: 41

This also brings to mind Hardt and Negri's *Empire* (2000), in which it is stated that justice for all people under the *Empire*'s guarantee is related to a measurement of virtue. Islam as the religion of justice and equality clearly defines the responsibilities of parts of the social body. Yet, today's bourgeoisie of Turkey and Islam are on the same page, which points out solutions to problems of inequality in terms of the social justice of the state (Yankaya, 2014: 17).

Concrete identities and belongings draw boundaries between groups of people according to sex, ethnicity, class, race, and the like. Group limits create their own narrations to create "generalized others" through the politics of morality (Jones, 1996: 85–86; Yuval-Davis, 2009). Judgement makes the boundaries and hierarchies between groups of people invisible, and it acquires dynamic content to unjust situations through the promised benefits and rights, subjecting it to structural conditions. Furthermore, "judgments of justice and injustice" (Young, 2001: 9) come to the fore in order to decipher the fact that justice is not about equality, even if equality refers to procedural justice (Young, 2001: 6–7).

That is to say, there are structural inequalities, which legitimise the justice of unjust privileges by relying on moral judgement. Therefore, risk factors differ depending on the population categories. If you are a woman, the spectrum of these risks extends in comparison to a man (Brown, 1995). It is clear that neoliberal risk society does not present the same life standards to, for example, the woman, man, black, young, old, homosexual, poor, or rich. Therefore, female or subaltern subjectivities are built on the awareness of risk factors that are more likely to be experienced. This is, for me, the internalisation of social happenings without asking why there are such risks at large, and why a woman has to care for herself more than a man does in particular.

In other words, our inequalities are taken for granted by ourselves and sometimes it is accepted that we do not have to be equal by wishing to be the best for ourselves. In the neoliberal understanding of female subjectivity, the woman is expected to be aware of the structural barriers against not only her career steps but also her individual emancipation to make personal choices. Although underdeveloped countries are regularly pointed to as those lacking in gender equality and equal opportunities, in developed countries we witness neoliberal feminist subjectivities that develop an ambitious aspect of overcoming gender inequality by accepting it as a personal problem instead of a structural problem (Rottenberg, 2013: 3; see also Young, 2001; Brown, 1995).

Within this neoliberal frame, gender equality turns into a goal by balancing out all social and gender roles at the same time and empowering the self. In the end, collective consciousness against gender inequalities loses its meaning, and in tandem with this missed insubordinate perspective collective actions are reduced to individual submissiveness in line with neoliberal rationality, leading to new moral values towards a work-life balance (Rottenberg, 2013; Fraser, 2012; Orgad and De Benedictis, 2015; Yuval-Davis, 2009). Eventually, the distribution of justice is unfair if cultural demands and consumption styles are taken into account. Justice finds its functional meaning if the social order is secured.

In this regard, gender justice needs to be thought about in terms of a social justice output that is about access to sources and rights. If I describe my own definition of justice, justice is contingent on equal access to life resources. I mean not the equal distribution of justice as a governmental technology, but indeed freedom without obstacles and even without intermediaries to reach resources and rights. Otherwise, if justice is defined as the equal distribution of rights, benefits, and the responsibilities to life and living together, this equality denotes the distribution of justice in line with sexual, cultural, class, race, and ethnic differences as well. Moreover, all prohibitions and inequalities demand the patience and collaboration of women, and so justice is not at stake at all. Gender justice distributes its benefits and concessions in accordance with the heteronormative social order embedded in family values (Young, 1996: 255–259). In other words, justice itself has expectations from individuals to protect and secure them from life's dangers. Therefore, "the question of social justice is recast in personal, individualized terms" (Rottenberg, 2013: 5).

François Ewald (1990) calls attention to norms with an explanation of the relation between law and discipline. For him, norms determine the common standard by which groups of the population can be fairly regulated in peace. Therefore, he argues that a norm is equal to consensus, which lends it a sense of equality. The norm is juridical instead of legal; therefore, it establishes the parameters of judgement (Ewald, 1990: 138–139). The norm appears in the juridical responses against cases, events, and relations between events. Therefore, Foucault regards punishment as a positive mechanism of justice by taking account of its corrective function and *political tactic* (1984c: 170–171). Justice serves as a security mechanism to discipline subjects and order according to moral norms. State interventions and punishments of justice for security purposes are legitimised (Chatterjee, 2004: 34; Ewald, 1990: 140). According to Chatterjee, this would be a reason why equality seems guaranteed by the state along with extensive surveillance mechanisms on individuals and population groups (Chatterjee, 2004: 34) because "governmentality always operates on a heterogeneous social field, on multiple population groups, and with multiple strategies. Here there is no equal and uniform exercise of the rights of citizenship" (Chatterjee, 2004: 60). That is to say, governmentality needs to produce population groups and classes loaded with moral values, which is the core of governmental politics (Chatterjee, 2004: 75). These population groups ultimately are subject to macro- and micro-community relations, which provide the "conduct of conduct" from the individual through the community to the population.

Now, the economy of power and moral values appears. Governmentality needs the matter of equality at a discursive level, but practically there must be different groups and classes to recognise criminality, violence, and marginality. Neoliberal reason must produce the standard by highlighting abnormalities and inequalities among groups. These kinds of classification give us the characteristic features of these groups. If the population divides gender categories as woman and man, other sexual orientations are left at the periphery of justice. Chatterjee says that womanhood is regulated by law, and women are under state security, but this is not practically true at all because women's behaviours and everyday practices are regulated by other authorities among community-based relations (Chatterjee, 2004: 77; Dean, 1994: 195,197). This is actually "life-conduct" based on specific knowledge in order to stimulate self-actualization (Dean, 1994: 211, 198–199).

Therefore, the woman's traditional gendered roles are legitimised with reference to her delicate nature. According to Gülay Toksöz, this perspective becomes an obstacle, discouraging woman to participate in business life and to have a job. While neoliberalisation already brings serious precarity, it leads to more precarious and risky life conditions for the woman by merging religiously conservative values with moral rules. In parallel with this governmental rationality, parental leave and unpaid leave open up an opportunistic way in which women are excluded from the job market on account of their 'obligatory' gendered roles, i.e. motherhood (Evrensel, 7 May2017; Acar-Savran, 2008; Toksöz, 2016; Dedeoğlu, 2009; Rottenberg, 2014). Justice finds its own moral merits by convincing women of 'the single way of life' wherein family, marriage, and mothering are her principal responsibilities and raison d'être (Acar-Savran, 2008).

Likewise, Ayşe Buğra (2014: 149) respond to the question as to "how neoliberalism can act in tandem with cultural conservatism to shape a social order in which traditional gender norms are reasserted and the parity of participation crippled". There are incentive policies to encourage women to work at home for very low pay. Traditional and conservative sensibilities regulate the motivation of women by convincing them about their exclusive responsibilities with respect to family care (Bugra, 2014: 152). Moreover, the increasing news about sexual harassment at the workplace points to the risks working women face. In a way, the risk of workplace harassment functions as a new *consent mechanism* to discourage women from working outside their home or neighbourhood.

Another driving force pushing women to stay at home is "helplessness" against the male-order of the public. There are set rules and limits women are expected to accept and normalise (Bugra, 2014: 152–153). Therefore, helplessness or learned helplessness is another mechanism concealed in conservative discursive practices. On the one hand, increasing conservative and restrictive values insistently give the recipe of ideal womanhood; on the other hand, it is a struggle to make a living under the precarious conditions imposed by neoliberalism. Under these circumstances, women in Turkey try to oscillate between "learned helplessness and life with dignity" in the face of working conditions, restrictions, earning a living, and personal ideals (Sert and Akkoyunlu-Wigley, 2015). Since the religiously conservative direction of society pushes women to care for her home and family duties, the woman at work life and its accomplishments are devalued (Sert and Akkoyunlu-Wigley, 2015: 73–74). Therefore, it may be said that Islamic references and control over women's behaviours and attire not only cultivate discriminatory and abusive public attitudes in general, but they also lead to collective pressure, through which the discursive practices in patriarchal language easily turn into humiliating jokes or unfair performance measures on the working woman (Sert and Akkoyunlu-Wigley, 2015: 73; Arat, 2010). Through the conservative and traditional image of ideal womanhood, successful working women in particular are left vulnerable and alone against the oppressive authoritarian mechanisms that have mushroomed (Sert and Akkoyunlu-Wigley, 2015; Arik, 2012; Fraser, 1989).

Referring once again to Buğra (2014: 154–155), religiously conservative values aim to produce the docile and obedient womanhood within a population whether she is a mother at home or a worker in a factory. The political project has successfully transformed public perception and expectations from the woman in general because the woman must 'act like a woman' (Hekman,

2014; Braidotti, 1994; Gioscia and Delacoste, 2013). The woman is expected to empower her practices of self-management and economic rationality by taking personal initiative and innovating (Iqtidar, 2011: 561–562; Rottenberg, 2013: 4–5). The woman should normalise inequality, and she needs to willingly mentor and transform her skills and perspective to take more responsibility and thereby happily do her best in unequal circumstances (Rottenberg, 2013: 7, 16).

Equality is regarded as the realisation of roles and responsibilities in line with the God-given life duties. The woman must comprehend that this filling of God-given duties is a prerequisite for social justice and peace. Yet, there is still a major disciplinary implementation of conservative values that Akgöz and Balta (2015: 11, 13) point out: i) just as homemaker women, who need to bring serenity to men's lives, conservative values discipline and motivate men against neoliberal precarity by exalting them as breadwinner-heroes. For these men, women and children become a reason to work vigorously; ii) 'women as an anti-anxiety agent' against neoliberal crises are used as *a buffer* in order to prevent social ruptures and the demise of the family. That is why with the help of conciliatory regulations and consulting services to keep women in the family unit, the responsibilities and roles of women are reproduced using any possible mechanism to gain consent or to make women accept her helplessness. To paraphrase Nadesan, biopower is quite a capable and seductive way to find new strategies and tactics to optimise the efficiency and productivity of individuals, families, market organizations, and states (Nasesan, 2008: 3; Valverde, 1996).

According to Wendy Brown (2018), with the economisation of relations and roles, justice and equality lose their meaning and functionality. For her, the soul is reconstructed, and new measures of virtues turn the tables on the wrongdoings and the normative failures of moral subjects. Equality and violence are defined in the same semantic field, indeed *competing with* each other (Brown, 2018: 27). In other words, justice and sustainability speak to the social responsibilities of the woman and man who need to have children and then work to make a home, both of which bond to national development (Brown, 2018: 28–29).

Nevertheless, it is essential to state how Brown defines the governmental rationality of neoliberalism in order to make clear how neoliberal subjects are morally motivated. For her, emotions replace rationality in order to develop a realistic perspective as to what we can have apart from a family and friendships. This is directly tied to the social status of ordinary subjects, because having a normative lifestyle around family relations has to do with self-care and self-esteem, as well as human capital (Brown, 2018: 37). This is the reason why human capital becomes more important than the just distribution of labour, because this blurs inequalities and injustices on the grounds of lack of cooperation and lack of entrepreneurial skills (Brown, 2018: 75).

By the same token, there is social justice, promising "equal inequality for all",[7] which is the main principle of neoliberal governmentality encouraging entrepreneurial subjects to find their own way of recognising their own problems and finding relevant solutions. Thereby, according to Brown, differences among entrepreneurial subjects are depoliticised by convincing them of the fact of equal inequality. For her, this is the reason why democracy is accepted as egalitarian, as well as the explanation for the existence of permanent under classes, risks, and poverty (Foucault, 2008: 143;Brown, 2003: 7; Brown, 2006: 695). Equal inequality opens a field to use our way of life freely so liberalism seeks to take advantage of gender, religious, ethnic, and class differences to generate "economic calculation, everything is in it" through which democratic values gain political manoeuvering instead of direct verdicts: i.e., true-false, bad-good (Brown, 2003: 8–9). That is why neoconservatism is a great accompaniment to neoliberalism, in that miscalculations of the populist promises of democracies can legitimise themselves (Brown, 2006: 295–297). In this way, the law turns into a tactical means to legitimise new norms, and regulations and religion becomes the main source of moral values for the neoconservatist political agenda and state power, which gain populism as well as the authoritarian impact on the masses (Brown, 2006: 296–297).

Brown deciphers the challenging togetherness of neoconservatism and neoliberalism by reformulating them in terms of governmental rationality: "market-political rationality (neoliberalism) and "moral-political rationality" (neoconservatism) (Brown, 2006). On the one hand, there are the self-care subjects of neoliberalism, and on the other hand, the self-sacrificing subjects of neoconservatism find their existential reasons around common values and attachments in which religion, morality, security, and market are built on an alternative order where justice and democracy have their own changeable calculations and remedies (Brown, 2006: 698–699). Because "justice in neoliberalism is not to maximize individual wealth or rights but it is centred upon developing and enhancing the capacity of individuals to share power and collaboratively govern themselves" (Brown, 2003: 20).

Therefore, while neoliberal political rationality explicitly highlights winners and losers, neoconservatism strongly suggests protecting what we have (Brown, 2006: 701). This is why the family turns into a property requiring

---

7   It is stated in one of Diyanet's articles which is actually in parallel with the main principle of neoliberal governmentality that *God does not equalise individuals, but it gives equal opportunities to them* (Göç, Kentleşme, ve Dinadarlık 2014: 53).

emotional investment to be maintained. For this, women are specifically urged to devote themselves to their families by augmenting risks and dangers outside the family. As a result, the woman is not free because she is confined to family relations and to her mothering role, but this irrational situation becomes rational through the neoconservative promise of development and happiness. On this point, Anthony Giddens (1992: 40–46) calls attention to love, which makes couples believe that they are created for each other and complete each other. In this sense, Giddens says well: "emotion and motivation are inherently connected" because emotions ground the motivation of the mind (Giddens, 1992: 201; Hartmann and Honneth, 2006: 42–43). As a result, the cultivation of happy marriages and well-matched spouses turn into a life career as a sign of self-esteem by excluding and devaluing singleness (Hartmann and Honneth, 2006: 56).

In order to stress family-individual relations, gender categories are brought to the fore because they provide a multidimensional opportunity so as to express our moral standpoints, and to prove our social capacities for cooperation with society and survive in life. Therefore, a *good life is to enjoy justice*. This normative life has its own policing mechanisms in order to monitor the conduct of others and to govern ourselves (Brown, 2018: 102–105). Gender categories are, thus, quite beneficial, and family is an unprecedented field to make woman and man components of governmentality by dispossessing their autonomous existence and seeking (Brown, 2018: 117).

Still, there is a devastating paradox which disregards the woman as human capital because moral values and expectations of high politics subject the woman to her family commitments and social loyalties. As such, the "invisible practices" of her daily life mean that the woman is derived from self-care and self-investment. As a result, the woman exists only in the family by being excluded from public life or by functioning as a complementary part of manhood (Brown, 2018: 121–122; Arat, 2010; Bugra, 2014). Therefore, gender inequality is deepened by neoliberalism and unsettled by conservative measures. When family care, elder care and child care are privatised, the woman is expected to take responsibility for these through demands on her emotional labour (Brown, 2018: 123; Bugra, 2014; Akgöz and Balta, 2015). Women are asked to stay at home and care for every generation of the family in order to reduce the financial burden of the state. Thus, these kinds of gendered responsibilities are linked to the life sphere of true womanhood through religious conservative expectations of moral rationality.

As a final result for this section, as mentioned in Woman-Man Equality Workshop of AKP (AK Parti, 2010), according to the Global Gender Gap Index report for 2009 published by World Economic Forum, Turkey ranked 129 out of 134 countries in terms of gender equality. Similarly, according to the same report, Turkey ranked 123 out of 130 countries in 2008, 121 in 2007, and 105 in 2006. It seems that there is progressive implementation in neither gender equality nor gender justice, because injustice comes from inequalities, and inequalities show themselves in structural injustice (Uygur, 2015: 131–132). Therefore, there must be awareness for promising clichés of both gender equality and justice (Uygur, 2015: 131–132).

4 The Exclusion and Inclusion of Women at the Intersection of Differences

Donna Harraway, in her seminal work *A Cyborg Manifesto*, signals all domineering relations based on male-based knowledge and the wrong consciousness of the woman as a collective object (Harraway, 1991). What I understand from the cyborg gender is an integrative fiction by which all hierarchies and inequalities due to men's access to knowledge and skills disappear through building true knowledge and competence. However, in our normative order, there are values and their counterbalances, both of which reconstruct selves and relations with others (Brown, 2018). In other words, we know that neoliberal rationality produces subjectivities, which conduct their power relations through their performances and choices. However, there is no single form of ideal behaviour and identity expressions because neoliberal rationality must legitimise itself in order to maintain order according to cultural, political and economical variables. Therefore, under neoliberal governmentality individuals have existential credit in that they can increase, spend or lose it. In other words, in line with variables of neoliberal rationality, values bring about credits to performances and existential forms in order to have respect and prestige in society (Brown, 2018). Linking to Harraway, fictional cyborgs may not challenge the patriarchal gendered order based on Islamic values in Turkey, but women who insist on living their own way and having equal opportunities are seen as fictional, such they may run into the exclusionary boundaries of the Islamic neoliberal order. However, there is no direct intervention to mark the unwanted woman's life sphere. Within freedom, individuals locate their subjectivities somewhere between the *"denaturalisation of secular life"* and the *"naturalisation of Islamic life"* (Tuğal, 2009: 452).

As mentioned (see Chapter 3), Şerif Mardin (1997) points to neighbourhood (*mahalle*) values, or the values of small groups, from which derive *moral-control* mechanisms and conduct through collective responsibility. The family and individuals become subjects of the neighbourhood, and through it bonding to society. The families and individuals of the neighbourhood, are subjected to specific rules and domineering relations of the neighbourhood that comprise their sense of social belonging. Therefore, "society was based on contract, and *mahalle* operated on ascriptive bases. Thus *mahalle* began to appear as a fund of traditional values which were hampering the expansion of human personality" (Mardin, 1997: 214–215).

From a similar perspective, governmental rationality composes its own local methods and practices to discipline and manage individuals and communities through the regulation of their consumption culture, including all practices around daily life(Gürkan, 2018b). Subjectivities are reconstructed around these practices, which includes *micro-tactics within the communities* in order to form a place of religious-cultural frames in the process of developing subjectivities (Ismail, 2011: 859), because social relations need to be changed by Islamic norm impositions. Within these social relations, "people learned how to establish dossiers, systems of marking and classifying, the integrated accountancy of individual records" (Foucault, 1980c: 71).

In light of this fact, honour produces plenty of mechanisms to shape identities. In Turkey, the headscarf is not only veiling; especially after the rise of political Islam, it turns into a symbol of belonging (İlyasoğlu, 2015;Toprak, 2008; Gökariksel and Secor, 2009). In post-2002 Turkey, I think, the veiling beyond its use as the headscarf gains new conservative closeness and intimacy through new symbols and performances. This new form of veiling succeeds to transform the behaviours of a woman and her intimate relations. Veiled dress and modest behaviours are the clearest clues, giving necessary information about lifestyles and belonging. To illustrate, the survey about "trust relations" shows that veiling is an important criterion to trust someone, and to understand her reliability. Likewise, symbols and locations referring to strong piety are deemed as honesty (Konda, 2012c).[8] In this sense, as veiling is connected to honesty and reliability, it would be regarded as an indicator of self-esteem for women.

---

8 However, the same survey provides another remarkable insight that the trust equally decreases when the income status, the neighbourhood and welfare situation decrease (Konda, 2012c). This shows that new Islamic bourgeoisie culture is no different from any other bourgeoisie despite veiling and other religious commitments because it seems that poor people are seen as unreliable and peripheral subjects, whom the bourgeoisie refuse to recognise. As a result, the new Islamic bourgeoisie needs to be studied in the context of neoliberal governmentality, which is an integral part of post-2002 Turkey. Referring to Foucault (1980g: 41), with the moral subject of populace, the dangerous must be dangerous for the society in any way.

Thus, I can argue that veiling and dress codes may be used as "everyday self-technologies of self" because the ""conduct of conduct" reflects a vast array of new technologies, new subjectivities, and new calculations" (Nadesan, 2008: 2). In other words, meanings and symbols around dress and behaviours create a model for ideal female subjectivity, in which even 'good' or 'bad' womanhood is panopticised through the Islamic suitability of dress codes and behavioural rules (Gökariksel and Secor, 2009). Veiling and modest clothes are actually the most practical way to show identity and belonging in post-2002 Turkey. Sennett says it well:

> A sense of political community can be built out of such acts of decoding. You look for details of behavior among the persons espousing one view or the other to decide which best corresponds with your sense of yourself. Those details become for you a revelation of the true character of the conflict; they symbolize what the conflict is about. As ideology becomes measured as to whether it is believable or not through these details of behavior, political struggle itself becomes more personal. Political language becomes miniaturized, little moments or events seeming of immense importance, because through these details you are learning who is fighting, and therefore on which side you belong.
> SENNETT, 1978: 238

Within the changing power relations and rationality of interventions into the public and private spheres, new subjectivities are reproduced and thereby new resistance models appear. It clarifies that while manhood is exalted and goaded into controlling the morality of life through the female body, womanhood is expected to be docile. For Susan Bordo (2010), this docility does not have to do with silence, but with accepting, enjoying, and understanding the position of womanhood among power relations. There is a road from "social conditioning" to "normalisation" around the agency of unstable subjectivities and bodies, and the normal or the misfit should be marked and separated by these bodily performances (Bordo, 2010: 254–255).

With biopolitics, as specified in different parts of the chapter, the security of the state becomes the problems of high politics gaining content with the security of democracy, equality, borders of the nation-state, terrorism, etc. To tackle these problems at a macro level seeks micro-problems in family life, womanhood, population, lifestyles, and children as the repercussions of macro problems. Within these sorts of macro-micro relations, exalted manhood and its protective duties in daily life therefore become a reflection of the masculine guardianship of the state (Dönmez, 2013). Under these circumstances, the social order targeting security and happiness for everyone turns into the bigotry in the hands of the overproud masculinity gaining its discursive practices from womanhood and the female body. As known, Foucault's power does not belong to any institution or any particular group. However, the process between normalisation and resistance shapes power relations by reconstructing subjectivities. The increase in self-surveillance and self-correction push individuals to find a place among differences. In a nutshell, as Bordo said, no one controls the rules of the game, but the players are not equal to win the game (Bordo, 2010: 253; Lemke, 2001: 200; see also Foucault, 1997f; 2003a; 1980d) This means some groups of women play the game for power or against it.

Islamic knowledge needs to gain ascetics upon subjectivities and boundaries through power relations. Bodily performances and lifestyles become indicators and even marks of difference. As Islam asks for a defined lifestyle and consumption ranging from what should be eaten to how we should be sitting, not only performances but also locations and spaces are changed and regulated. All these reconstruct life itself, and individuals identify themselves according to their choices and visibilities within practices of life. Today there is also an Islamic culture industry, working as "homogenizing production of Muslim woman" through "political corrective" mechanisms, i.e., political actors and experts of Islamism (Gökarıksel and Maclarney, 2010: 1–6; Madi, 2014; Hier, 2008; Foucault, 2001d; Dean, 1994; Rabinow and Rose 2006). The social status and personal values, cultural belongings and worldview are directly related to consumption behaviours. The religious lifestyle of the new Islamic bourgeoisie moves further as a counteraction against secular choices. It gains its own place to transform and motivate individuals around similar transformative symbols, cultures, and places (Aygül and Öztürk, 2016: 193–194).

To illustrate, new restaurants where one can find Halal foods, and gender-segregated hotels, shopping centres, and beaches have been opened. These changing consumption behaviours inevitably produce and widen transformative elements of a new culture through which individuals can identify and exclude each other practically (Aygül and Öztürk, 2016: 193–198; Madi, 2014). Aygül and Öztürk (2016: 198) elucidate the religious transformation of all these consumption behaviours and places by pointing to the "sterilization" of the modern and popular Western style of consumption culture. For Aygül and Öztürk (2016: 198), this sterilisation is remarkably highlighted by pointing to "*tesettür* (veiling) hotels", where it is believed that people are protected from forbidden sexual relations even during their holidays. It is clear that all regulations related to locations and places are based on intimate relations between women and men. Relatedly, dress codes of women and family life in referring to male protection follow the woman's sexuality and performance in the direction of the Islamic lifestyle and identity. This inevitably renders the ideal woman as the mother, having a family and children, and dreaming of a holiday at one of the conservative hotels by force of the Islamic bourgeoisie. However, Alev Çınar makes an important point:

> The veil operates to redraw the public-private boundaries upon the body, thereby challenging the established norms of publicness and privacy. This function of the veil was used both by the founding elite when they unveiled the female body toward the establishment of a modern, West-oriented public sphere where a modern national subject was constructed, and by the Islamists of the 1990s, who reveiled the female body so as to insert new, Islamic norms of privacy in the secular public sphere, thereby disrupting the authority of secularism.
>
> ÇINAR, 2005: 169

The public sphere is an important arena to generate and regulate differences, exclusions, and inclusions through not only imperative and warning descriptions of 'how' of behaviours, but also 'how' of visibilities through only images and performances of bodies (Çınar, 2008: 895–896). Therefore, the public has its own norms that are composed of control points of power through the public gaze. The power created its own public gaze in order to categorise and regulate the diversities and differences in a very homogeneous way, which also means "subjugation" (Çınar 2008: 896). The hierarchies between public subjects inevitably, appear and some subjects are in the public gaze than others, such as women or the unveiled (Çınar, 2008: 896). Surely there are differences between Islamic women themselves in terms of class, ethnicity, veil-unveil, single or married, mother or not. However, the attention of governmentality is not uniquely geared towards individuals, lands, or things, but instead the interests of the population and circulation and production of goods, more importantly, the risk analysis and capability of foreseeing are required by biopolitics (McMahon, 2015: 147; Foucault, 2001e: 219). Therefore, self-esteem should be emphasized as new politics and a new set of social relations in order to encourage subjects to think further about their social possessions, i.e., honour and reputation.

Diyanet supports this argument, saying that *everyone needs to have an aim in this life, which shows the self-esteem and self-respect* (Çekin, 2006: 29). *The individual is a meaningful existence and must realise her or his existential reason.* It does not mean *that individualism is good; on the contrary, individualised responsibilities compose families and communities* without alienating the individual from religious and traditional values (Aydın, 2008: 20–23). This looks like what Cihan Tuğal (2002: 109) describes as "individualist spiritualities in the realm of religion", which create a new Islamic image, in which an autonomous individual takes his or her own decisions in the interest of society.

It is clear that "the political use of religion creates an artificial barrier" (Patel, 2005: 206) but still, secular conservatism before 2002 Turkey redrew the boundaries between women through 'state feminism', which is actually regulated by gender experts in line with state behaviours towards gender equality and relations (Kantola and Squires, 2012: 383–384). With neo-Kemalists' adaptation into market feminism in the 1980s, well-educated women and working women under the emphasis of definitive state feminism were wrongly presented as a success of secularism. This is true but the missing point is that the 1980s' ideal womanhood denoted the Kemalist bourgeoisie (Arat-Koç, 2007: 50). This is why the womanhood of the Kemalist bourgeoisie excluded *other* womanhoods, which were represented rural and Anatolian traditional values. Therefore, in post-2002 Turkey, the "collective subject position" of Islamic womanhood is produced against a secularised model of woman, which turns into the main object of "moral panic" in society (Hier, 2008: 174). So to speak, a "folk devil" is produced in secularism in order to ground the necessitated transformation (Hier, 2008: 174). Likewise, the scientific education of the woman is devalued with religious conservatism, and the commitment to family values of society is regarded as a sign of self-esteem (Çarkoğlu and Kalaycıoğlu, 2009: 47). This is the reason why self-esteem through conservative commitments practically labels and excludes working and unveiled women.

Self-esteem obviously works as a technology underlying discursive practices because it aims to impede subjects with self-governance and endurance against social problems ranging from crime to poverty (Cruikshank, 1993: 328). More clearly, self-esteem is accepted as a criterion for compatible and fruitful private and public relations; otherwise, lack of self-esteem poses threat and exclusion due to anti-social behaviours (Cruikshank, 1993: 330). It is important here to keep in mind that technologies of neoliberal governmentality always try to persuade subjects to act as self-controlled and self-educated individuals in accordance with the needs of market rationality under the guise of 'social order' for the sake of cooperation and *honour.* Namely, self-esteem is the main access to human capital for managing the population and creating more active citizens for society. In a neoliberal sense, this does not have anything to do with overconfidence and arrogance. Self-esteem has somehow pastoral meanings like internal dialogues and self-questioning regarding existence (Cruikshank, 1993).

This, in a way, shall be the path to pointless solidarity concealed again within market rationality to encourage being good subjects. This is why the state of esteem cannot be reduced to mere modal status and possessions. It has to do with high motivation (Cruikshank, 1993). This self-esteem and the state of esteem are observed on performance and pleasure as new forms of surveillance and control of neoliberal subjects.

The development of psychiatric power and medicine is extensively discussed in order to highlight the significant place of knowledge concerning body and mind for better pursuance of the conduct and government of the population and individual by producing the most persuasive rationality of government for creating common sense as to what is true or false, what is normal or abnormal, what is successful or unsuccessful (Foucault, 2003b). In this sense, knowledge-power naturally became the driving force behind the figure of "personal enterprise", which was gradually constructed by combining the psychological conception of the human being, the new economic norm of competition, the representation of the individual as "human capital", the cohesion of the organisation by means of "communication", and the social bond as a "network" (Dardot and Laval, 2013: 285). Therefore, "enterpreneurial self-governmentality" intrinsically meets the purport of "enterprise culture", which must include the "naturalization of risks and all possibilities" not only in working life but also in private relations (Dardot and Laval, 2013: 261–264). This means to be successfully able to keep up one's guard against 'life' and to be confidently open and positive toward those with whom the individual lives and works. This is the way in which the individual strengthens her performance and motivation to steer 'her life' because this strong performance, in all aspects, brings satisfaction and more accountability and compatibility to the society. The social and working norms of the subject take yet another twist, which is no longer balanced or average but veers towards maximum performance, whereby self-restructuring is mandatory and far from conformism (Dardot and Laval, 2013: 283).

Following these theoretical insights, Sevinç Doğan's book, *The AKP in the Neighbourhood* (Mahalledeki AKP) sheds light on the AKP's party organisations in the neighbourhoods and *political alienation*, in which the interests of a party are regarded as general interests of society. Likewise, the expectations and hopes of people are one way or another interconnected to the interests of the AKP(Doğan, 2017a; Foucault, 2007: 63). In neighbourhoods, there are associations, foundations, and party branches, putting attention on especially women to the party works (Doğan, 2017a: 75–76). That is to say, women are the definitive element to reflect the identity of the party. Therefore, all women have a similar style of behaviour and dress according to the party's specification, so the majority is veiled. As mentioned above, headscarf/veiling is not the only reference to religion, but also it is a good means of identifying the different class backgrounds and cultural factors by which womanhood can be performed. In either case, forms of veiling are related to "presentation of femininity" (Doğan, 2017a: 75–76).

In other words:

> The JDP(AKP) women are keen on underlining that they are not against change and modernity but that this change should take place while preserving essential social values'which make us what we are'. Thus, it is important to understand how, in practice, the conservatism aspect of conservative democracy strikes a balance between tradition and change regarding women question.
> ÇITAK AND TUR, 2008: 463

As in Doğan's inquiry, the resignation and loyalty to religion are highlighted in order to give a modest and obedient tone to the party's promises. Moreover, Doğan points to "family" as a unit of the "right-centered hegemonic project", by which family and community-based family relations obviously form the governmental rationality of party to successfully permeate into the micro-sphere and to reach even the unborn. That is why the family is a strategic unit (see Chapter 3). The roles of women and men in the party organisation run parallel to the gendered roles in their family relations. That is to say, party organisations are kind of schools to teach ideal motherhood and womanhood to its female members (Doğan, 2017a: 82). In parallel with gender roles, it is quite normal that lifestyles show similarities as well because the party itself is a big family. There is a single lifestyle model by which party practices can transform personal lives as well (Doğan, 2017a: 91–92). It means the collective identity of the party is actually an assembly of similar individual identities.

Obviously, Islam itself does not accept individual survival, which is seen as loneliness and selfishness. Individualism is against the nature of Islamic society, in which everyone has a duty and role, gifted by God. However, the classical definition of liberalism points to the necessity of individual autonomies to have their own decision (Kaya, 2004: 111). Additionally, neoliberal rationality underlines the importance of freedom, but it forms an obstacle to freedom by reminding the public of risk factors. Concisely, Islamic neoliberal rationality seeks to motivate entrepreneurial subjects to gain consciousness about their social and gender responsibilities in order to connect them to community-based family relations.

According to a survey about "lifestyles" (Konda, 2015), there are two maps of the social rationality of the people in post-2002 Turkey: one is about personal lives and the second is about life with others. The survey evaluates this in reference to challenging the mismatch between *true* values and established practices. Universal and local values challenge each other as local values are politicised and polarised between dichotomies in post-2002 Turkey (Konda, 2015). This impacts relations between individuals as well. According to Binnaz Toprak, the liberal legal system in Turkey theoretically creates room to tolerate the differences between groups; however, traditional references and religious knowledge determine prohibitions and boundaries, which force individuals to live parallel lives between their intimate relations and public relations (2008: 4). Private and public spheres intersect each other in Islamic choices, so individual and collective choices intertwine, too. Therefore, the interaction and intersection of the public and private spheres need to be analysed through manifold transformation in the context of religious values (Yankaya, 2014: 254–255).

The Islamic lifestyle is reconstructed in connection with issues of taste and preference, which leaves open a path by which Islamic morality actually demands performance in line with economic and political interests because the conservative performance of Islamic morality means happiness and prestige through the Islamic transformation (Yankaya, 2014: 251). Islamic choices refer to the rational and strategic, maybe sometimes conformist, but always expecting social and economic profits as well (Yankaya, 2014: 251). Therefore, the measures of Islamic belonging point to the private sphere as well, but the private sphere expects to see Islamic subjectivities being well integrated into the transformative conditions of the public (Yankaya, 2014: 256–257). As argued at several points, marriage and maternal duties, as the private roles of the woman, are publicised as a category of the population. Motherhood, thus, becomes the very core element of Islamic neoliberal female subjectivity in post-2002 Turkey. Additionally, motherhood becomes a differential feature in order to include the woman in the 'collective womanhood' of Islamic neoliberal subjectivity.

Furthermore, the "deprivatisation of religion" is the conditional way of living in public (Razavi and Jenichen, 2010; Bugra and Savaşkan, 2014), therefore the freedom to wear the headscarf and other religiously conservative demands publicise the gendered roles in the family. Additionally, the ideal Islamic lifestyle is presented by a new Islamic bourgeoisie. This Islamic bourgeoisie, relying on the AKP's state power, describe a comfortable life in which highly secured residential family estates reconstruct the cultural codes belonging to comfort, richness, and taste (Doğan, 2017a: 246).

Justice, as mentioned above, is a governmental model which is independent of injustice and inequality; this is why social inequalities are re-defined and regulated through state services; in this way, everybody is convinced that they will reach welfare conditions one day (Doğan, 2017a: 260). That is to say, the comfortable living conditions of high party members are a sort of promise to those who work for the party. The proximity to the party through symbols and lifestyles opens a way to the Islamic bourgeois lifestyle. Therefore, even though not every member of the party can equally enjoy *life*, the desires and hopes of the people give them a status and motivate them to work in the AKP's direction. As a result, an Islamic bourgeoisie culture expands its influence on individuals' choices, which does not directly change the class status of its members, but life aspirations bring satisfaction and self-esteem with the help of party status and power (Doğan, 2017a: 208–209). For Islamist strategies and practices, the "market as an alternative engine" is employed to produce discursive practices and generate moral and political impacts (Iqtidar, 2011: 536).

Therefore, just as the market promotes selfish desires and individuality, it also provides a domain for moral choices to be rewarded and punished (Iqtidar, 2011: 536). The market plays a crucial role in the "conduct of conduct" to practice the moral and religious values and differences between people (Iqtidar, 2011: 560). What you drink, how you dress and what you consume in your daily life cannot be thought of independently from political and religious settings because these choices form Islamic social identities and roles. Therefore, the Islamist worker and the Islamist bourgeoisie are best identified through their consumption (Iqtidar, 2011: 562–563). The shift to conservative and traditional practices in post-2002 Turkey, for example, constructs itself by standing against Westernised secular values. Skipping anti-imperialist voices, the social and cultural fears regarding moral decay inevitably want to mould sexuality and family relations through a woman (Cooper, 2008: 27–28). In order to transform population groups through common values, religious sensitivities have become the most plausible and practical way of bringing everyone under the same party roof because:

> Religion, as a powerful source of identity, is frequently utilised both to promote intra group cohesion and to mobilise inter-group differences and conflict. It can serve as a source of legitimacy for national leaders who are developing new political institutions, or who are trying to bolster their legitimacy in times of crisis. In addition, dominant religious institutions can also have a strong bearing (often more than political parties) on citizens' political choices, and are therefore important the 'larger national cause', and in the end abandoned altogether.
>
> RAZAVI AND JENICHEN, 2010: 838

Inevitably, Islamic modernity has sought social integration into a neoliberal market order, which makes new Islamic women from different class-based hierarchies. That is to say, the new Islamic individualism converts the backward meaning of headscarves and anti-consumerism of Islamic fundamentalism (Özyeğin, 2009: 107). The neoliberal rationality of Turkey produced its own Islamic individuals, having their own way to demand their religious, gender and human rights within the context of Turkish modernity embedded in traditional and religious sensitivities.

In any case, veiling is the most important indicator of the boundaries against the immorality as a kind of defence mechanism. To put it bluntly, Kemalist secularism excluded the headscarf from the public, and now Islamists try to develop cultural boundaries against secular lifestyles without using political and cultural force regarding the use of the headscarf. A new pious identity for the woman is built on conflicts between secular and Islamic gender rules revolving around women's sexuality, maternal roles, and bodily performance (Özyeğin, 2009: 119; Çınar, 2008: 904). In other words, the norms and boundaries of the public have a great potential to restructure and reconstruct the boundaries of the private in line with moral values. The private includes bodily privacy and intimacy as well, thus headscarf is a strong indicator of the boundaries of private, public and morality through the body (Çınar, 2008: 903–904).

The socialisation of the woman is based on the virtues that shape the boundaries between her nature and public life. The private and public subjectivity of a woman constitutes her socialisation, so her nature suggests that she stay at home as a housewife and good mother (Aktaş, 1991: 251). Looking at the connection between the socialisation of a woman and secular values, the social practices around her empowerment and gender equality also produced another causality for the ideal place of a woman. For example, Islamists claim that motherhood or marriage is obstacles to economic independence by secularists. Commitment to family and husband were seen as indicators of lack of freedom. The home was described as captivity, which also devalued motherhood (Aktaş, 1991: 251). However, now these maternal and womanly performances and possession are regarded as 'value-giving' abilities to differentiate the good woman and bad woman from each other.

Similarly, a single woman and the woman who does not want to be a mother are seen as irresponsible, selfish and unwilling to take responsibility (Sancar, 2014: 231). Religiously conservative values boldly draw the boundaries, belongings, and possessions of women. Additionally, the increasing rates of violence push women into the private sphere and into homosocial relations. As a result, women may compete with each other over their maternal abilities and their feminine competences (Özyeğin, 2011; Özbay, 2011). On the other hand, the working conditions for the woman are truly heavy. Housewifery has become a new feature of the Islamic bourgeoisie, and working women are excluded from the dominant culture (Buğra, 2015: 18–19). It is worth reiterating that social differences are not limited to secular and Islamist, but are also measured in terms of class, age, marital status, maternal status, family status, education degree, and the like. However, it is clear that free, single, and childless women are exposed more to "the potential gaze of the other" (Sancar 2014: 231, Foucault, 2014: 145).

Being an ideal subject is about having a personal reputation and the issue of prestige (Yankaya, 2014). Therefore, power relations prompt the production of "imaginations against the realities" by making a public show of being happy and free (Doğan, 2017b: 20–21). Social honour comes to the fore once again in order to balance out "social costs" and "collective control" because in order for someone to win, someone else must lose (Sen, 2005: 51). Therefore, the intersection of differences sheds light particularly on the advantages and disadvantages of groups of women. This is why Susan Hekman puts forward the category of "woman" by which "some women are more 'woman' than others"; therefore, "the woman" upholds hierarchies among women by pointing to the idealised features of womanhood (Hekman, 2014). As mentioned above, this idealisation of womanhood between inclusionary and exclusionary conservative values opens a path towards "gendered governmentality" wherein the true woman and her sense of belonging are socially, politically, and economically framed and regulated (Erol, 2016).

"The normalising gaze" is invisible, but the subject knows of being gazed upon (Smith, 2000: 289; Foucault, 1984a: 197). Awareness of social norms and their adoption are transformative even if the subject does not feel it. This is the reason why power is omnipresent, and why we are talking about a "panoptisized society" under expert knowledge (Fraser, 1989: 49). However, this is beyond a reason as to how we need civil society to shape the moral collectivity. Namely, moral and civic entrepreneurs are the other ways to develop self-governing skills through an active populace (O'Malley, 2004: 75). In the Foucauldian vein, power cannot be divided and shared between population groups, but it is circulated and passed through individuals and networks. Thereby, the individual is a "power-effect" (Foucault, 2003a: 29–30; 1980e: 174). However, power ultimately became the representation of the bourgeoisie in that its values lead the mechanisms of power (Foucault, 2003a: 32). The new Islamic bourgeoisie is a tool to garner the interest of all population groups by refashioning modern populist religious values against wild capitalism, but with the same mechanisms (Tuğal, 2002: 86).

According to Diyanet, *everybody is responsible for each other because their good is our goodness* (Ünal, 2008: 44). However, there is a nuance between secular women's responsibilities and Islamic women's responsibilities:

> They [*secular women*] underlined the importance of responsible individualism as opposed to communally defined responsibilities. Islamist women, on the other hand, challenged the secular concept of equality with their insistence on male-female complementarity of roles and their equivalence in Islam. They sought equal status and individualism within these complementary roles. Their search for a religiously defined identity caused them to defy the secular codes of the Republic. One important implication of this defiance was their challenge of the prevailing concept of secularism, which was under the surveillance of a paternalist state.
> ARAT, 1998: 129, italics added

Secularists and Islamists judge each other along the same lines: Each thinks the other is authoritarian. This causes "exclusionary polarization" that blocks each possible dialogue to break and transform prejudices against each other (Arat, 2005: 5). Both Islamic and secular women draw boundaries between them without showing a will to break with patriarchal norms and masculine control, which actually widens the distance between them. With the neoliberalisation of Islamism, the moral boundaries of Islam turn into democratic and humanitarian boundaries as well (Arat, 1998: 126). This forms the ways in which the ideal society is defined and worked towards. Relying on moral boundaries, the virginity of the female body, the veiling of the female body, the modest behaviour and dress of the woman, marriage, maternal status, and motherhood become the first and foremost national identity of woman-subjects in post-2002 Turkey. Representations and symbols based on ideal womanhood turn into surveillance, forming "the demarcation between ingroup and outgroup mores" (Özyeğin, 2009: 111). Moral boundaries help to generate common values, around which Islamic identity becomes a cultural identity by blurring Sunni-Islam dominant principles. This is the reason why the private is publicised and the maternal roles of the woman are subjected to public measures.

All in all, in post-2002 Turkey we have to recognise the new Islamic female subjectivity that has arisen in secular-republican Turkey, by internalising new authoritarian and traditional values built on honour and self-esteem and relying on maternal roles and pure family belongings.

5 Concluding Remarks

State feminism under Kemalist governments situated the ideal middle-class woman in urbanised family relations. Her features were self-sacrificing and loyal to her family and class values. Therein, the high-class woman was caricatured as selfish and Westernised, straying too far from Turkish traditions and morality. In addition to these two types of women, rural women were portrayed as ignorant, oppressed, and abnormal (Dönmez, 2013: 9). Among these images of different women, Islam as backwardness and dogmatism relied heavily on the rural women. At the state level, there were no obstacles preventing women from having a decent education regardless of class background. Turkish modernity with Republican principles resulted in progressive economic growth and gained strength by inviting everyone's support from the old to the young. Therefore, for the woman's empowerment, education was crucial to make her aware of her civil rights, representation, and working rights. Surely, there were patriarchal mechanisms to suppress the woman within gender relations just as there were legal rights for women. However, at least, a woman was expected to know about the materiality of economic independence.

With the neoliberalisation of Islamism in post-2002 Turkey, high politics is viewed as always encouraging women's empowerment, but when we look at the restrictions and the limits of the micro, women are not allowed to empower themselves within Islamic patriarchal mechanisms. The "family related division of labor" prevents women from accessing resources on the grounds of their maternal duties, lack of time and money (Durusoy, 2013: 36). On the one side, flexible production and the demand for cheaper labour trap the woman in a precarious life; on the other side, "the superwoman", who can both be a good mother and have an outstanding career, is exposed to devaluation from ideal womanhood (Durusoy, 2013: 40).

Within this scenario, the uneducated woman is advantaged in providing safety to her family under masculine protection. In parallel, the divorced woman is subject to discrimination upon attempting to (re)enter the workforce or by being targeted by sexual harassment due to her marital status. Therefore, it is not a coincidence that state interventions and regulations exist to direct women towards home-centred works and care services. It is not an accident, therefore, that neoliberal politics decline the cost of social security and insurance for women in Turkey.

Additionally, Diyanet states that *religion separates the legitimate and the illegitimate from each other*. If it is said that *I am free and this life is mine, this produces an unmanageable subject "who dirties the society". This subject cannot be controlled under freedom* (Balaban, 2008: 35). Wendy Brown conceptualises this as "freedom turning to self-sacrificing" encouraging "collective devotion" for the goodness of society (Brown, 2018: 239). According to neoliberal rationality, freedom intrinsically controls subjects by internalising them through "moralization of consequences of this freedom" to *police the health of the social body* (Brown, 2003: 7; see Foucault, 1980e). Therefore, the neoliberal subject must know what is good for her- or himself, and what polishes her or his prestige and status (Brown, 2018: 128). Along with the religious conservative values of the power regime under AKP rule, loyal, docile and self-sacrificing mothers are granted with the top status of being a so-called true woman of Islamic neoliberal subjectivity, who is responsible for the *hygiene* and *health* of society.

CHAPTER 6

Conclusions
Resistance for the Better

In concluding this book, I would like to state the results of the study in two different contexts, and then relate them to one another. I aim to disclose how they form a unique theory and a case study, and further how they offer a new theoretical and analytical lucidity in the field of gender and biopolitics.

The first context is that Foucauldian analytics gives us various useful roadmaps. The literature of biopolitics offers a critical and challenging way of exploring how omnipresent power works. In the introduction of this study, I explored the issue of the government's problems with society, humans, the individual, and nature. Providing a theoretical explanation, I have mapped out how governments use these problems to letigimise interventions. In other words, I have pointed out that problematisations, reflected and regulated by the actors and agencies within a specific language, are indeed the discursive practices employed by governmental rationality to find its own route, and to smoothly proceed in times when power relations are fragile and transforming. When starting to analyse what these problematisations indicate and how they should be solved, the sources of knowledge-power that these problematisations feed on leads us to realise where neoliberal rationality acquires its legitimatisation of dominance and transformation. To study these specific knowledge-power sources has helped me to explain how such rationality of power governs the daily lives of individuals themselves, and further how these individuals govern themselves in accordance with the desires of power. Through these problematisations, I have explored this line of thinking in Foucauldian literature and offered methodological grounds to examine a case study; this serves as a contribution to the literature.

As for the second context, which is actually gender and politics in Turkey, to critically re-problematise the life spheres of womanhood falsified by the government not only contributes to Foucault's work on gender, but also to studies about Turkey and its people. In addition, starting with the analysis of the life spheres of womanhood in post-2002 Turkey, I have shown that instead of *defending the society* in line with the truth of the power regime in post-2002 Turkey, there is however a need *to defend the life of the woman*, and to re-problematise the government's issues with woman and womanhood. To put it more clearly, the changing definition of womanhood must be studied with the consequences of this change by correlating them with the new truth of the power regime under AKP rule. This truth of the AKP power regime has constituted an unprecedented synthesis of Islamism and neoliberalism. This political synthesis successfully found its social and economic correspondence in the global and local contexts, becoming a new truth regime with which to respond to these problems in. Likewise, there have been idealisations for which the truth of the power regime has produced its own discursive language, as well regulatory and disciplinary mechanisms in aiming to transform society as part of the Islamic neoliberal project. In order to generate the fundamental mechanisms of this new truth regime for the human and social fabric of the imagined population, the AKP needed to highlight key domains. In this book, I approached womanhood as one of these broad domains in order to reveal the emplacements of these power relations in the life spheres of the woman. In other words, womanhood as a domain enabled me to pinpoint problems of the power regime with respect to the life of the woman, which connected to the life of the society and population as a whole. Looking at it from this angle, the woman's sexuality, her position in the family, the reasons for violence against the woman, and finally essential components of Islamic neoliberal female subjectivity have led me to contend with the other face of religious, conservative and neoliberal promises of the new truth regime in post-2002 Turkey. I have argued that these promises based on problematisations of the new truth regime also must be reproblematised by comparing the reasons for and results of this political transformation through womanhood.

In this respect, the two contexts mentioned above – namely my theoretical approach and the analysis of the political transformation in Turkey through studying the woman – contribute to social sciences literature by combining not only political science and gender disciplines but also by reiterating various neoliberal values both at a local and global scale. I believe that to construe the governmental rationality of Islamic neoliberal Turkey – which melts all the components of Eastern and Southern cultures into the same pot – and to argue that womanhood is the most politicised aspect of society through religion and tradition, are useful insights to all the social sciences.

What I mean is that I agree that Foucault's perspective that observing and analysing the developments and consequences of only American, French, and German neoliberalism does not suffice to define the experiences societies that have been obliged to adopt increasingly conservative forms of neoliberalism via authoritarian interventions and military coups. This is the reason that I utilise governmentality as an approach for the exclusive governmental mechanisms and tools of neoliberal rationality in Turkey in this book. To understand how religion and tradition sometimes are embedded with 'community' life and turn into an institutional rationality, and to be able to disclose the mechanisms and discursive practices through which they become integrated with our lives and even minds, I believe that it is academically necessary to differentiate between Foucauldian neoliberalism and authoritarian neoliberalism in post-2002 Turkey.

When defining power relations, Foucault similarly indicated patriarchal relations as a part of this rationality. Even though this has led him to be marked as gender blind in the feminist literature, his work still enables us to comprehend that the sovereign rationality of neoliberalism shapes patriarchal relations in its own way. Indeed, the fact that neoliberalism repetitively defines gender roles as fields of political manoeuvre and attributes values and duties is exactly related to what I discussed. Still, I have insistently opted to take womanhood as a mechanism, a point of resistance and category of population because of the necessity for it to be clarified in the governmentality literature. In other words, the gender regime is a reflection of the state in which wide-ranging governmental practices function as an effect on power and power relations in microspheres. Furthermore, the gender regime itself is the fundamental domain of state knowledge related to the population and its groups. During these transformative times, administrative rules and legal structure gain functionality and legitimacy through the conduct of womanhood. In other words, strategies of the state form problematisations of government; and governmentalisation of the state leads its tactics and acts to the woman and life spheres of womanhood in order to solve these established problems, and to take preventive measures. In doing so, idealised images carve out the essence of problem-solving mechanisms by relying on the knowledge-power of biopolitical authority, ranging from scientific expertise to religious and traditional wisdom.

The crucial aspects that need to be underlined are the governmental strategies and interventions that begin with the realisation of problems and then get individuals' consent to participate in the problem-solving process. In this interwoven context of Foucault's perspective and gender-politics in post-2002 Turkey, the life spheres of womanhood caused me to develop conceptual and analytical grounds to reveal the transformative position of the woman, and also to explore the instruments and means produced by idealised womanhood and the female body. In doing so, I believe that the paradoxical and interrelated life spheres of womanhood lead us to identify the political and economic route that the Islamic neoliberal rationality of the power regime in post-2002 Turkey has taken.

In order to detail my points and strengthen arguments, in the second chapter, I have analysed how the woman's sexuality, which is both a hidden and an open issue, shapes and rationalizes the intimacy and publicness of womanhood by placing the woman at the centre of politics and the social order. Again, in the second chapter, a specific discussion has been presented about the government's expectations from the gender regime, and how the social and public performances of the woman should be in Islamic understanding of the social body. In addition, I have elaborated on how the sexuality and virginity of the woman can politically turn into a governmental problem through moral values, public consciousness, and order. More specifically, I have aimed to argue that the government dominates and governs the woman's body through religious values, but also has observed that the contradictions of the government may become political and economic tools. Each point in this chapter scrutinised the body politics and biopolitics of Islam through sexuality in a broad framework to grasp the building of womanhood that is gradually getting more concrete and structured in post-2002 Turkey. Specifically, the two major results that I expect to convey are that male authority strengthens with the help of sexuality and that woman is socially pacified in a similar manner. The most interesting result in this chapter is that sexual relations not only control the woman's body via such rules as bearing so-called physical results, but also that the government today assigns representations of the woman and decides her visibility and bodily performativity.

Disciplining and regulating sexuality as a life sphere takes us to other life spheres of womanhood such as marriage and family. Here, I have indicated how family – as the smallest unit of the society – constitutes a nation and how the state mobilises individuals through common values using national- and moral development. In this light, I have examined the corrective, healing, and even punishing duties of the family via womanhood. This womanhood has readily helped us look into the interrelated roles in motherhood, fertility, and being a wife. To handle womanhood as a population category has enabled me to pinpoint how the woman is attributed with institutional, statistical, and instrumental values. For this, it has become clear that the woman, beyond her reality of being an individual, is a social and biological carrier of national family values, where her duties and goals are generaliszed as a representation of a collective role. Therefore, we come to see that internal family problems and violence, or other triggers for divorce, are ignored through such excuses as family values and giving the woman a secure life. More precisely, even though divorce theoretically seems to be a legal right, moral values hinder it by constantly and systemically reminding the woman of her attitudes, perseverance, and more importantly vulnerability against risk in public. For this reason, violence turns into a daily question of family life.

Not surprisingly, violence itself refers to an entrenched gender question in Turkey, but I wanted to re-problematise it as another life sphere of the woman, which regulates and disciplines her everyday life. In this chapter on violence, I first pointed out that social persuasion and conceding that the phenomenon of violence itself is simply a part of life are the government's expected normality. Thus, the reasons for violence and the violence itself turn into an inseparable part of life for those who cannot achieve the desired womanhood. In other words, the possibility of being exposed to violence or not suddenly becomes the most normal criminal element of life in the risk society shaped by neoliberalism. Concomitantly, male protection and gendered mediation turn again into a consent mechanism by taming the woman with violence. Violence is, therefore, a political problem beyond the gender question, and it is essential to define violence and to repoliticise it. The phenomenon of the man resorting to violence, the high rates of violence, and violence itself should be abnormalised; it should be viewed as deviant, but also as a category independent of the issue of women's clothes and behaviours, which can be weaponised in the name of tradition.

Lastly, from the beginning of this book, among these life spheres, the subjectivity of the woman in accordance with Islamic neoliberal values has provided us with the basis for discussion on the broadest life sphere of the woman. In the final chapter, I aimed to show that religious-cultural elements in Turkey have always fuelled, enlivened and palliated every kind of political manoeuver, with my further focus on the Islamisation of neoliberalism in post-2002 Turkey, because it is a pivotal point to highlight that governmental mechanisms of Islamism are pretty much rational and even legitimate. As we have seen in the post-2002 case, a gradually authoritarian neoliberal governmentality has affected not only politics but also society with increasing rates of violence. In addition, this disciplinary and sovereign government has also had an increasing influence on the individual and the population due to its security concerns and controls. Moreover, religious references re-regulate the woman through a discourse of justice, and through these conservative values in Islamic neoliberal governmentality, they confine her to the family, which is seen to be the safest place. Religious or secular identities are, therefore, valued according to the truth of the power regime in post-2002 Turkey, and their public differentiations are performed by the woman. Likewise, exclusionary and inclusionary elements of secularism and Islamism on the woman not only indicate the proximity or the distance to the power regime but they also make them gain or lose strength from the private to the public no matter if religious or secular. And this specifically creates a conflictual sphere which religiously fed neoliberalism can exclusively make use of in Turkey. As a result, womanhood becomes a moral subjectivity by defining 'others' in parallel with their own Islamic neoliberal subjectivity in practice.

When this book is taken as a whole, the results and attained insights are as follows: First of all, for many reasons, it would be an academically challenging attempt to problematise what is religious and traditional, and to analyse it governmentally. For this reason, throughout the whole book, I have never had the intention to question religious knowledge itself. But on the other hand, I have not affirmed either that religion should become institutionalised in the direction of the truth of the power regime in post-2002 Turkey, and this further should affect the life of the woman deeply. While one of the most pivotal questions in the introduction of the book is said to be the social problems resulting from religious insufficiencies, the fact that traditional and religious references gain political rationality, and that more interventions are directed towards people's lives, makes sense regarding 'what the government fingers as the problem' and 'what gets solved'. However, in parallel with this, not only gender-based violence but also an increasing rate of criminality is at stake in general terms. It seems that the problems and suggestions that have arisen under this power regime do not have to do with moral degeneration and religion at all, both of which sought to lay problems and solutions on the woman's sexuality and family values.

Secondly, there is the question of whether the existence of disciplinary and regulatory consent mechanisms at the government level really constitutes consent, or whether the woman's deep silence over such issues is taken as consent. There is also the issue of the woman being left vulnerable. These issues beg careful explanation. I believe that governmentality has a crisis here. That domestic violence is on the rise in parallel to escalating poverty, and that the man has the power to destroy the whole family indicate that not only the woman but also the man are left helpless and desperate. In other words, even though family life is understood as the least risky place under conditions of insecurity, another perspective from empowered gendered relations indicates that these are actually symptomatic of a gender crisis of governmental failures. It is clear that indeed worsening financial life conditions 'destroy the family'. This is not an issue I specifically touch upon in the book, but this crisis actually results from the Islamic neoliberal rationality of post-2002 Turkey. As a result, this drastic problem cannot be tackled by keeping the woman silent and docile under masculine authority. In other words, here the political and social root of this problem is not related to the demise of the family and modernity. It has to do with the precariousness of neoliberal promises against the rising influence of the Islamic bourgeoisie's values, wherein a strict gender division of labour cannot equally appeal to the class position of every family.

As the third point, the tendency towards greater daily engagement with the family in post-2002 Turkey is a result of individuals' quest for happiness and peace imposed by this power as a risk society. Similarly, that the woman is expected to get involved more with the home results from the fact the current limited and unequal economic opportunities forces men into working life. Not surprisingly, neoliberalism directs its attention to spiritual values in such times of crisis with a focus on justice. This is because the idea of equality is already against the nature of neoliberalism and so gender justice; the discursive practices in pursuit of social justice do not bring equality among population groups. Ranging from gender categories to class differences, the Islamic principles of justice bind the unequal groups together with a belief in social harmony. In this context, I see that the neoliberal art of government and an Islamist image of society not only complement each other in the macro-sphere but also disburden the ambivalence of their governmental rationalities in the micro-sphere.

As the fourth point, gender categories and class differences become diversified components of this sacred harmony, in which inequality is equally divided into determined groups. These categories help to discipline bodies, and to regulate them for the economy of power through common societal values. In order to remind population groups of their categorical differences and risks, the analytic relation between security and freedom develops problem-solving skills and mechanisms with the help of constructive norms generated from religious and social values. What I want to emphasise is that civil society became an apparatus of the state, but the motivation of civil society is formed in line with governmental problems of the state. This negatively influenced the life of the woman because the goodness of society is tied to the goodness of the woman and the protection of the female body. This is why security mechanisms and the risks of the public developed by pointing to family, sexuality, and woman. In line with this, violence is depoliticised as a daily life problem for any woman. It is expected to promote the woman's problem-solving skills against gender-based violence instead of taking the increasing risks of violence and crimes as the result of the Islamic-neoliberal insistence on social harmony.

As the fifth point, gender categories depoliticise the political reality of violence against the woman too. The truth of the new gender regime provides an intersectional domain where the macro level of the state and the micro level of its effects can be observed through idealised performances of the female body, falsified womanhood and gendered relations between woman and man. The gender regime carries the social and political repercussions of power regime in order to rationalise its conservatism, authority, and hierarchies. In post-2002 Turkey, docile and self-sacrificing womanhood reconstructs the perception of the public in the direction of male-dominant gender regime. As a result, the parliamentarian and public representation of the woman stayed under the domineering shadow of the man in politics. This opened a debatable domain in which the state can easily generate the problems and problematisations, ranging from mixed-education, the collective intimacy of the woman, gender-mixed public life, women's rights, sexual freedom, contraception, abortion, and the like. With these discussions and problematisations, the power regime in post-2002 Turkey reinforced the gaps between the woman's sexual freedom, her consent, and her intimacy. In other words, the governmental practices of the state found their own way to permeate into these gaps in life spheres to conduct firstly the woman and then to transform society through her.

As the sixth point, on the one hand, this theoretical and case study of post-2002 Turkey aims to respond to the discussions on increasing 'authoritarian populism' at the global level by examining knowledge-power sources. On the other hand, I believe it also opens up more crucial debates such as, 'Is this really populism?' or 'Is neoliberalism itself in a crisis of survival?' with its answers lying in the discussion about the woman and womanhood. Here I would like to specifically make it clear that authoritarian populism is not a concept that I can only employ, and that can never take me to the result of this book without taking into account the oppressive interventions of the authoritarian governments against rising inequalities due to neoliberalism. Neoliberalism itself reaches individuals by using a populist and depoliticised language in order to blur the real problems of societies and individuals. This is why I think that in the 21st century neoliberalism is becoming more authoritarian and controlling life spheres in order to keep its unique and reproducible authority over the woman.

Lastly, without dissolving women's political reality in any populist regime – this would exactly be what the neoliberal governmentality desires – I want to bring up a major point which governmental rationality misses by breaking all the religious and traditional knowledge-power chains. This point is that even though secularity and secular life do not end patriarchy, they still protect women and bestow them several social rights. Namely, a secular public life free from religion and tradition at least as a political value protects women's rights, bodies, and lives; this is the most crucial result and strongest argument I have observed for the case of post-2002 Turkey. I argue that the Islamic neoliberal transformation since 2002 has rendered the life of the woman as a political problem against secularism.

Michel Foucault (2003a: 54) expects us to be focused on "a growing rationality" when highlighting the history of the present. In such a life there are riots, brute facts, the weaknesses of the other, accidents, victories, fears, courage, bodies, passions, ambitions, blood, tears, exiles, and undeserved deaths, yet

CONCLUSIONS   213

there is always life. For Foucault, whatever has been happening is exactly the rationality that governs us today.

The sociopolitical context of post-2002 Turkey did not develop in isolation; the present has built on the riots, heartbreaks, passions, forced migrations, and deaths of the past, with the influence of every Anatolian civilisation that has come before it. For this reason, the first limitation of this book is that it centralises the woman as the most important transformer to the exclusion of other events and structures of daily and political life that would help us to decipher the transformations in governmental rationality in post-2002 Turkey. There are three reasons for such a limitation: The first is that books are intrinsically required to have a scope and framework, which limits the possible avenues to pursue. The second is that the woman is the main actor of traditional and religious knowledge, and that motivates action in times of political and social transformation. That is, governmental practices are the most visible faces of the truth of the woman and womanhood. Third but most important is that this limitation allows us to crystallise the place and importance of the woman in the history of the present. Thus, the final limitation is actually not a limitation of this book, to read a period of the woman in order to decipher the rationality between life and death; indeed, this is a point which I do not want to leave aside.

Still, this reading of the period necessitates articulating another limitation. The transformations in post-2002 period is not complete. Rationality continues to grow with the same political actors in the same neoliberal economic vein. Therefore, every question and claim within this book can be mirrored in future analyses and research, since we are still living this process and it is neither scientifically possible to definitively answer these questions, nor do I have such an intention. What I intended instead was to develop a methodology that facilitated thinking outside the box on this topic, since manhood, male power, violence, sexuality, and family issues will require further thought within various contexts, together with neoliberalism and authoritarianism.

More specifically, I hope that each question and claim that I offer in this book will shed light on future studies on women's resistance and struggle in Turkey. The continued urgency of women's resistance and refusal to be intimidated by the increasing authoritarian governmentality of the power regime in post-2002 Turkey shows that, while the transformation is still trying to 'transform', it is having difficulty doing so.

References

Books and Articles

Abadan-Unat, Nermin. 1986.*Women in the Developing World: Evidence from Turkey*. Denver: University of Denver.

Abou-Zeid, Ahmed. 1965."Honour and Shame among the Bedouins of Egypt". In *Honour and Shame. The Values of Mediterranian Society*. Ed. J.G. Peristiany. 243–260. London: Weidenfeld and Nicolson.

Abu-Odeh, Lama. 2014."Arap Toplumlarında Namus Cinayetleri ve Toplumsal Cinsiyetin İnşası". In *Müslüman Toplumlarda Kadın ve Cinsellik*. Ed. Pınar İlkkaracan. 243–264. İstanbul: İletişim Yayınları.

Acar-Savran, Gülnur.1994. "Feminist Teori ve Erkek Şiddeti".*Defter*. No. 21. 45–55.

Acar-Savran, Gülnur. 2011. "Özel/Kamusal, Yerel/Evrensel: İkilikleri Aşan Bir Feminizme Doğru".*Praksis*. Vol. 8. 255–306.

Ackelsberg, Martha A. and Lyndon-Shanley, Mary.1996. "Privacy, Publicity, and Power: Feminist Rethinking of the Public-Private Distinction". In *Revisioning the Political: Feminist Reconstructions of Traditional Concepts in Western Political Theory*. Ed. Nancy J. Hirschmann and Christine Di Stefano. 213–233. Colo: Westview Press.

Agamben, Giorgio.1998. *Homo Sacer: Sovereign Power and Bare Life*. Stanford: Stanford University Press.

Agamben, Giorgio. 2009. *What is an Apparatus? And Other Essays*. Stanford: Stanford University Press.

Agathangelou, Anna M. 2004. *The Global Political Economy of Sex: Desire, Violence, and Insecurity in Mediterranean Nation States*. New York: Palgrave Macmillan.

Ahmad, Feroz. 1999. *Modern Türkiye'nin Oluşumu*. İstanbul: Kaynak Yayınları.

Ahmed, Sara. 2010. *The Promise of Happiness*. Durham: Duke University Press.

Ahmed, Sara. 2014. *The Cultural Politics of Emotion*. Edinburg: Edinburg University Press.

Akdoğan, Yalçın. 2004. *AK Parti ve Muhafazakâr Demokrasi*. Alfa: Istanbul.

Akgöz, Görkem and Balta, Ecehan. 2015. "Kapitalizmin Krizine Toplumsal Cinsiyet Perspektifinden Bakmak: Analitik Bir Çerçeve Önerisi". *Hacettepe Üniversitesi Sosyolojik AraştırmalarE-Dergisi*. 1–17. Retrieved from: http://www.sdergi.hacettepe.edu.tr/?page=makaleler.

Aktaş, Cihan.1991. "Kadının Toplumsallaşması ve Fitne".*Journal of Islamic Research*. Vol. 5. No. 4. 251–259.

Altınay, Ayşe Gül. 2004. *The Myth of the Military-Nation: Militarism, Gender, and Education in Turkey*. New York: Palgrave Macmillan.

Altınay, Ayşe Gül and Arat, Yeşim. 2007. *Türkiye'de Kadına Yönelik Şiddet*. İstanbul: Punto Baskı Çözümleri.

Aradau, Claudia. 2010. "Security That Matters: Critical Infrastructure and Objects of Protection".*Security Dialogu*.Vol. 41. No. 5. 491–514.

Arat, Yeşim.1998. "Feminists, Islamists, and Political Change in Turkey".*Political Psychology*. Vol. 19. No. 1. 117–131.

Arat, Yeşim.2000. "From Emancipation to Liberation: The Changing Role of Women in Turkey's Public Realm".*Journal of International Affairs*. Vol. 54. No. 1. 107–123.

Arat, Yeşim. 2005. *Rethinking Islam and Liberal Democracy: Islamist Women in Turkish Politics*. Albany: State University of New York Press.

Arat, Yeşim. 2010. "Religion, Politics and Gender Equality in Turkey: Implications of a Democratic Paradox?".*Third World Quarterly*. Vol. 31. No. 6. 869–884.

Arat-Koç, Sedef. 2007. "(Some) Turkish Transnationalism(s) in an Age of Capitalist Globalization and Empire: "White Turk" Discourse, the New Geopolitics, and Implications for Feminist Transnationalism".*Journal of Middle East Women's Studies*. Vol. 3. No. 1. 35–57.

Arendt, Hannah. 1961. *Between Past and Future: Six Exercises in Political Thought*. New York: The Viking Press.

Arik, Hülya. 2012. "Speaking of Women? Exploring Violence against Women through Political Discourses: A Case of Headscarf Debates in Turkey".*e-cadernos CES (Online)*. No. 16. 10–31.

Aslan Akman, Canan. 2008".Sivil Toplumun Yeni Aktörleri Olarak İslami Eğilimli Kadın Dernekleri".*Toplum ve Demokrasi*. Vol. 2. No. 4. 71–90.

Aslan-Akman, Canan. 2013. "Islamic Women's Ordeal with the New Face(s) of Patriarchy in Power: Divergence or Convergence over Expanding Women's Citizenship". In *Gendered Identities: Criticizing Patriarchy in Turkey*. Ed. Rasim Özgür Dönmez and Fazilet Ahu Özmen. 113–145. UK: Lexington Books.

Aslan, Özlem and Gambetti, Zeynep. 2011".Provincializing Fraser's History: Feminism and Neoliberalism Revisited". *History of the Present: A Journal of Critical History*. Vol. l. No. 1. 131–147.

Atasoy, Yıldız. 2007. "The Islamist Ethic and Spirit of Turkish Capitalism Today". In *Socialist Register 2008: Reactions to Imperialism and Neoliberalism*. Ed. L. Panitch and C. Leys. Monthly Review Press: New York.

Ayata, Ayşe and Tütüncü, Fatma.2008. "Party Politics of AKP (2002–2007) and the Predicaments of Women at the Intersection of the Westernist, Islamist and Feminist Discourses in Turkey". *British Journal of Middle Eastern Studies*. Vol. 35. No. 3. 363–384.

Aygül, Hasan Hüseyin and Öztürk, Özgür. 2016. "Dini Çoğulculuk ve Kamusal Alanda Dindar Tüketim Kültürü".*Hacettepe Üniversitesi İletişim Fakültesi Kültürel Çalışmalar Dergisi*.Vol. 3. No.1. 190–206.

Aytaç, Ahmet Murat. 2015. *Ailenin Serencamı: Türkiye'de Modern Aile Fikrinin Oluşması*. Ankara: Dipnot Yayınları.

Barlas, Asma. 2002. "Believing Women". In *Islam: Unreading Patriarchal Interpretations of the Qur'an*. Austin: University of Texas Press.
Baroja, Julio Caro. 1965. "Honour and Shame: A Historical Account of Several Conflicts". In *Honour and Shame. The Values of Mediterranian Society*. Ed. J.G. Peristiany. 79–138. London: Weidenfeld and Nicolson.
Bayraktar, Sevi. 2011. *Makbul Anneler Müstakbel Vatandaşlar: Neoliberal Beden Politikalarında Annelik*. Ankara: Ayizi Kitap.
Bedirhanoğlu, Pınar. 2013. "Türkiye'de Neoliberal Otoriter Devletin Adalet ve Kalkınma Parti'li Yüzü". In *AKP Kitabı Bir Dönüşümün Bilançosu*. Ed. İlhan Uzgel and Bülent Duru. 40–65. Ankara: Phoenix Yayınevi.
Bell, Vikki. 1993a. "Governing Childhood: Neo-liberalism and the Law". *Economy and Society*. Vol. 22. No. 3. 390–405.
Bell, Vikki. 1993b. *Interrogating Feminism: Feminism, Foucault and the Law*. London and New York: Routledge.
Bell, Vikki. 2006. "Performative Knowledge". *Theory, Culture & Society*. Vol. 23. No. 2/3. 214–217.
Berkes, Niyazi. 1998. *The Development of Secularism in Turkey*. London: Hurst&Company.
Berktay, Fatmagül. 2012. *Tarihin Cinsiyeti*. Istanbul: Metis Yayınları.
Bora, Aksu. 2010. "Hatırlananlar ve Unutulanlar: İslam Coğrafyasında Modernleşme ve Kadın Hareketleri". *Bilig*. No. 53. 51–66.
Bora, Aksu and Günal, Asena (ed.). 2014. *90'larda Türkiye'de Feminizm*. Istanbul: İletişim Yayınları.
Bordo, Susan. 2004. "The Body and the Reproduction of Femininity". In *The Gendered Society Reader*. Eds. Michael S. Kimmel and Amy Aronson. 309–326. New York and Oxford: Oxford University Press.
Bordo, Susan. 2010. "Feminism, Foucault and the Politics of the Body". In *Feminist Theory and the Body: A Reader*. Eds. J. Price and M. Shildrick. 246–257. New York: Routledge.
Bostan-Ünsal, Fatma. 2014. "Müslüman Kadınlar "İdeal Aile"yi Nasıl Tanımlıyor, Nasıl Sorguluyor? AK Parti'de Aile Anlayışı". In *Başka Bir Aile Anlayışı Mümkün Mü?*. Eds. Ulrike Dufner and Semahat Sevim. 22–25. İstanbul: Heinrich Böll Stiftung.
Bouhdiba, Abdelwahab. 2008. *Sexuality in Islam*. London and New York: Routledge.
Braidotti, Rosi. 1994. *Nomadic Subjects: Embodiment and Sexual Difference in Contemporary Feminist Theory*. New York: Columbia University Press.
Brook, Barbara. 1999. *Feminist Perspectives on the Body*. London and New York: Longman.
Brown, Wendy. 1995. *States of Injury: Power and Freedom in Late Modernity*. Princeton: Princeton University Press.
Brown, Wendy. 2003. "Neo-liberalism and the End of Liberal Democracy". *Theory&Event*. Vol. 7. No. 1. 1–25.
Brown, Wendy. 2006. "American Nightmare: Neoliberalism, Neoconservatism, and De-Democratization". *Political Theory*. Vol. 34. No. 6. 690–714.

Brown, Wendy. 2018. *Halkın Çözülüşü: Neoliberalizmin Sinsi Devrimi*. Istanbul: Metis Yayınları.

Bugra, Ayse. 2014. "Revisiting the Wollstonecraft Dilemma in the Context of Conservative Liberalism: The Case of Female Employment in Turkey".*Social Politics*. Vol. 21. No. 1. 148–166.

Buğra, Ayşeand Savaşkan, Osman. 2014. *New Capitalism in Turkey: The Relationship between Politics, Religion and Business*. Cheltenham: Edward Elgar.

Burchell, Graham. 1996. "Liberal Government and Techniques of the Self". In *Foucault and Political Reason: Liberalism, Neo-liberalism, and Rationalities of Government*. Eds. P. Miller and N. Rose. 19–36. Chicago: University of Chicago Press.

Butler, Judith. 2002. *Gender Trouble: Feminism and the Subversion of Identity*. New York and London: Routledge.

Butler, Judith. 2004a. *Undoing Gender*. New York and London: Routledge.

Butler, Judith. 2004b. *Precarious Life: The Powers of Mourning and Violence*. London and New York: Verso.

Butler, Judith. 2011. *Bodies That Matter: On Discursive Limits of "Sex"*. London and New York: Routledge.

Chatterjee, Partha. 2004. *The Politics of the Governed: Reflections on Popular Politics in Most of the World*. New York: Columbia University Press.

Cinar, Alev. 2006. "Secularism and Islamic Modernism in Turkey".*Etnografica*. Vol. x. No. 1. 85–96.

Cindoğlu, Dilek. 1997. "Virginity Tests and Artificial Virginity in Modern Turkish Medicine".*Women's Studies International Forum*. Vol. 20. No. 2. 253–261.

Cindoğlu, Dilek and Zengirci, Gizem. 2008. "The Headscarf in Turkey in the Public and State Spheres".*Middle Eastern Studies*. Vol. 44. No. 5. 791–806.

Connell, Raewyn W. 2005. *Masculinities*. Berkeley and Los Angeles: University of California Press.

Connell, Raewyn W. 2009. *Gender In World Perspective*. Cambridge: Polity Press.

Connors, Jane. 2005. "United Nationas Approaches to 'Crimes of Honours'". In *'Honour': Crimes, Paradigms and Violence against Women*. Eds. Lynn Welchman and Sara Hossain. 22–41. Australia and New Zealand: Zed Books/Spinifex Press.

Coomaraswamy, Radhika. 2005. "Violence against Women and 'Crimes of Honour'". In *'Honour': Crimes, Paradigms and Violence against Women*. Eds. Lynn Welchman and Sara Hossain. XI-XIV. Australia and New Zealand:Zed Books/Spinifex Press.

Cooper, Melinda. 2008. "Orientalism in the Mirror: The Sexual Politics of Anti-Westernism".*Theory, Culture & Society*.Vol. 25. No. 6. 25–47.

Cruikshank, Barbara. 1993. "Revolutions Within: Self-government and Self Esteem". *Economy and Society*. Vol. 22. No. 3. 327–344.

Cruikshank, Barbara. 1998. "Moral Disentitlement: Personal Autonomy and Political Reproduction". In *Displacement of Social Policies*. Ed.Haennien Sakari. 145–171. SoPhi: University of Jyvaskyla.

Cürül, Burçak and Dönmez, Rasim Özgür. 2013. "Transexuals in Turkey: Between Disciplining and Eradicating". In *Gendered Indentities: Criticizing Patriarchy in Turkey*. Eds. R.Ö. Dönmez and F.A. Özmen. 67–77. UK: Lexington Books.

Çağlar-Gürgey, Fatma İrem. 2015. "Ev-İçi Şiddet Davalarında Yargıcın Tarafsızlığı". *Ankara Barosu Dergisi*. No. 4. 55–76.

Çakmak, Diren. 2009. "Türkiye'de Çocuk Gelinler". Birinci Hukukun Gençleri Sempozyumu-Hukuk Devletinde Kişisel Güvenlik. 20–21 March 2009.Ankara Üniversitesi.

Çarkoğlu, Ali and Kalaycıoğlu, Ersin. 2009. *The Rising Tide of Conservatism in Turkey*. New York: Palgrave Macmillan.

Çınar, Alev. 2005. Modernity, *Islam and Secularism in Turkey: Bodies, Places and Time*. Minneapolis:University of Minnesota Press.

Çınar, Alev. 2008. "Subversion and Subjugation in the Public Sphere: Secularism and the Islamic Headscarf". *Journal of Women in Culture and Society*. Vol. 33. No. 4. 891–913.

Çitak, Zana and Tür, Özlem. 2008. "Women Between Tradition and Change: The Justice and Development Party Experience in Turkey". *Middle Eastern Studies*. Vol. 44. No. 3. 455–469.

Dardot, Pierre and Laval, Christian. 2013. *The Way of the World: On Neoliberal Society*.trans. Gregory Elliott. London and New York: Verso.

Dean, Mitchell. 1994. *Critical and Effective Histories: Foucault's Methods and Historical Sociology*. London and New York: Routledge.

Dean, Mitchell. 1995. "Governing the Unemployed Self in an Active Society". *Economy and Society*. Vol. 24. No. 4. 559–583.

Dean, Mitchell. 1998. "Risk, Calculable and Incalculable".*Soziale Welt*.Vol. 49. No. 1. 25–42.

Dean, Mitchell. 2002. "Liberal Government and Authoritarianism". *Economy and Society*. Vol. 31. No. 1. 37–61.

Dedeoğlu, Saniye. 2009. "Eşitlik mi Ayrımcılık mı? Türkiye'de Sosyal Devlet, Cinsiyet Eşitliği Politikaları ve Kadın İstihdamı". *Çalışma ve Toplum*. Vol. 2. 41–54.

Deleuze, Gilles. 1992. "Postscript on the Societies of Control". *October*. Vol. 59. 3–7.

Devellioğlu, Ferit. 2005. *Osmanlıca Türkçe Ansiklopedik Lugat*. Ankara: Alkım Kiyabevi Yayınları.

Direk, Zeynep. 2009. "Judith Butler: Toplumsal Cinsiyet ve Bedenin Maddeleşmesi". In *Cinsiyetli Olmak: Sosyal Bilimlere Feminist Bakışlar*. Ed. Zeynep Direk. 67–84. İstanbul: YKY.

Doğan, Sevinç. 2017a. *Mahalledeki AKP: Parti İşleyişi, Taban Mobilizasyonu ve Siyasal Yabancılaşma*. İstanbul: İletişim Yayınları.

Doğan, Sevinç. 2017b. "Otoriterliğin Gölgesinde: Taraftarlık ve Muhaliflik Sınırları Değişirken". *Birikim-Aylık Sosyalist Kültür Dergisi*. No. 337. 16–25.

Doğan, Recep. 2016. "Namus", "Töre" ve Eril Şiddet. Ankara: Ütopya Yayınları.

Donzelot, Jacques. 2008. "Michel Foucault and Liberal Intelligence".*Economy and Society*. Vol. 37. No. 1. 115–134.

Dönmez, Rasim özgür. 2013. "Coup d'Etats and the Masculine Turkish Political Sphere: Modernisation without Strong Democratization". In *Gendered Indentities: Criticizing Patriarchy in Turkey*. Eds. R.Ö. Dönmez and F.A. Özmen. 1–32.UK: Lexington Books.

Dumrul, Candan and Karabacak-Danacı, Huriye. 2015. "Kadın ve Kız Çocuklarına Karşı İşlenen Cinsel Şiddet Suçlarında Cezasızlık Sorunu Raporu". *Ankara Barosu Dergisi*. Vol. 4. 255–291.

Durusoy, Serap. 2013. "The Unknown Reality of Women in Turkey: Economic Violence". In *Gendered Indentities: Criticizing Patriarchy in Turkey*. Eds. Rasim Özgür Dönmez and Fazilet Ahu Özmen. 33–50. UK: Lexington Books.

Duva, Özlem. 2015. "Mitostan Logos'a Yargının Cinsiyetlendirilmesi ve Hukukun Eril İnşası".*Ankara Barosu Dergisi*. No. 4. 27–44.

Düzkan, Ayşe and Ahıska, Meltem.1994".'80'li Yıllarda Türkiye'de Feminizm".*Defter*. Vol. 7. No. 21. 145–167.

Erol, Maral. 2016. "Anticipation, Choice, and Personal Responsibility: Medicalisation of Menopause as Gendered Governmnetality". In *The Making of Neoliberal Turkey*. Eds. C. Özbay, M. Erol, and A. Terzioğlu, Z.U. Türem. Ashgate Publishing Company.

Ewald, Francois. 1990. "Norms, Disciplinei and the Law". *Representations, Special Issue: Law and the Order of Culture*. No. 30. 138–161.

Foucault, Michel. 1980a. "The History of Sexuality". In*Power/Knowledge: Selected Interviews and Other Writings 1972–1977*. Eds. C. Gordon, L. Marshall, J. Mepham and K. Soper. 183–193. New York: Pantheon Books.

Foucault, Michel. 1980b. "Two Lectures". In*Power/Knowledge: Selected Interviews and Other Writings 1972–1977*. Eds. C. Gordon, L. Marshall, J. Mepham and K. Soper. 78–109. New York: Pantheon Books.

Foucault, Michel. 1980c. "Truth and Power". In *Power/Knowledge: Selected Interviews and Other Writings 1972–1977*. Eds. C. Gordon, L. Marshall, J. Mepham and K.Soper. 109–133. New York: Pantheon Books.

Foucault, Michel. 1980d. "Power and Strategies". In *Power/Knowledge: Selected Interviews and Other Writings 1972–1977*. Eds. C. Gordon, L. Marshall, J. Mepham and K. Soper. 134–145. New York: Pantheon Books.

Foucault, Michel. 1980e. "The Politics of Health in the 18th Century". In *Power/Knowledge: Selected Interviews and Other Writings 1972–1977*. Eds. C. Gordon, L. Marshall, J. Mepham and K. Soper. 166–182. New York: Pantheon Books.

Foucault, Michel. 1980f. "The Eye of Power". In *Power/Knowledge: Selected Interviews and Other Writings 1972–1977*. Eds. C. Gordon, L. Marshall, J. Mepham and K. Soper. 146–165. New York: Pantheon Books.

Foucault, Michel. 1980g. "Prison Talk". In*Power/Knowledge: Selected Interviews and Other Writings 1972–1977*.Eds. C. Gordon, L. Marshall, J. Mepham and K. Soper. 37–54. New York: Pantheon Books.

Foucault, Michel. 1980h. "Body/Power". In *Power/Knowledge: Selected Interviews and Other Writings 1972–1977*.Eds. C. Gordon, L. Marshall, J. Mepham and K. Soper. 55–62. New York: Pantheon Books.

Foucault, Michel. 1980i. Questions on Geography. In *Power/Knowledge: Selected Interviews and Other Writings 1972–1977*. Eds. C. Gordon, L. Marshall, J. Mepham and K. Soper. 63–77. New York: Pantheon Books.

Foucault, Michel. 1984a. "The Means of Correct Training". In *The Foucault Reader*. Ed. P. Rabinow. 188–205. New York: Pantheon Books.

Foucault, Michel. 1984b. "Docile Bodies". In *The Foucault Reader*. Ed. P. Rabinow. 179–187. New York: Pantheon Books.

Foucault, Michel. 1984c. "The Body of Condemned". In *The Foucault Reader*. Ed. P. Rabino. 170–178. New York: Pantheon Books.

Foucault, Michel. 1986. *The History of Sexuality: The Care of the Self. Volume III* .R. Hurleys (trans.). New York: Pantheon Books.

Foucault, Michel. 1990. *The History of Sexuality: The Use of Pleasure. Volume II* .R. Hurleys (trans.). New York: Vintage Books.

Foucault, Michel. 1997a. "Polemics, Politics, and Problematisations". In *Ethics: Essentials Works of Foucault 1954–1984 Volume One*. Ed. P. Rabinow, R. Hurley and the others (trans). 111–120. New York: The New Press.

Foucault, Michel. 1997b. "Technologies of Self". In *Ethics: Essentials Works of Foucault 1954–1984 Volume One*. Ed. P. Rabinow, R. Hurley and the others (trans). 223–252. New York:The New Press.

Foucault, Michel. 1997c. "The Hermeneutic of the Subjects". In *Ethics: Essentials Works of Foucault 1954–1984 Volume One.*Ed. P. Rabinow, R. Hurley and the others (trans). 90–108. New York: The New Press.

Foucault, Michel. 1997d. "The Abnormals". In*Ethics: Essentials Works of Foucault 1954–1984 Volume One*. Ed. P. Rabinow, R. Hurley and the others (trans). 51–58. New York: The New Press.

Foucault, Michel.1997e. "Subjectivity and Truth". In*Ethics: Essentials Works of Foucault 1954–1984 Volume One*. Ed. P. Rabinow, R. Hurley and the others (trans). 87–92. New York: The New Press.

Foucault, Michel. 1997f. "The Ethics of the Concern for Self as a Practice of Freedom". In *Ethics: Essentials Works of Foucault 1954–1984 Volume One*. Ed. P. Rabinow, R. Hurley and the others (trans). 281–302. New York:The New Press.

Foucault, Michel. 1995. *Discipline and Punish: The Birth of Prison*.A. Sheridan(trans), New York: Vintage Books.

Foucault, Michel. 1998.*The History of Sexuality: The Will to Knowledge, Volume 1*.R. Hurleys (trans.). London: Penguin Books.

Foucault, Michel. 2001a. "The Subject and Power". In *Power: Essential Works of Foucault 1954–1984 Volume Three*, Ed. J.D. Faubion. 328–348. New York: New York Press.

Foucault, Michel. 2001b. "The Political Technology of Individuals". In *Power: Essential Works of Foucault 1954–1984 Volume Three*. Ed. J.D. Faubion. 403–417. New York: New York Press.

Foucault, Michel. 2001c. "Questions of Method". In *Power: Essential Works of Foucault 1954–1984 Volume Three*. Ed. J.D. Faubion. 328–348. New York: New York Press.

Foucault, Michel. 2001d. "Truth and Juridical Forms". In *Power: Essential Works of Foucault 1954–1984 Volume Three*. Ed. J.D. Faubion. 1–89. New York: New York Press.

Foucault, Michel. 2001e. "Governmnetality". In*Power: Essential Works of Foucault 1954–1984 Volume Three*. Ed. J.D. Faubion. 201–222. New York: New York Press.

Foucault, Michel.2003a. *Society Must be Defended: Lectures at College De France 1975–76*. eds. M. Bertani and A. Fortana. New York: Picador.

Foucault, Michel. 2003b. *Abnormal: Lectures at the College de France 1974–1975*. Ed. Arnold Davidson, Graham Burchell(trans.). London and New York: Verso.

Foucault, Michel. 2007.*Security Territory Population Lectures at the College de France 1977–1978*.G. Burchell(trans.). New York: Palgrave Macmillan.

Foucault, Michel. 2008.*Birth of Biopolitics*. G. Burchell (trans.). New York: Palgrave Macmillan.

Foucault, Michel. 2014. *Wrong-doing, Truth-telling: The Function of Avowal in Justice*.F. Bion and B. Harcourt (Eds.). (S. Sawyer, Trans.). Chicago: University of Chicago Press.

Fraser, Nancy. 1989. *Unruly Practices: Power, Discourse, and Gender in Contemporary Social Theory*. Minneapolis: University of Minnesota Press.

Fraser, Nancy. 2000. "Rethinking Recognition". *New Left Review*. 107–120.

Fraser, Nancy. 2012. "Feminism, Capitalism, and the Cunning of History: An Introduction".*Working Paper Series*.No. 17. Paris: Fondation Maison des sciences de l'homme.

Gambetti, Zeynep. 2009. "İktidarın Dönüşen Çehresi: Neoliberalizm, Şidddet ve Kurumsal Şiddetin Tasfiyesi".*İ.Ü. Siyasal Bilgiler Fakültesi Dergisi*. No. 40. 145–166.

Garland, David. 1996. "The Limits of the Sovereign State: Strategies of Crime Control in Contemporary Society". *The British Journal of Criminology*. Vol. 36. No. 4. 445–471.

Giddens, Antony. 1992. *The Transformation of Intimacy: Sexuality, Love and Eroticism in Modern Societies*. Stanford, CA:Stanford University Press.

Gioscia, Laura and Delacoste, Gabriel. 2013. "On Critical Thought Today. An Interview with Wendy Brown".*Revista Pleyade.* Vol. 12 (December).233–240.

Gökariksel, Banu and Secor, Anna J. 2009. "New Transnational Geographies of Islamism, Capitalism and Subjectivity: The Veiling-Fashion Industry in Turkey". *Area.* Vol. 41. No. 1. 6–18.

Gökarıksel, Banu and McLarney, Ellen. 2010. "Muslim Women, Consumer Capitalism, and the Islamic Culture Industry".*Journal of Middle East Women's Studies.* Vol. 6. No. 3. 1–18.

Göle, Nilüfer. 2011. *Melez Desenler. İslam ve Modernlik Üzerine.* İstanbul: Metin Yayınları.

Göle, Nilüfer. 2016. *Modern Mahrem: Medeniyet ve Örtünme.* İstanbul: Metis Yayınları.

Grewal, Inderpal. 2006. "'Security Moms' in the Early Twentieth-Century United States: The Gender of Security in Neoliberalism".*Women's Studies Quarterly.* Vol. 34. No. 1/2. 25–39.

Grewal, Inderpal. 2013. "Outsourcing Patriarchy". *International Feminist Journal of Politics.* DOI:10.1080/14616742.2012.755352.

Günaydın, Ayça and Özdoğan, Zeynep. 2014. ""Biz Büyük Bir Aileyiz": Aile ve Sosyal Politikalar Bakanlığı Kamu Spotları". *Kültür ve Siyasette Feminist Yaklaşımlar.* No. 22. 53–84.

Gür, Deniz Ali. 2016. *Bilginin Dinselleştirilmesi: Yeni Ümit Dergisi Örneği.* Ankara: NotaBene Yayınları.

Gürkan, Ceyhun. 2016. "Braudel and Foucault on Structure and Event: Towards a New Approach to (Neo)Liberalism and Capitalism". *InterDisciplines: Journal of History and Sociology.* Vol. 7. No. 2. 63–94.

Gürkan, Ceyhun. 2018a. "Halkın Çözülüşü: Neoliberalizmin Sinsi Devrimi". *Mülkiye Dergisi.* Vol. 42. No. 2. 293–310.

Gürkan, Ceyhun. 2018b. "Foucault, Public Finance and Neoliberal Governmentality: A Critical Sociological Analysis".*Yönetim ve Ekonomi.* Vol. 25. No. 3. 1–11.

Haeri, Shahla. 2014. "İran'da Geçici Evlilik ve Devlet: Kadın Cinselliği Üzerine İslami bir Söylem". In *Müslüman Toplumlarda Kadın ve Cinsellik.* Ed. Pınar İlkkaracan. 151–174. İstanbul: İletişim Yayınları.

Hardt, Michael and Negri, Antonio. 2000. *Empire.* Cambridge: Harvard University Press.

Harraway, Donna. 1991. *A Cyborg Manifesto: Science, Technology, and Socialist Feminism in the Late Twentieth Century.* New York: Routledge.

Hartmann, Heidi. 1981. "The Family as the Locus of Gender, Class, and Political Struggle: The Example of Housework".*Signs.* Vol. 6. No. 3. 366–394.

Hartmann, Martin and Honneth, Axel. 2006. 'Paradoxes of Capitalism'.*Constellations.* Vol. 13. No. 1. 41–58.

Hartsock, Nancy. 1989/1990. Postmodernism and Political Change: Issues for Feminist Theory. *Cultural Critique.* No. 14. The Construction of Gender and Modes of Social Division. 15-33.

Harvey, David. 2006. "Neoliberalism as Creative Destruction". *Georg. Ann.* 88B: 2. 145–158.
Hekman, Susan. 2014. *The Feminine Subject*. Cambridge: Polity Press.
Heyes, Cressida. J. 2007. *Self-Transformations: Foucault, Ethics, and Normalized Bodies.* Oxford: Oxford University Press.
Hier, Sean P. 2008. "Thinking beyond Moral Panic: Risk, Responsibility, and the Politics of Moralization".*Theoretical Criminology*. Vol. 12. No. 2. 173–190.
Hoyek, Danielle and Rafif Rida Sidawi. 2005. "Murders of Women in Lebanon: 'Crimes of Honour' between Reality and the Law". In *'Honour': Crimes, Paradigms and Violence against Women*. Eds. Lynn Welchman and Sara Hossain, Australia and New Zealand: Zed Books/Spinifex Press. 111–136.
Hughes-Rinker, Cortney. 2013. "Responsible Mothers, Anxious Women: Contraception, Modernization, and Neoliberalism in Morocco".*Arab Studies Journal*. Vol. 21 (2013). 97–121.
Imam, Ayesha M. 2014. "Müslüman Dinsel sağ ("köktendinciler") ve cinsellik". In *Müslüman Toplumlarda Kadın ve Cinsellik*. Ed. Pınar İlkaracan. 75–94. İstanbul: İletişim Yayınları.
Iqtidar, Humeira. 2011. "Secularism Beyond the State: The 'State' and the 'Market' in Islamist Imagination". *Modern Asian Studies*. Vol. 45. No. 3. 535–564.
Ishkanian, Armine. 2014. "Neoliberalism and Violence: The Big Society and Changing Politics of Domestic Violence in England". *Critical Social Policy*. 1–20.
Ismail, Salwa. 2011. "Authoritarian Government, Neoliberalism and Everyday Civilities in Egypt". *Third World Quarterly*. Vol. 32. No. 5. 845–862.
İlkkaracan, Pınar. 2014. "Giriş: Müslüman toplumlarda kadın ve cinsellik". In *Müslüman Toplumlarda Kadın ve Cinsellik*. Ed.Pınar İlkaracan. 11–32. İstanbul: İletişim Yayınları.
İlyasoğlu, Aynur and Durakbaşa, Ayşe. 2001. "Formation of Gender Identities in Republican Turkey and Women's Narratives as Transmitters of 'Herstory' of Modernisation".*J Soc Hist.*Vol. 35. No.1. 195–203.
İlyasoğlu, Aynur.2015. *Örtülü Kimlik: Islamcı Kadın Kimliğinin Oluşum Öğeleri*. İstanbul: Metis Yayınlar.
İnceoğlu, Yasemin and Kar, Altan. 2010. *Dişilik, Güzellik ve Şiddet Sarmalında KAdın ve Bedeni*. İstanbul: Ayrıntı Yayınları.
Jones, Kathleen. 1996. "What is Authority's Gender". In *Revisioning the Political. Feminist Reconstructions of Traditional Concepts in Western Political Theory*. Eds. Nancy Hirschmann and Christine Di Stefano. 75–93. Oxford: Westview Pres.
Kandiyoti, Deniz. 1987. "Emancipated but Unliberated? Reflections on the Turkish Case".*Feminist Studies*. Vol. 13. No. 2. 317–339.
Kandiyoti, Deniz. 1988. "Bargaining with Patriarchy". *Gender and Society*. Vol. 2. No. 3. 274–290.

Kandiyoti, Deniz. 1991. *Women, Islam and the State*. London: Macmillan.
Kantola, Johanna and Squires, Judith. 2012. "From State Feminism to Market Feminism?". *International Political Science Review/ Revue internationale de science politique*. Vol. 33. No. 4. 382–400.
Kara, İsmail. 2014. "Diyanet İşleri Başkanlığı: Devletle Müslümanlar arasında bir kurum". In *Modern Türkiye'de Siyasi Düşünce: Islamcılık*. Vol. 6. Istanbul: Iletişim Yayınları. 178–184.
Karahanoğulları, Yiğit. 2018."Kitap Eleştirisi: Yeni İslami Burjuvazi, Türk Modeli". *Kültür ve İletişim*. No. 42. 233–239.
Kaya, İbrahim. 2004. *Social Theory and Later Modernities: The Turkish Experience*.Liverpool University Press.
Keskin, Ferda. 2016. "Hükümranlıktan Yönetimselliğe".*Felsefelogos*. No. 63 71–80.
Koğacıoğlu, Dicle. 2004. "The Tradition Effect: Framing Honor Crimes in Turkey".*Differences: A Journal of Feminist Cultural Studies*. Vol. 15. No. 2. 118–151.
Koğacıoğlu, Dicle. 2007. "Gelenek Söylemleri ve İktidarın Doğallaşması: Namus Cinayetleri Örneği". *Kültür ve Siyasette Feminist Yaklaşımlar*. No. 3.1–32.
Larner, Wendy. 2000a. "Post-Welfare State Governance: Towards a Code of Social and Family Responsibility". *Social Politics: International Studies in Gender, State & Society*. Vol. 7. No. 2. 244–265.
Larner, Wendy. 2000b. "Neoliberalism: Policy, Ideology, Governmentality".*Studies in Political Economy* 63. 5–25.
Lavee, Einat. 2015. "The Neoliberal Mom: How a Discursive Coalition Shapes Low-Income Mothers' Labor Market Participation".*Community, Work & Family*. 1–18.
Leite, Marianna. 2013. "(M)othering: Feminist Motherhood, Neoliberal Discourses and the Other". *Studies in the Maternal*. Vol. 5. No. 2. 1–23.
Lemke, Thomas. 2001. " 'The Birth of Biopolitics': Michel Foucault's Lecture at the College de France on Neo-liberal Governmentality' ".*Economy and Society*. Vol. 30. No. 2. 190–207.
Lemke, Thomas. 2007. "An Indigestible Meal? Foucault, Governmentality and State Theory". *Distinktion: Scandinavian Journal of Social Theory*. Vol. 8. No. 2. 43–64.
Lemke, Thomas. 2011. *Biopolitics: An Advanced Introduction*. New York and London: New York University Press.
Lemke, Thomas. 2012. *Foucault, Governmentality and Critique*. Boulder and London: Paradigm Publishers.
Lundgren, Eva. 2012. *Şiddetin Normalleştirilme Süreci*. İstanbul: Mor Çatı Kadın Sığınağı Vakfı Yayınları.
Mack, Ashley Noel. 2016. "The Self-Made Mom: Neoliberalism and Masochistic Motherhood in Home-Birth Videos on YouTube". *Women's Studies in Communication*. Vol. 39. No.1. 47–68.

Mackinnon, Catherine A. 1991. *Toward a Feminist Theory of the State*. London and Cambridge: Harvard University Press.

Madi, Ozlem. 2014. "From Islamic Radicalism to Islamic Capitalism: The Promises and Predicaments of Turkish-Islamic Entrepreneurship in a Capitalist System (The Case of İGİAD)". *Middle Eastern Studies*.Vol. 50. No. 1. 144–161.

Mahmood, Saba. 2001. "Feminist Theory, Embodiment, and the Docile Agent: Some Reflections on the Egyptian Islamic Revival".*Cultural Anthropology*. Vol. 16. No. 2. 202–236.

Mardin, Şerif. 1997. "Religion and Secularism in Turkey". In *Atatürk: Founder of a Modern State*.Eds.A. Kazancigil and E.Özbudun. London: Hurst&Company, 191–219.

McMahon, J. 2015. "Behavioral Economics as Neoliberalism: Producing and Governing 'Homo-economicus".*Contemporary Political Theory*. Vol. 14. No. 2. 137–158.

McNay, Lois. 2000. *Gender and Agency: Reconfiguring the Subject in Feminist and Social Theory*. Cambridge: Polity Press.

McNay, Lois. 2009. "Self as Enterprise Dilemmas of Control and Resistance in Foucault's *The Birth of Biopolitics*".*Theory, Culture & Society*.Vol. 26. No. 6. 55–77.

Mernissi, Fatima. 1991. *The Veil and the Male Elite: A Feminist Interpretation of Women's Rights in Islam*.Perseus Books Publishing.

Mernissi, Fatima. 2014a. "Islamda aktif kadın cinselliği anlayışı". In *Müslüman Toplumlarda Kadın ve Cinsellik*. Ed. Pınar İlkaracan. 33–54. İstanbul: İletişim Yayınları.

Mernissi, Fatima. 2014b. "Bekaret ve Ataerki". In *Müslüman Toplumlarda Kadın ve Cinsellik*. Ed. Pınar İlkaracan. 99–114. İstanbul: İletişim Yayınları.

Miller, Ruth A.2007. *The Limits of Bodily Integrity: Abortion, Adultery, and Rape Legislation in Comparative Perspective*. Aldershot: Ashgate Publishing.

Mutluer, Nil. 2014. "Yapısal, Sosyal ve Ekonomi Politik Yönleriyle Diyanet İşleri Başkanlığı". In *Sosyo-Ekonomik Politikalar Bağlamında Diyanet İşleri Başkanlığı*. İstanbul: Helsinki Yurttaşlar Derneği. 4–66.

Nadesan, Majia H. 2008. *Governmentality, Biopower, and Everyday Life*. New York and London: Routledge.

Najmabadi, Afsaneh. 2000. "(Un)veiling Feminism", *Social Text* 64, Vol. 18, No. 3, 29–45.

Navaro-Yaşın, Yael. 2000. "Evde Taylorism: Türkiye Cumhuriyeti'nin ilk yıllarında evişinin rasyonelleşmesi (1928–40)".*Toplum ve Bilim*. No. 84.51–74.

Oksala, Johanna. 2010. "Violence and the Biopolitics of Modernity". *Foucault Studies*. No. 10. 23–43.

Oksala, Johanna. 2011. "Violence and Neoliberal Governmentality". *Constellations*. Vol. 18. No. 3. 474–486.

O'Malley, Pat. 1992. "Risk, Power and Crime Prevention".*Economy and Society*. Vol. 21. No. 3. 252–275.

O'Malley, Pat. 1999. "Governmentality and the Risk Society".*Economy and Society*. Vol. 28. No.1. 138–148.

O'Malley, Pat. 2004. *Risk, Uncertainty and Government*.GlassHouse Press.

Orgad, Shani and De Benedictis, Sara.2015. "The 'Stay-at-home' Mother, Postfeminism and Neoliberalism: Content Analysis of UK News Coverage".*European Journal of Communication*, Vol. 30, No. 4. 418–436.

Öncü, Ahmet. 2014. "Turkish Capitalist Modernity and the Gezi Revolt". *Journal of Historical Sociology*. Vol. 27. No. 2. 151–176.

Öncü, Ahmet. 2018. "Hakk or Right: A Veblenian Narration of the Differences between the Justice Notions in Western Europe and Turkey".*J Hist Sociol.*1–16.

Özbay, Cenk; Erol, Maral; Terzioğlu, Ayşecan and Türem, Z.Umut (Eds.). 2016. *The Making of Neoliberal Turkey*. Ashgate Publishing Company.

Özbay, Ferhunde. 2014. "Demografik Dönüşüm Sürecinde İktidar, Kadın ve Aile". In *Başka Bir Aile Anlayışı Mümkün Mü?*. Ed. Ulrike Dufner ve Semahat Sevim. 106–111. İstanbul: Heinrich Böll Stiftung.

Özbay, Ferhunde. 2015. *Dünden Bugüne Aile, Kent ve Nüfus*. İstanbul: İletişim Yayınları.

Özbudun, Sibel. 2016. *Kadınlar: İslam, AKP ve Ötesi*. Ankara: Ütopya Yayınevi.

Özçetin, Burak. 2011. "Making of New Islamism in Turkey Transformation of the Islamist Discourse from Opposition to Compliance". Middle East Technical University.Ph.D. Ankara.

Özdalga, Elisabeth. 2015. *İslamcılığın Türkiye Seyri*. İstanbul: İletişim Yayınları.

Özkan-Kerestecioğlu, İnci. 2014. "Mahremiyetin Fethi: İdeal Aile Kurgularından İdeal Aile Politikalarına". In *Başka Bir Aile Anlayışı Mümkün Mü?*. Ed. Ulrike Dufner ve Semahat Sevim. 10–21. İstanbul: Heinrich Böll Stiftung.

Özkazanç, Alev. 2013.*Cinsellik, Şiddet ve Hukuk: Feminist Yazılar*. Ankara: Dipnot Yayınları.

Özyeğin, Gül. 2009".Virginal Facades Sexual Freedom and Guilt among Young Turkish Women". *European Journal of Women's Studies*.1350–5068. Vol. 16. No. 2. 103–123.

Özyeğin, Gül.2011. "Arzunun Nesnesi Olmak: Romans, Kırılgan Erkeklik ve Neoliberal Özne". In *Neoliberalizm ve Mahremiyet: Türkiye'de Beden, Sağlık ve Cinsellik*.151–178. İstanbul: Metis Yayınları.

Parla, Ayşe. 2001. "The Honor of the State: Virginity Examinations in Turkey". *Feminist Studies*.Vol. 27. No.1. 65–88.

Patel, Vinhuti. 2005. "Fundamentalism, Communalism and Gender Justice". In *Religion, Power and Violence Expression of Politics in Contemporary Times*. Ed. Ram Puniyani. 191–207. New Delhi and london: Sage Publications.

Pitt-Rivers, Julian. 1965. "Honour and Social Status". In *Honour and Shame. The Values of Mediterranian Society*. Ed. J.G. Peristiany. 19–78. London: Weidenfeld and Nicolson.

Pollack, Shoshana and Rossiter, Amy. 2010. "Neoliberalism abd the Entrepreneurial Subject: Implications for Feminism and Social Work". *Canadian Social Work Review / Revue canadienne de service social*, Vol. 27. No. 2. 155–169.

Rabasa, Angel and Larrabee, F. Stephen. 2008. *The Rise of Political in Turkey*.National Defense Research Instute.

Rabinow, Paul and Rose, Nikolas. 2006. "Biopower Today".*BioSocieties*. Vol. 1. 195–217.

Razavi, Shahra and Anne Jenichen. 2010. "The Unhappy Marraige of Religion and Politics: Problems and Pitfalls for Gender Equality". *Third World Quarterly*. Vol. 31. No. 6.833–850.

Repo, Jemima. 2016. *Biopolitics of Gender*. Oxford University Press.

Rose, Nikolasand Miller, Peter. 1992. "Political Power beyond the State: Problematics of Government". *The British Journal of Sociology*. Vol. 43. No. 2. 173–205.

Rose, Nikolas. 1999. *Governing the Soul: The Shaping of the Private Self*.2nd Edition. London and New York: Free Association Books.

Rose, Nikolas. 2000."Government and Control". *British Journal of Criminology*. 40. 321–339.

Rose,Nikolas and O'Malley, Pat and Valverde, Mariana. 2006. "Governmentality".*Annual Review of Law and Social Science*. Vol. 2. 83–104.

Rottenberg, Catherine. 2013. "The Rise of Neoliberal Feminism",*Cultural Studies*.1–20.https://doi.org/10.1080/09502386.2013.857361.

Rottenberg, Catherine. 2014. "Happiness and the Liberal Imagination: How Superwoman Became Balanced".*Feminist Studies*.Vol. 40. No. 1.144–168.

Saktanber, Ayşe and Çorbacıoğlu, Gül. 2008. "Veiling and Headscarf-Skepticism in Turkey", *Social Politics: International Studies in Gender, State and Society*. Vol. 15. No. 4. 514–538.

Sallan-Gül, Songül. 2013. *Türkiye'de Kadın Sığınma Evleri: Erkek Şiddetinden Uzak Yaşama Açılan Kapılar mı?*. İstanbul: Bağlam Yayıncılık.

Sancar, Serpil.2014. *Türk Modernlesmesinin Cinsiyeti. Erkekler Devlet, Kadınlar Aile Kurar*. İstanbul: İletisim Yayınları.

Scott, Joan W. 2010. "Toplumsal Cinsiyet: Faydalı Bir Tarihsel analiz Kategorisi".*Kültür ve Siyasette Feminist Yaklaşımlar*. Vol. 12. 112–138.

Selek, Pınar. 2002. "Ataerkil ve Şiddet Kültürü". In *Kadına Yönelik Şiddet ve Hekimlik Sempozyumu*. Ankara: Ankara Tabip Odası. 17–24.

Sen, Purna. 2005. " 'Crimes of Honour'. Value and Meaning". In *'Honour': Crimes, Paradigms and Violence against Women*. (Eds.) Lynn Welchman and Sara Hossain, Australia and New Zealand: Zed Books/Spinifex Press. 42–63.

Sennett, Richard. 1978. *The Fall of Public Man*. London: Penguin Books.

Sert, Özlem and Akkoyunlu-Wigley, Arzu. 2015. "Öğrenilmiş Çaresizlik ve Onurlu Yaşam Arasında: Bezdiri ve Kadın". in *Kadına Yönelik Şiddetin Ekonomi Politiği*.Ed. Derya Güler-Aydın. Ankara: Hacettepe Üniversitesi Yayınları.71–91.

Shalhoub-Kevorkian, Nadera. 2005. "Researching Women's Victimisation in Palestine: A Socio-Legal Analysis". In *'Honour': Crimes, Paradigms and Violence against Women*. (Eds.) Lynn Welchman and Sara Hossain, Australia and New Zealand: Zed Books/Spinifex Press. 160–180.

Shalhoub-Kevorkian, Nadera. 2014. "Tecavüzün Kültürel bir Tanımına Doğru: Filistin Toplumunda Tecavüz Mağdurlarıyla Çalışırken Karşılaşılan İkilemler". In *Müslüman Toplumlarda Kadın ve Cinsellik*. (Ed.) Pınar İlkaracan, İstanbul: İletişim Yayınları. 207–242.

Shier, Allie and Shor, Eran. 2016. "'Shades of Foreign Evil": "Honour Killings" and "Family Murders" in the Canadian Press".*Violence Against Women*, Vol. 22. No. 10. 1163–1188.

Siddiqi, Dina M. 2005. "Of Consent and Contradiction: Forced Marriages in Bangladesh". In *'Honour': Crimes, Paradigms and Violence against Women*. Eds. Lynn Welchmann and Sara Hossain. 282–307. Australia and New Zealand: Zed Books/Spinifex Press.

Sirman, Nükhet. 1988/1989. "Turkish Feminism: A Short History".*Dossier*.5/6. Aralık-Mayıs. 20–25.

Sirman, Nükhet. 2004. "Kinships, Politics and Love: Honour in the Postcolonial Contexts – The Case of Turkey". In*Violence in the Name of Honour/ Theoretical and Political Challenges*. Eds. Shahrzad Mojab and Nahla Abdo. 39–56. Istanbul Bilgi University Press.

Sirman, Nükhet. 2006. "Writing the Gender Regime of Republican Turkey". In *Writing Turkey/Explorations in Turkish History, Politics, and Cultural Identity*. Ed. Gerald Maclean. 41–54. Middlesex University Press.

Smith, Carole. 2000. "The Sovereign State v. Foucault: Law and Disciplinary Power". *Sociological Review*.Vol. 48. 283–306.

Taylor, Dianna. 2013. "Resisting the Subject: A Feminist-Foucauldian Approach to Countering Sexual Violence". *Foucault Studies*. No. 16. 88–103.

Tekeli, Şirin. 1984. "Faşizm ve Kadınlar". *İstanbul Üniversitesi İktisat Fakültesi Mecmuası*. Vol. 38. No. 3-4. 405–429.

Tekeli, Şirin (ed.). 2011. *1980'ler Türkiyesi'nde Kadın Bakış Açısından Kadınlar*. İstanbul:İletişim Yayınları.

Tibi, Bassam. 1995. "Culture and Knowledge: The Politics of Islamisation of Knowledge as a Postmodern Project? The Fundamentalist Claim to De-Westernizaticn".*Theory, Culture & Society*.Vol. 12. 1–24.

Toksöz, Gülay. 2016. "Kadın'dan Aileye Geçiş AKP Döneminin İstihdam Politikalarının Toplumsal Cinsiyet Açısından Analizi".*VIII. Sosyal İnsan Hakları Ulusal Sempozyumu*. 111–121.

Toprak, Binnaz. 1982. "Türk kadını ve din". In *Türk Toplumunda Kadın*. Ed. Nermin Abadan-Unat. 361–373. İstanbul: Araştırma Eğitim Ekin Yayınları.

Toprak, Binnaz. 1996. "Civil Society in Turkey". In *Civil Society in the Middle East*. Ed. A. R. Norton. 87–118. Leiden: E.J. Brill.

Toprak, Binnaz. 2005. "Islam and Democracy in Turkey". *Turkish Studies*. Vol. 6, No. 2, 167–186.

Toprak, Binnaz. 2006. *Değişen Türkiye'de Din, Toplum ve Siyaset*. İstanbul: TESEV Yayınları.

Toprak, Binnaz. 2008. "Türkiye'de Farklı Olmak, Din ve Muhafazakarlık Ekseninde Ötekileştirilenler".İ. Bozan, T. Morgül and N. Şener (Project Coordinators). Boğaziçi Üniversitesi: İstanbul.

Tuğal, Cihan. 2002. "Islamism in Turkey: Beyond Instrument and Meaning".*Economy and Society*.Vol. 31. No. 1. 85–111.

Tuğal, Cihan. 2009. "Transforming Everyday Life: Islamism and Social Movement Theory". *Theor Soc*. No. 38. 423–458.

Türkmen, Buket. 2009. "A Transformed Kemalist Islam or a New Islamic Civic Morality? A Study of 'Religious Culture and Morality' Textbooks in Turkish High School Curricula". *Comparative Studies of South Asia, Africa and the Middle East*. Vol. 29. No. 3. 181–197.

Türkmen, Buket. 2012. "Toplumsal Proje ve Kadinlik Deneyimi: Islamci Kadin Tarafindan Tanimlanan Mahrem". In *Cinsiyetli olmak: Sosyal Bilimlere Feminist Bakislar*. Ed. Zeynep Direk. 130–156. Yapi Kredi Yayinlari: Istanbul.

Türkmen, Buket. 2014. "The New Islamist Domination in Turkey: Occidentalism Toppled". In *Turkey between Nationalism and Globalisation*. Ed. Riva Kastoryano. 107–122. London: Routledge.

Uygur, Gülriz. 2015. "Toplumsal Cinsiyet ve Adalet: Hukuk Adaletsizdir".*Ankara Barosu Dergisi*. No. 4. 121–132.

Valverde, Mariana. 1996. 'Despotism' and ethical liberal governance, *Economy and Society*, 25:3, 357–372.

Vergin, Nur. 1985. "Social Change and the Family in Turkey". *Current Anthropology*. Vol. 26. No. 5. 571–574.

Yankaya, Dilek. 2014. *Yeni İslami Burjuvazi Türk Modeli*. Istanbul: İletişim Yayınları.

Yavuz, M. Hakan. 2003. *Islamic Political Identity in Turkey*. Oxford and New York: Oxford University Press.

Young, Iris Marion. 1994. "Gender as Seriality: Thinking about Women as a Social Collective".*Signs*. Vol. 19. No. 3. 713–738.

Young, Iris Marion. 2001. "Equality of Whom? Social Groups and Judgments of Injustice".*Journal of Political Philosophy*. Vol. 9. No. 1. 1–18.

Young, Iris Marion. 2003. "The Logic of Masculinist Protection: Reflections on the Current Security State". *Journal of Women in Culture and Society*. Vol. 29. No. 1. 1–25.

Young, Iris Marion. 1996. "Reflections on Families in the Age of Murphy Brown: On Gender, Justice, and Sexuality". In *Revisioning the Political: Feminist Reconstructions of Traditional Concepts in Western Political Theory*. Ed. Nancy J. Hirschmann and Christine Di Stefano. 251–270. Oxford: Westview Press.

Yuval-Davis, Nira. 2009. "Women, Globalisation and Contemporary Politics of Belonging".*Gender, Technology and Development*. Vol. 13. No. 1. 1–19.
Walby, Sylvia. 1997. *Gender Transformation*. London and New York: Routledge.
Walby, Sylvia. 2004. "The European Union and Gender Equality: Emergent Varieties of Gender Regime". *Social Politics*. Vol. 11. No. 1. 4–29.
Welchman, Lynn and Sara Hossain.2005. "Honour, Rights and Wrongs". In *'Honour': Crimes, Paradigms and Violence against Women*. Eds. Lynn Welchman and Sara Hossain. 1–21. Australia and New Zealand: Zed Books/Spinifex Press.
West, Candace and Zimmermann, Don H. 2004. "Doing Gender". In *The Gendered Society Reader*. Ed. Michael S. Kimmel and Amy Aronson. 150–168. New York and Oxford: Oxford University Press.
Wood, Julia T. 2009. *Gendered Lives: Communication, Gender, and Culture*. Wadsworth: Congage Learning.
Zürcher, Eric Jan. 2009. *Modernleşen Türkiye'nin Tarihi*. İstanbul: İletişim Yayınları.

Primary Sources

AIRB (Aile İrşat ve Rehberlik Bürolorı). 2013 (August 28). T.C. Diyanet İşleri Başkanlığı. No: 69097877–204.
Akçay-Civriz, Gülşah. 2017. "Sağlıklı Sınırlarla Sağlıklı Bireyler Olmaya Doğru". In *Nesil Emniyeti*. Diyanet Monthly Journal: Aile (April). 12–17.
AK Parti. 2007. Genel Seçimleri Seçim Beyannamesi (2007). Tanıtım ve Medya Başkanlığı-Şubat 2015.
AK Parti. 2011. Genel Seçimleri Seçim Beyannamesi (2011). Tanıtım ve Medya Başkanlığı-Şubat 2015.
AK Parti. 2012. Political Vision of AK Parti 2023 Politics, Society and the World.
AK Parti Kadın Kolları. 2010. "Kadın Erkek Eşitliği Çalıştay Raporu".
Albayrak, Ahmet. 2016. "Gençlik Psikolojisi Perspektifiyle Hayatı Sonlandırma, İntihar". In *İntihar ve Töre Cinayetleri Bağlamında Sosyal Sorunlar ve İslam*.DIB Yayınları: İstanbul. 53–60.
Alpaydın, Yusuf. 2012. Evlilik Öncesi Eğitimi Eğitici Kitabı. T.C. Aile ve Sosyal Politikalar Bakanlığı. İstanbul.
Altıntaş, Ramazan. 2016. "Intıhar ve Töre Cinayetlerini Önlemede Dini İnancın Rolü". In *İntihar ve Töre Cinayetleri Bağlamında Sosyal Sorunlar ve İslam*. İstanbul: Diyanet İşleri Başkanlığı Yayınları. 93–104.
Arslan, Elif. 2014. Ailemde Merhamet İstiyorum. DIB Yayınları. Ankara.
Arslan, Elif. 2015. "Mütevazı Bir Aile Mektebi". In *Bilgiden Hikmete Uzanan Yolda*. Diyanet Monthly Journal. No. 300. 38–41.

Aydın, M. Şevki. 2008. "Bireyin Kendi dindarlığını Oluşturma Yeteneği". In *Bireycilik, Diğerkamlık*. Diyanet Monthly Journal (November). No. 215. 20–23.

Balaban, Ayfer. 2005. "Aile içi Şiddet". In *Şiddetin Karmaşık Dünyası*. Diyanet Monthly Journal (February). No. 170. 21–24.

Balaban, Ayfer. 2008. "Prof. Dr. Hayrettin Kahraman İle "Temiz Hayat, Temiz Toplum". In *İslam ve İnsan Hakları*. Diyanet Monthly Journal (February). No. 206. 32–35.

Başbakanlık- Çocuk ve Kadınlara Yönelik Şiddet Hareketleriyle Töre ve Namus Cinayetlerinin Önlenmesi İçin Alınacak Tedbirler (2006/17). Offical Gazette, 26218, 04.07.2006.

Bayraktar-Karahan, Fatma. 2015. "Mekandan Daha Fazlası Ev". In *Mekandan Daha Fazlası Ev*. Diyanet Monthly Journal: Aile (September). 4–9.

Bayraktar-Karahan, Fatma. 2016. "Ailece Sınanmak". In *Ailece Sınanmak*. Diyanet Monthly Journal: Aile (March). 6–11.

Beder Şen, Rahime. 2005. "Aile Birliğinin Parçalanması: Boşanma". In *Modern Çağda Müslüman Kimlik*. Diyanet Monthly Journal (November). No. 179. 53–54.

Beder Şen, Rahime. 2007. "Ailede Anne ve Baba Rolleri". In *Modernliğin Alaca Karanlığında Dini Hayat*. Diyanet Monthly Journal (March). No. 195. 39–41.

Beder Şen, Rahime. 2007b. "Çocuk İstismarı ve İhlali". Diyanet İşleri Başkanlığı. Şiddet Bu kadar Yanımızdayken... Diyanet Monthly Journal (January). No. 193. 42–45.

Bilgiç-Selman, Şule. 2012. Üreme Sağlığı ve Sağlıklı Annelik. T.C. Aile ve Sosyal Politikalar Bakanlığı. İstanbul.

Canel, Azize Nilgün. 2012a. Aile Yaşam Becerileri. T.C. Aile ve Sosyal Politikalar Bakanlığı. İstanbul.

Canel, Azize Nilgün. 2012b. Evlilik ve Aile Hayatı. T.C. Aile ve Sosyal Politikalar Bakanlığı. İstanbul.

Canel, Azize Nilgün. 2012c. Evlilikte İletişim ve Yaşam Becerileri. T.C. Aile ve Sosyal Politikalar Bakanlığı. Ankara.

Ceceli-Alkan, Nurten. 2004. "Mutlu, Başarılı ve Sağlıklı Bir toplum İçin Önce Aile". In *Önce Aile*. Diyanet Monthly Journal (September). No. 165. 5–7.

CEID (Cinsiyet Eşitliği İzleme Derneği). 2014. Kadına Yönelik Şiddetle Mücadele Mekanizması: İzleme Modeli.

Çapçıoğlu, İhsan. 2015. "Ailede Merhamet ve Merhametin Yansımaları". In *Bir İnsanlık Sorunu Merhametsizlik*. Diyanet Monthly Jorunal (November). No. 299. 30–33.

Çekin, Ahmet. 2006. "Varolmanın Anlamı". In *Ahlak Eğitimi*. Diyanet Monthly Journal (April). No. 184. 26–29.

Çekin, Ahmet. 2009. "Örnek Alma, Örnek Olma". In *Hayatın Nevbaharı Gençlik ve Sorunları*. Diyanet Monthly Journal (September). No. 225. 13–15.

Çiftçi, Ali. 2009. "Sorunlar Yumağında Gençliğimiz". In *Hayatın Nevbaharı Gençlik ve Sorunları*. Diyanet Monhly Journal (September). No. 225. 4–6.

"Çocuk İstismarına Yönelik Rapor". 2016. http://imdat.org/wp-content/uploads/2016/05/çocuk-istismarina-yönelik-rapor.pdf.

Demirkan, Semra. 2006. "Boşanmanın Çocuklar Üzerindeki Etkisi". In *Büyük İç Dünya, Küçük Benlik Gönül İnsanı Olmak*, Diyanet Monthly Journal (December). No. 192. 34–37.

Demirkan, Semra. 2007. "Ana Ailenin Harsıdır". In *Toplumsal Sorumluluğun Dini Temelleri*.Diyanet Monthly Journal (December). No. 204. 47–49.

Demirkan, Semra. 2008. "Aile Değeri". In *Bireycilik Diğerkamlık*.Diyanet Monthly Journal (November). No. 215. 32–35.

Demirkan, Semra. 2009. "Gençliğin Toplumsallaşmasında Ailenin Rolü". In *Hayatın Nevbaharı Gençlik ve Sorunları*. Diyanet Monthly Journal (September). No. 225. 10–12.

Dönmez, Fatma. 2014. "Onlar Bize Emanet". In *Ailede Samimiyet*. Diyanet Monthly Journal: Aile Eki. No. 288 (December). 14–17.

Deniz, Mehmet Bülent and Göral, Ö. Sevgi. 2012. Aile Hukuk Rehberi. T.C. Aile ve Sosyal Politikalar Bakanlığı. İstanbul.

Friday Khutbah. (07.03.2008). İslamda Kadın Hakları.

Friday Khutbah. (10.07.2009). Nikah ve Düğünlerimiz.

Friday Khutbah. (05.03.2010). İslamda Kadın Hakları.

Friday Khutbah. (25.11.2011). Eşimiz, Evladımız, Annemiz: Kadın.

Friday Khutbah. (02.03.2012). İslamın Kadına Verdiği Değer.

Friday Khutbah. (08.06.2012). Çocuklarımıza Karşı Sorumluluklarımız.

Friday Khutbah. (02.11.2012). İslamda Edep ve Haya.

Friday Khutbah. (28.06.2013). İslami Bir Değer: Edeb.

Friday Khutbah. (23.08.2013). İnsanın Katli, İnsanlığın Katlidir.

Friday Khutbah. (08.03.2013). Bir Kul Olarak Kadın.

Friday Khutbah. (22.08.2014). Haya Hayattır.

Friday Khutbath. (12.09.2014). Bilgi Ahlakı.

Friday Khutbah. (31.07.2015). İnsan: Akıllı ve Sorumlu Varlık.

Friday Khutbah. (20.02.2015a). Kadına El Kalkmaz.

Friday Khutbah. (20.02.2015b). Her Can Kutsaldır ve Dokunulmazdır.

Friday Khutbah. (06.03.2015). Allah, Aşırı Gidenleri Sevmez.

Friday Khutbah. (08.05.2015). Cana Can Olmak: Aile.

Friday Khutbah.(01.04.2016). Öfkeye Hakim Olabilmek.

Friday Khutbah. (13.05.2016). Huzur ve Muhabbet Ocağı: Ailemiz.

Friday Khutbah. (20.05.2016). Mahremiyeti Yitirmek Mahrumiyettir.

Göç, Kentleşme ve Dindarlık. 2014. Diyanet Monthly Journal (August). No. 284.

Görgülü, Faruk. 2015. "Dini Dergicilik ve Süreli Yayınlarımız". In*Bilgiden Hikmete Uzanan Yolda*. Diyanet Monthly Journal (December). No. 300. 24–27.

Görgülü, Ülfet. 2017. "Nesil Emniyeti". In *Nesil Emniyeti*. Diyanet Monthly Journal: Aile (April). 4–9.

Güner-Özduygu, Filiz. 2016. "Intiharlar Töre Namus Cinayetleri ve Krizler". In *İntihar ve Töre Cinayetleri Bağlamında Sosyal Sorunlar ve İslam*. İstanbul: Diyanet İşleri Başkanlığı Yayınları.105–112.
İlmihâl Volume 2. İslam ve Toplum. Diyanet İşleri Başkanlığı.
Istanbul Convention- Council of Europe Convention on Preventing and Combating Violence against Women and Domestic Violence.2011. İstanbul. 11.05.2011.
"Kadına Yönelik Şiddet Raporu". (2011). İnsan Hakları Derneği İstanbul Şubesi, İstanbul.
Kahraman, Fikret. 2006. "Çocuk Aile ve Toplumun Emanetidir". In *Ahlak Eğitimi*. Diyanet Monthly Journal (April). No. 184. 20–23.
Karslı, İbrahim Hilmi. 2016. "Güvenli Topluma Giden Yol". In *Fitneye Karşı Güven Toplumu*. Diyanet Monthly Journal (November). No. 311. 6–9.
Koç, Mustafa. 2013. "Aile Yaşamında Farklılıklarda Uzlaşmak ve Ortak Noktalarda Buluşmak". In *Gösteriş ve Reklam Kültürü*. Diyanet Monthly Journal (December). No. 276. 43–46.
Konda. 2015. "Hayat Tarzları". Konda Araştırma.
Konda. 2014. "Diyanet Algı, Memnuniyet ve Beklentiler Araştırması".Konda Araştırması.
Konda. 2012a. "Ayıp, Günah ve Suç Algı Tanımları". Konda Araştırma.
Konda. 2012b. "Gündelik Hayatta Mutluluk".Konda Araştırma.
Konda. 2012c. "Gündelik Hayatta Güven".Konda Araştırma.
Koytak, Necla. 2004. "Duygu Okulu Olarak Aile". In *Önce Aile*. Diyanet Monthly Journal (September). No. 165. 18–21.
Kök, Tülay. 2016. "Evleneceğimiz Kişiyi Nasıl Daha iyi Tanıyabiliriz?". İn *Diyanet İşleri Başkanlığı*(2016). Ailece Sınanmak, *Diyanet* Monthly Journal: Aile (March). 22–25.
Kurt, Abdurrahman. 2016. "Toplumsal Güven İhtiyacı". Diyanet İşleri Başkanlığı (2016d). Fitneye Karşı Güven Toplumu. *Diyanet* Monthly Journal (November). No. 311. Ankara.20–23.
Law No. 4787.2003. Aile Mahkemelerinin Kuruluş, Görev ve Yargılama Usullerine Dair Kanun. T.C. Resmi Gazete, 24997. 18.01.2003.
Law No. 5326. 2005. Kabahatler Kanunu. T.C. Resmi Gazete. 25772. 31.03.2005.
Law No. 6284. 2012. Ailenin Korunması ve Kadına Karşı Şiddetin Önlenmesine Dair Kanun. T.C. Resmi Gazete. 28239. 08.03.2012.
Law No. 633. 1965. Diyanet İşleri Başkanlığı Kuruluş ve Görevleri Hakkında Kanun. T.C. Resmi Gazete. 12038. 22.06. 1965.
Law No. 5237 Türk Ceza Kanunu. 2004. T.C. Resmi Gazete. 25611. 12.10.2014.
Law No. 4721. 2001. Türk Medeni Kanunu. T.C. Resmi Gazete. 24607. 8.12.2001.
Martı, Huriye. 2013. "Söyleşi". In *Diyanet İşleri Başkanlığı* (2013). Cami, Kadın ve Aile, Diyanet Monthly Journal (October). No. 274. P.34.
Martı, Huriye (ed.). 2014. Ailem. DIB Yayınları: Ankara.
Martı, Huriye (ed.). 2015. Diyanet İşleri Başkanlığının Aile Koruması ve Kadına Yönelik Şiddetin Önlenmesi Konusunda Görüş ve Yaklaşımları. DIB Yayınları: Ankara.

Okumuş, Ejder. 2006. "Çocuk Suçluluğunun Önlenmesinde Islam Maneviyatının Önemi". In *Ahlak Eğitimi*. Diyanet Monthly Journal (April). No. 184. 17–19.

Okumuş, Ejder. 2007. "Toplumsal Çöküşte Kötü Ahlakın Rolü". In *Toplumsal Sorumluluğun Dini Temelleri*. Diyanet Monthly Journal (December). No. 204. 15–18.

Okumuş, Ejder. 2009. "İslam ve Kadın". In *Hayatın Nevbaharı Gençlik ve Sorunları*. Diyanet Monthly Journal (September). No. 225. 34–36.

Özbudun, Nazlı. 2014. "Evet Demeden Önce Evlilik". In *Evet Demeden Önce Evlilik*, Diyanet Monthly Journal: Aile (July). Ankara. 4–9.

Özbuğday, Şükrü. 2004. "İslam'da Aile Hayatı ve Türk Aile Yapısının Geleneksel Özellikleri". In *Önce Aile*. Diyanet Monthly Journal (September). No. 165. 12–15.

Özkan, Ayşenur. 2014. Ailem Dağılmasın. Ankara.

Özüdoğru-Erdoğan, Halide. 2016. "Çalışan Kadın İkilemi". In *Ailece Sınanmak*, Diyanet Monthly Journal: Aile (March). Ankara. 26–27.

Piyade, Özgül. 2014. "İyi İnsan; İyi Gelin, İyi Kayınvalidedir". In *Biriktirilemeyen Bir Kaynağın; Zamanın Yönetimi*. Diyanet Monhtly Journal: Aile (October). No. 286 Ankara. 20–22.

Ramazanoğlu, Yıldız. 2013. "Camiyle Kadın Arasında Kırılgan Tecrübemiz". In *Cami, Kadın ve Aile*. Diyanet Monthly Journal (October). No. 274. 19–23.

Sarısaman-Yıldırım, Nuriye. 2015. "Medyanın Özgürleştiremediği Kadın". In *Medya ve Din Algısı*. Diyanet Monthly Journal (August). No. 296. 55–57.

Sönmez, Özden Zehra. 2016. "Anne Olmak". In *Adabımuaşeret*. Diyanet Monthly Journal: Aile (May). Ankara. 26–27.

Subaşı, Necdet. 2016. "Çağımızda Sosyal Değişim ve Yansımaları". In *İntihar ve Töre Cinayetleri Bağlamında Sosyal Sorunlar ve İslam*, İstanbul: Diyanet İşleri Başkanlığı Yayınları. 35–42.

Şentürk, Lütfi. 2013. "Zina ve Fuhuş Toplumun Temelini Sarsar". In *Örnek Vaazlar-1*. Diyanet İşleri Başkanlığı: Ankara. 280–287.

Şiddet Önleme ve İzleme Merkezleri Hakkında Yönetmelik. 2016. Official Gazette-29656 (17.03.2016). http://www.resmigazete.gov.tr/eskiler/2016/03/20160317-8.htm.

T.C. Türkiye Büyük Millet Meclisi İnsan Haklarını İnceleme Komisyonu (2011). Kadına ve Aile Bireylerine Yönelik Şiddet İnceleme Raporu, 24. Dönem 2. Yasama Yılı. https://www.tbmm.gov.tr/komisyon/insanhaklari/docs/2012/raporlar/29_05_2012.pdf.

T.C.Başbakanlık, Kadın Statüsü Genel Müdürlüğü (2008). Kadına Yönelik Aile İçi Şiddete İlişkin Hukuksal Durum ve Uygulama Örnekleri.

T.C.Başbakanlık, Kadın Statüsü Genel Müdürlüğü (2009). Türkiye'de Kadına Yönelik Aile İçi Şiddet, Ankara.

T.C. Türkiye Büyük Millet Meclisi, Constitution of the Republic of Turkey.

T.C. Türkiye Büyük Millet Meclisi (2015). Kadına Yönelik Şiddetin Sebeplerinin Araştırılarak Alınması Gereken Önlemlerin Belirlenmesi Amacıyla Kurulan Meclis Araştırması Komisyon Raporu. Vol. 1. No. 717. 08.05.2015.

T.C. Türkiye Büyük Millet Meclisi (2015). Kadına Yönelik Şiddetin Sebeplerinin Araştırılarak Alınması Gereken Önlemlerin Belirlenmesi Amacıyla Kurulan Meclis Araştırması Komisyon Raporu. Vol. 2. No. 717. 08.05.2015.

T.C. Aile ve sosyal Politikalar Bakanlığı (n.d.). Kadına Yönelik Şiddetle Mücadele Ulusal Eylem Planı (2007–2010), Ankara.

T.C. Kalkınma Bakanlığı (2015). Onuncu Kalkınma Programı (2014–2018). Ailenin ve Dinamik Nüfus Yapısının Korunması Programı Ulusal Eylem Planı, Ankara.

T.C. Aile ve sosyal Politikalar Bakanlığı (2012). Kadına Yönelik Şiddetle Mücadele Eylem Planı (2012–2015), Ankara.

Toprak, Hicret K. 2006."Eğitimde Sevgi Prensibi ve Şiddetin Yeri". In *Ahlak Eğitimi*. Diyanet Monthly Journal (April). No. 184, Ankara. 41–44.

Uysal, Asım. 1999. Evlilik ve Cinsel Hayat. Konya: Uysal Kitabevi.

Ünal, İ. Hakkı. 2008. "Aile Sorumluluğu". In *İslam ve İnsan Hakları*. ...Diyanet Monthly Journal (February). No. 206. 43–44.

Üresin, Emel. 2007. "Kadına Karşı Şiddet". In *Şiddet Bu kadar Yanımızdayken*. Diyanet Monthly Journal (January). No. 193. 17–18.

Yenen, Halide. 2009. "Yeni Roller ve Yeni Sorumluluklarıyla Kadın". In *Hayatın Nevbaharı Gençlik ve Sorunları*. Diyanet Monhly Journal (September). No. 225. 37–39.

Yılmaz, Hakan. 2012. Türkiye'de Muhafazakarlık: Aile, Cinsellik, Din". Açık Toplum Vakfı and Boğaziçi Üniversitesi: İstanbul.

Newspaper Articles

Acar-Savran, Gülnur. 2008. "Kadın düşmanlığının yeni yüzü", Sendika.Org Emeğin ve Direnişin Gündemi. (20 March 2008). http://sendika63.org/2008/03/kadin-dusmanliginin-yeni-yuzu-gulnur-acar-savran-radikal2–19201/.

Bianet. (5 March 2019). "Bianet Şiddet, Taciz, Tecavüz Çetelesi Tutuyor". https://bianet.org/kadin/bianet/133354-bianet-siddet-taciz-tecavuz-cetelesi-tutuyor.

Bianet.(19 November 2018). "Kadınlar Mücadele Ediyor, Erkek Şiddeti Yargılanıyor". (B.Baki and E.Kepenek-Reporters) https://bianet.org/english/toplumsal-cinsiyet/202671-kadinlar-mucadele-ediyor-erkek-siddeti-yargilaniyor

Bianet. (22 February 2018). "AKP 2004'te Suç Haline Getiremediği Zinayı Yeniden Gündemine Aldı". https://m.bianet.org/bianet/insan-haklari/194571-akp-2004-te-suc-haline-getiremedigi-zinayi-yeniden-gundemine-aldi.

Bianet. (9 May 2017). "Yıkılan Sadece Bir Genelev Değil". https://m.bianet.org/biamag/kadin/186298-yikilan-sadece-bir-genelev-degil.

REFERENCES

Bianet. (11 October 2017). "Genelevler Kapatılıyor, Kayıtdışı Alan Büyüyor". (Ç. Tahaoğlu Reporter) https://m.bianet.org/bianet/kadin/190499-genelevler-kapatiliyor-kayitdisi-alan-buyuyor.

Bianet. (3 March 2016). "Kadınlar Mücadele Ediyor, Erkek Şiddeti Yargılanıyor" https://m.bianet.org/bianet/print/172646-kadinlar-mucadele-ediyor-erkek-siddeti-yargilaniyor.

Bianet. (16 February 2015). "Özgecan Aslan Eyleminde Bir Kız Çocuğu Cezasız Kalan Tecavüzü Anlattı". (S. Kara-Reporter) http://bianet.org/bianet/kadin/162316-ozgecan-aslan-eyleminde-bir-kiz-cocugu-cezasiz-kalan-tecavuzu-anlatti.

Bianet. (14 July 2014). "Erdoğan'dan Kadın Öğrencilere: Çok Seçici Olmayın, Evlenin". https://bianet.org/bianet/toplumsal-cinsiyet/157312-erdogan-dan-kadin-ogrencilere-cok-secici-olmayin-evlenin.

Bianet. (8 December 2010). "'Akademik' Aile Konferasından Nefret Söylemi Çıktı". https://m.bianet.org/bianet/siyaset/126481-akademik-aile-konferasindan-nefret-soylemi-cikti.

BirGün. (28 July 2017). "AKP Çocukların 'gelin' olmasında ısrarcı". https://www.birgun.net/haber-detay/akp-cocuklarin-gelin-olmasinda-israrci-171977.html.

BirGün. (28 April 2017). "Alcohol ban in Turkey's tourism hub Antalya". https://www.birgun.net/haber-detay/alcohol-ban-in-turkeys-tourism-hub-antalya-157378.html.

Case, Holy. 2017. "The New Authoritarians", aeon. (7 March 2017). https://aeon.co/essays/the-new-dictators-speak-for-the-complainer-not-the-idealist.

CNN Türk. (21 November 2016). "İşte çocuk gelin haritası". https://www.cnnturk.com/turkiye/iste-cocuk-gelin-haritasi.

CNN Türk. (17 March 2015). "Özgecan Aslan'ın son görüntüleri". https://www.cnnturk.com/video/turkiye/ozgecan-aslanin-son-goruntuleri.

CNN Türk. (5 March 2015). "Son 7 yılda kadına şiddet yüzde 1400 arttı". https://www.cnnturk.com/haber/turkiye/son-7-yilda-kadina-siddet-yuzde-1400-artti.

CNN Türk. (28 July 2014). "Bülent Arınç: "Kadın herkesin içinde kahkaha atmayacak"". https://www.cnnturk.com/haber/turkiye/bulent-arinc-kadin-herkesin-icinde-kahkaha-atmayacak.

Cumhuriyet. (7 September 2017). "16 yıl sonar... 'Evin reisi' döndü". (E. Kaplan-Reporter). http://www.cumhuriyet.com.tr/haber/egitim/818271/16_yil_sonra...__Evin_reisi__dondu.html.

Cumhuriyet. (8 March 2017). "Toplu tecavüz mağduru: Vazgeçmeyin lütfen ... Başka kadınlar için". http://www.cumhuriyet.com.tr/haber/turkiye/693326/Toplu_tecavuz_magduru__Vazgecmeyin_lutfen..._Baska_kadinlar_icin.html#.

Deutsche Welle. (07 February 2019). "Şule Çet davasında Sanık Avukatlarına tepki". https://www.dw.com/tr/%C5%9Fule-%C3%A7et-davas%C4%B1nda-san%C4%Bık-avukatlar%C4%Bına-tepki/a-47410615.

Deustche Welle. (15 November 2013). "Erdoğan wants to snop in student bedrooms". https://www.dw.com/en/erdogan-wants-to-snoop-in-student-bedrooms/a-17230991.

Diken. (5 January 2018). "Kampanyacı erkek, imzacı erkek: 'Kadınlar pembe otobüse binip rahat etsin' ". http://www.diken.com.tr/kadinlar-pembe-otobuse-binip-rahat-etsin-kampanyaci-erkek-imzaci-erkek/.

Evrensel. (23 November 2017). "Rakamlarla, Kadınların Uğradığı Şiddet ve Eşitsizlik Tablosu". (H. Tok Reporter). https://www.evrensel.net/haber/338724/rakamlarla-kadinlarin-ugradigi-siddet-ve-esitsizlik-tablosu.

Evrensel. (7 May 2017). "Daha fazla güvencesizlik çok daha düşük ücret". (D. Kayacan and B. Yıldırım-Reporters) https://www.evrensel.net/haber/318683/daha-fazla-guvencesizlik-cok-daha-dusuk-ucret.

Evrensel Gazetesi. (26 February 2017). "AKP ile Kadınların Çelişkili İlişkisi". (Rep. Örnek, Gizem and Tok, Hilal). https://www.evrensel.net/haber/309821/akp-ile-kadinlarin-celiskili-iliskisi.

Evrensel. (19 March 2015). "Ceza indirimine yeni bahane: Mağdurun' psikolojisi düzeldi!" https://www.evrensel.net/haber/108292/ceza-indirimine-yeni-bahane-magdurun-psikolojisi-duzeldi.

Evrensel. (22 April 2012). "Fethiye Davası'nda Hukuka da Tecavüz". https://www.evrensel.net/haber/27928/fethiye-davasinda-hukuka-da-tecavuz.

Gazete Yolculuk. (25 May 2016). "Adana'da kadın cinayeti: Reddedilen erkek, eski sevgilisini öldürdü" http://gazeteyolculuk.net/adanada-kadin-cinayeti-reddedilen-erkek-eski-sevgilisini-oldurdu.

Gazete DuvaR. (13 December 2018). "Yargıtay cezayı onadı: Bir kadın, istediği saatte dışarı çıkar!". https://www.gazeteduvar.com.tr/gundem/2018/12/13/yargitay-cezayi-onadi-birkadin-istedigi-saatte-disari-cikar/.

Gazete duvaR. (14 July 2018). " 'Mini etekli yolcu var' diye halk otobüsünü karakola çektirdi!". https://www.gazeteduvar.com.tr/gundem/2018/07/14/mini-etekli-kadin-var-diye-halk-otobusunu-karakola-cektirdi/.

Haberler.com. (22 October 2015). "Davutoğlu, Evlenemeyen Gençlere Eş Bulma Vaadinde Bulundu". https://www.haberler.com/basbakan-davutoglu-sanliurfa-da-7805017-haberi/.

Haberler.com. (22 February 2014). "Erdoğan: Bahçeli Aile ve Çocuk Nedir Bilmez". https://www.haberler.com/basbakan-erdogan-sivas-ta-konusuyor-5701862-haberi/.

HaberSol. (13 February 2019). "Şule Çet dosyasında o raporu yazan adli tıp uzmanına soruşturma açılacak". http://haber.sol.org.tr/turkiye/sule-cet-dosyasinda-o-raporu-yazan-adli-tip-uzmanina-sorusturma-acilacak-256581.

HaberSol. (25 May 2013). " 'Bunlar ahlaksız' diyerek 'öpüşen eylemcilere' saldırdılar" http://haber.sol.org.tr/kent-gundemleri/bunlar-ahlaksiz-diyerek-opusen-eylemcilere-saldirdilar-haberi-73599.

HaberSol. (17 January 2013). "N.Ç. davasında utanç kararı: Mahkeme 'rızası var' diyerek sanıklara alt sınırdan ceza verdi!. http://haber.sol.org.tr/kadinin-gunlugu/nc-davasinda-utanc-karari-mahkeme-rizasi-var-diyerek-saniklara-alt-sinirdan-ceza.

HaberSol. (22 May 2013). "Ankara Metrosunda 'ahlaklı olun' anonsu". http://haber.sol.org.tr/kent-gundemleri/ankara-metrosunda-ahlakli-olun-anonsu-haberi-73442.

HaberSol. (24 April 2011). "İETT şoförünü öpüşerek protesto ettiler". http://haber.sol.org.tr/devlet-ve-siyaset/iett-soforunu-opuserek-protesto-ettiler-haberi-41813.

HaberTürk. (12 November 2017). "Ombudsman, boşanan çiftler ve çocuklar için önerdi: 'Aile buluşma noktası' ". https://www.haberturk.com/ombudsman-bosanan-ciftler-ve-cocuklar-icin-onerdi-aile-bulusma-noktasi-1710327.

HaberTürk. (06 November 2017). "CHP 'Türkiye'de sosyal Bozulma' Raporu Hazırladı". https://www.haberturk.com/chp-turkiyede-sosyal-bozulma-raporu-hazirladi-1701648#.

HaberTürk. (14 February 2015). "Özgecan Aslan Ölüme Böyle Direnmiş". https://www.haberturk.com/gundem/haber/1043120-ozgecan-aslan-cinayetinde-korkunc-detaylar-ortaya-cikti#.

HaberTürk. (26 June 2012). "Tebrikler kızınız hamile"https://www.haberturk.com/ekonomi/makro-ekonomi/haber/753536-tebrikler- kiziniz-hamile.

HaberTürk. (2 June 2012). "Çocuğun ne suçu var, anası kendisini öldürsün!". https://www.haberturk.com/polemik/haber/747352-cocugun-ne-sucu-var-anasi-kendisini-oldursun-.

Hürriyet. (14 July 2018). "Otobüste mini etekli kıza tepki gösterdi, sürücüden aracı karakola çekmesini istedi". http://www.hurriyet.com.tr/otobuste-mini-etekli-kiza-tepki-gosterdi-suruc-4089714.

Hürriyet. (02 January 2015). "Sağlık Bakanı Müezzinoğlu: Annelik bir kariyerdir". http://www.hurriyet.com.tr/gundem/saglik-bakani-muezzinoglu-annelik-bir-kariyerdir-27882199.

Hürriyet. (23 August 2013). "Genç hakim adayı Yaylalı intihar etti". hürriyet. http://www.hurriyet.com.tr/gundem/genc-hakim-adayi-yaylali-intihar-etti-24575440.

Hürriyet. (25 May 2013). "Ankara metrosunda "öpüşme" eylemi". http://www.hurriyet.com.tr/gundem/ankara-metrosunda-opusme-eylemi-23368283.

Hürriyet. (11 March 2011). "Örtüsüz kadın perdesiz eve benzer". http://www.hurriyet.com.tr/gundem/ortusuz-kadin-perdesiz-eve-benzer-17238959.

Hürriyet Daily News. (5 November 2013). "Turkish government to act on accommodation housing female and male students". http://www.hurriyetdailynews.com/turkish-government-to-act-on-accommodation-housing-female-and-male-students-57392.

Hürriyet. (14 January 2008). "Başbakan'dan "türban" çıkışı". http://www.hurriyet.com.tr/gundem/basbakandan-turban-cikisi-8024104.

Hürriyet Daily News. (26 May 2012). "Abortion is 'murder,' says Turkey's PM". http://www.hurriyetdailynews.com/abortion-is-murder-says-turkeys-pm-21665.

Hürriyet Daily News. (28 May 2013). "Drink at home, Turkish PM tells booze regulation critics". http://www.hurriyetdailynews.com/drink-at-home-turkish-pm-tells-booze-regulation-critics-47764.

Hürriyet Daily News. (03 January 2013). "Turkish PM Erdoğan reiterates his call for three children". http://www.hurriyetdailynews.com/turkish-pm-erdogan-reiterates-his-call-for-three-children-38235.

Independent. (6 June 2016). "Turkey's President Erdoğan says childless women are 'deficient' and 'incomplete' ". https://www.independent.co.uk/news/world/europe/turkeys-president-erdogan-says-childless-women-are-deficient-and-incomplet-a7067126.html.

İleri Haber. (18 November 2016). "Bozdağ utanç önergesini böyle savundu:Tecavüz değil, küçüğün rızasıyla gayri resmi evlilik". https://ilerihaber.org/icerik/bozdag-utanc-onergesini-boyle-savundutecavuz-degil-kucugun-rizasiyla-gayri-resmi-evlilik-63272.html.

Kadın Cinayetlerini Durduracağız Platformu. (23 January 2014). "K. T'ye sahip çıkıyoruz". http://kadincinayetlerinidurduracagiz.net/davalarimiz/972/k-tye-sahip-cikiyoruz.

Milliyet. (24 November 2014). "Kadın ile erkeği eşit konuma getiremezsiniz çünkü o fıtrata terstir". http://www.milliyet.com.tr/erdogan-batsin-bu-dunya-siyaset-1974189/.

Milliyet. (19 July 2012). " 'Çocuk gelin'e 47 bıçaklı son". http://www.milliyet.com.tr/-cocuk-gelin-e-47-bicakli-son-gundem-1568857/.

Milliyet. (20 July 2009). "Erdoğan'dan şoke eden 'Münevver' yorumu!". http://www.milliyet.com.tr/erdogan-dan-soke-eden--munevver--yorumu--siyaset-1119465/.

NBC News. (08 June 2016). "Turkey's President Erdogan Calls Women Who Work 'Half Persons' ". https://www.nbcnews.com/news/world/turkey-s-president-erdogan-calls-women-who-work-half-persons-n586421.

NTV. (02 April 2018). "Özgecan Aslan'ın Babasından Nihat Doğan'a Tepki". https://www.ntv.com.tr/kadina-siddet/ozgecan-aslanin-babasindan-nihat-dogana-tepki,cOjHRbx7F0SHYX9bZjJeXA.

NTV. (26 October 2016). "Hemşire Ayşegül Terzi'ye otobüste tekme atan sanık tahliye oldu". https://www.ntv.com.tr/turkiye/hemsire-aysegul-terziye-otobuste-tekme-atan-saniktahliye-oldu,j0lvp6pUFUGzd0olwruOTw.

Presidency of the Republic of Turkey. (27 September 2017). "First Lady Erdoğan: "We should Launch a Mobilization to Reduce C-Section Rates". https://www.tccb.gov.tr/en/news/542/83673/emine-erdogan-sezaryen-oranlarini-dusurmek-icin-seferberlik-baslatmaliyiz.

Radikal. (24 May 2008). "Prof. Şerif Mardin: 'Mahalle baskısı gözleyerek yapılıyor'". http://www.radikal.com.tr/turkiye/prof-serif-mardin-mahalle-baskisi-gozleyerek-yapiliyor-879310/.

Sabah. (12 May 2011). "Ayşe Paşalı davasında karar çıktı". https://www.sabah.com.tr/gundem/2011/05/12/ayse-pasali-davasinda-karar-verildi.

Sendika.org. (4 June 2016). "İstanbul'da kadınlardan eylem: Aile dışında hayat var, gel bir nefes alalım". http://sendika63.org/2016/06/istanbulda-kadinlardan-eylem-aile-disinda-hayat-var-gel-bir-nefes-alalim-355124/.

Sönmez, Berrin. 2018. "Yeni Mücadele Alanı Uzlaştırmaya Direnmek", Gazete duvar. (15 November 2018). https://www.gazeteduvar.com.tr/yazarlar/2018/11/15/yeni-mucadele-alani-uzlastirmaya-direnmek/.

Sputnik Türkiye. (8 March 2018). "Binlerce Kadın 8 Mart için Sokağa Çıktı: İtaat Etmiyoruz". https://tr.sputniknews.com/turkiye/201803081032559787-binlerce-kadin-8mart-icin-sokaga-cikti-itaat-etmiyoruz/.

Sputnik Türkiye. (16 May 2018). "Bakan Eroğlu annelere seslendi: 'Uyusun de büyüsün demeyin, 'hedef 2071' diye ninni söyleyin". https://tr.sputniknews.com/turkiye/201805161033464310-veysel-eroglu-anneler-ninni/.

Star Gazetesi. (31 October 2013). "O gün neler yaşamıştı? İşte Merve Kavakçı olayı!". https://www.star.com.tr/politika/o-gun-neler-yasamisti-iste-merve-kavakci-olayi-haber-802075/.

T24 Bağımsız İnternet Gazetesi. (23 November 2018). "Erdoğan'dan kadın hakları açıklaması: Batı dünyasını baz alırsak doğru yere varamayız". https://t24.com.tr/haber/erdogandan-kadin-haklari-aciklamasi-bati-dunyasini-baz-alirsak-dogru-yere-varamayiz,754816.

T24 Bağımsız İnternet Gazetesi. (5 November 2013). "Başbakan: Kızlı erkekli kalınan evlerde karmakarışık her şey olabiliyor, adım atmaya mecburuz!". http://t24.com.tr/haber/basbakan-kizli-erkekli-kalinan-evlerde-karmakarisik-her-sey-olabiliyor,243338.

T24 Bağımsız Internet Gazetesi. (11 August 2012). "Yargıtay 'bekareti bozulmadı' dedi, tecavüzcünün cezasında indirim istedi". http://t24.com.tr/haber/yargitay-bekareti-bozulmadi-dedi-tecavuzcunun-cezasinda-indirim-istedi,210663.

T24 Bağımsız İnternet Gazetesi. (30 September 2008). "İslam kadın-erkek eşitliğini kabul etmez". (N. Düzel-Reporter). https://t24.com.tr/haber/islam-kadin-erkek-esitligini-kabul-etmez,9526.

The Guardian. (30 May 2016). "Recep Tayyip Erdoğan: no Muslim family can accept birth control". https://www.theguardian.com/world/2016/may/30/recep-tayyip-erdogan-no-muslim-family-can-accept-birth-control.

The Guardian. (24 November 2014). "Recep Tayyip Erdoğan: 'women not equal to men'". https://www.theguardian.com/world/2014/nov/24/turkeys-president-recep-tayyip-erdogan-women-not-equal-men.

140Journos. (1 March 2017). "Dünden Bugüne Başörtüsü Yasağı". https://140journos.com/d%C3%BCnden-bug%C3%BCne-kadar-ba%C5%9F%C3%B6rt%C3%BCs%C3%BC-yasa%C4%9F%C4%B1-5845cf7aa049.

Websites

AK Party https://www.akparti.org.tr/.
Archive-Friday Khutbahs https://www2.diyanet.gov.tr/DinHizmetleriGenelMudurlugu/sayfalar/hutbelerlistesi.aspx.
Kadın Adayları Destekleme Derneği http://ka-der.org.tr/.
Kadın Cinayetlerini Durduracağız Platformu (Women's Murders Stopping Platform) http://kadincinayetlerinidurduracagiz.net/.
Mor Çatı Kadın Sığınağı Vakfı (Purple Roof) https://www.morcati.org.tr/tr/.
T.C. Atatürk Kültür, Dil ve Tarih Yüksek Kurumu, Türk Dil kurumu http://www.tdk.gov.tr/.
T.C. Cumhurbaşkanlığı Diyanet İşleri Başkanlığı https://birimler.diyanet.gov.tr/.

Index

AKP   vii, ix, 1, 7, 8, 20, 22, 27, 40, 45, 47, 48, 50, 54, 55, 55n.8, 56, 56n.9, 57, 67, 74, 79, 81, 97, 157, 159, 160, 162, 164, 166, 168, 169, 170, 173, 176, 182, 183, 189, 196, 197, 198, 199, 204, 206, 216, 217, 220, 227, 229, 236, 237, 238
authoritarian   10, 22, 51, 94, 136, 137, 139, 156, 157, 160, 166, 169, 170, 173, 174, 176, 178, 186, 188, 202, 206, 209, 212

biopolitical authorities   6, 25, 26, 27
biopolitics   2, 5, 8, 9, 10, 11, 13, 15, 24, 41, 74, 82, 89, 92, 120, 124, 128, 132, 155, 157, 172, 174, 175, 178, 192, 194, 205, 208
biopolitics of Islamism   24
biopower   2, 3, 15, 22, 81, 89, 92, 128, 157, 166, 174, 187
body politics   28, 38, 39, 60, 208

collective subject position   195
common values   16, 44n.6, 68, 77, 105, 108, 117, 178, 188, 199, 202, 208
conduct of conduct   4, 23, 42, 159, 185, 192, 199
conservative democracy   67, 156, 171, 197
corrective mechanisms   75, 156
criminality   2, 5, 34, 124, 126, 175, 185, 210

disciplinary power   2, 3, 15, 81, 124, 145, 157, 164, 171, 172, 173, 174
discursive practices   2, 6, 9, 11, 13, 14, 28, 33, 36, 48, 49, 50, 52, 54, 63, 65, 75, 77, 92, 158, 171, 174, 186, 193, 195, 199, 205, 207, 211
dispositif   112, 124, 152
divorce   41, 106, 107, 150
Diyanet   ix, 15, 15n.1, 16, 17, 17n.4, 18, 19, 19n.5, 19n.6, 56, 58, 74, 75, 76, 77, 81, 82, 86, 92, 93, 94, 95, 104, 105, 106, 107, 108, 113, 117, 154n.6, 176, 180, 188n.7, 194, 202, 203, 225, 226, 231, 232, 233, 234, 235, 236, 242

economy of power   2, 22, 108, 185, 211
Erdoğan   55n.8, 57, 67, 68, 79, 80, 83, 92, 96, 98, 138, 166, 180, 235, 236, 237, 238, 239, 240, 241

family   viii, 1, 5, 7, 16, 17n.4, 19, 20, 22, 25, 26, 29, 31, 32, 33, 34, 37, 38, 40, 41, 42, 45, 47, 48, 49, 52, 54, 55, 55n.8, 58, 59, 62, 65, 66, 67, 68, 69, 70, 71, 71n.1, 72, 73, 74, 75, 76, 76n.2, 76n.3, 77, 77n.4, 78, 79, 80, 81, 82, 83, 84, 85, 86, 87, 87n.5, 88, 89, 90, 91, 92, 93, 94, 95, 97, 99, 100, 101, 102, 103, 104, 105, 106, 107, 108, 109, 110, 111, 114, 116, 117, 119, 127, 128, 130, 131, 132, 133, 137, 138, 139, 141, 143, 144, 146, 147, 148, 150, 151, 152, 153, 154, 157, 159, 167, 170, 175, 176, 180, 181, 184, 185, 186, 187, 188, 189, 190, 192, 193, 195, 197, 198, 199, 200, 201, 202, 203, 206, 208, 209, 210, 211, 213, 229, 241
family values   16, 55, 70, 71, 72, 75, 76n.3, 81, 100, 105, 144, 146, 148, 152, 184, 195, 208, 210
feminism   37, 39, 40, 44, 50, 53, 94, 179, 183, 195, 203, 224, 229
Foucault   2, 3, 4, 5, 7, 8, 9, 10, 11, 12, 13, 14, 15, 18, 32n.5, 64, 71n.1, 72, 76, 77n.4, 80, 81, 82, 86, 89, 92, 95, 103, 120, 124, 126, 127, 131, 134, 136, 145, 155, 156, 157, 172, 174, 176, 177, 184, 188, 191, 191n.8, 193, 194, 196, 201, 204, 205, 206, 207, 212, 217, 218, 219, 220, 221, 222, 223, 225, 226, 229

gender justice   21, 41, 42, 157, 178, 179, 180, 181, 184, 190, 211
gender regime   3, 5, 20, 24, 33, 34, 39, 40, 42, 47, 48, 54, 58, 65, 75, 176, 207, 208, 211
gender-based crimes   16, 20, 21, 111, 114, 120, 130, 143, 147, 150, 153
gender-based violence   3, 10, 20, 21, 23, 118, 135, 136, 139, 146, 151, 210, 211
gendered society   150
good life   63, 189
governmental rationality   1, 6, 11, 13, 19, 22, 27, 40, 47, 70, 99, 157, 171, 180, 185, 187, 188, 191, 197, 205, 206, 212, 213

happiness   3, 7, 8, 18, 21, 45, 69, 71, 89, 91, 92, 93, 99, 102, 106, 108, 113, 135, 168, 169, 189, 193, 198, 210

headscarf   44n.6, 45, 49, 50, 54, 56, 56n.9, 57, 58, 139, 182, 191, 196, 198, 200
health   3, 19n.5, 28, 82, 96, 98, 100, 102, 123, 125, 128, 140, 141, 143, 165, 204
heteronormativity   35
honour   128, 129, 131, 144, 215, 217, 218, 224, 227, 228, 229, 231

ideal womanhood   v, 1
intimacy   8, 20, 24, 25, 27, 43, 43n.6, 44, 45, 47, 48, 49, 50, 52, 54, 58, 59, 60, 62, 65, 66, 70, 75, 84, 103, 117, 127, 131, 150, 154, 166, 191, 200, 207, 212
Islamic body politics   39
Islamic neoliberal subjectivity   22, 168, 198, 204, 209
Islamisation   42, 44, 52, 53, 156, 158, 166, 167, 169, 171, 178, 209, 229
Islamism   1, 9, 10, 15n.1, 22, 33, 52, 55, 56, 84, 114, 135, 155, 156, 158, 160, 164, 165, 167n.5, 168, 169, 171, 173, 174, 178, 179, 193, 202, 203, 206, 209, 223, 227, 230

justice   ix, 1, 39, 42, 105, 119, 123, 149, 151, 166n.4, 178, 184, 185, 198, 219, 227, 230

Kemalism   52, 167n.5, 169
knowledge-power   10, 11, 12, 13, 14, 15, 16, 18, 22, 92, 97, 126, 136, 196, 205, 207, 212

life   viii, 1, 2, 3, 5, 6, 8, 10, 11, 14, 16, 17n.4, 18, 19, 20, 21, 22, 25, 26n.1, 27, 28n.3, 29, 30, 31, 32, 33, 37, 38, 39, 41, 45, 46, 48, 51, 55, 55n.8, 57, 58, 59, 61, 62, 64, 65, 66, 67, 68, 69, 71, 72, 73, 74, 75, 76, 77, 78, 79, 80, 81, 82, 83, 87, 88, 91, 92, 93, 94, 95, 98, 99, 100, 103, 106, 107, 108, 110, 111, 112, 113, 114, 115, 116, 118, 120, 124, 126, 127, 128, 130, 131, 134, 136, 144, 145, 146, 147, 149, 150, 151, 152, 153, 156, 157, 158, 159, 160, 161, 162, 163, 164, 168, 170, 171, 172, 173, 176, 177, 178, 179, 180, 183, 184, 185, 186, 188, 189, 190, 191, 192, 193, 194, 196, 197, 198, 199, 200, 203, 205, 207, 208, 209, 210, 211, 212, 213, 230
lifestyles   18, 19, 33, 43, 50, 71, 72, 81, 101, 127, 135, 137, 152, 154, 158, 159, 171, 173, 176, 178, 191, 192, 193, 197, 199, 200

manhood   10, 19, 32, 39, 69, 95, 102, 113, 118, 131, 139, 144, 145, 146, 148, 153, 154, 189, 192, 213
market-society   84, 126, 158, 179
marriage   19, 20, 21, 26n.1, 29, 30, 32, 33, 34, 36, 37, 38, 39, 41, 42, 44, 45, 49, 54, 59, 62, 66, 68, 70, 73, 74, 78, 83, 84, 91, 94, 95, 101, 105, 106, 107, 108, 109, 114, 131, 134, 141, 142, 143, 149, 150, 154, 173, 177, 186, 198, 200, 202, 208
morality   13, 15, 15n.1, 25, 29, 31, 34, 36, 38, 40, 41, 47, 48, 50, 58, 59, 61, 62, 64, 72, 74, 81, 82, 93, 100, 101, 102, 112, 116, 117, 119, 130, 131, 135, 144, 152, 158, 164, 167, 169, 173, 174, 179, 183, 188, 192, 198, 200, 203
motherhood   88, 93, 96, 179, 198, 225

neoconservatism   15, 42, 85, 139, 175, 188
neoliberal governmentality   9, 14, 15, 22, 41, 47, 76n.3, 89, 99, 131, 136, 139, 155, 156, 168, 171, 178, 188, 188n.7, 190, 191n.8, 195, 209, 212
neoliberal rationality   2, 7, 8, 14, 23, 67, 68, 74, 81, 84, 96, 126, 135, 136, 137, 153, 164, 175, 184, 190, 197, 200, 204, 205, 206, 207, 210
neoliberalism   1, 2, 8, 10, 15, 21, 22, 23, 42, 48, 50, 55, 85, 89, 94, 95, 99, 107, 115, 126, 135, 137, 139, 153, 155, 156, 157, 163, 164, 165, 167n.5, 169, 170, 171, 173, 174, 175, 179, 180, 186, 187, 188, 189, 206, 207, 209, 211, 212, 213, 226
norm imposition   70, 156
norms   2, 3, 5, 9, 12, 14, 20, 27, 30, 32, 34, 36, 39, 41, 42, 43, 44, 46, 47, 48, 51, 52, 53, 54, 58, 59, 61, 62, 64, 65, 68, 69, 70, 75, 76, 77, 85, 86, 88, 89, 92, 99, 102, 103, 106, 109, 118, 119, 120, 126, 132, 133, 136, 139, 141, 144, 151, 153, 155, 159, 167, 169, 175, 176, 178, 179, 184, 186, 188, 194, 196, 200, 201, 202, 211

passion   74, 108, 115, 128, 130, 131, 132, 133n.2, 134, 135
performativity   208
population   1, 3, 5, 6, 8, 9, 10, 11, 12, 16, 20, 23, 24, 26, 32, 35, 40, 47, 53, 55n.8, 61, 67, 69, 71, 77, 77n.4, 81, 82, 86, 88, 93, 94, 97,

99, 102, 103, 109, 115, 120, 127, 128, 145, 147, 153, 155, 162, 168, 169, 170, 172, 173, 174, 175, 177, 178, 179, 183, 184, 185, 186, 192, 194, 195, 196, 198, 199, 201, 206, 207, 208, 209, 211

rape   114, 119, 128, 226
rationality   2, 4, 5, 7, 8, 11, 13, 14, 19, 20, 27, 31, 33, 48, 60, 61, 67, 69, 71, 74, 85, 98, 103, 120, 126, 133, 136, 137, 147, 151, 167, 172, 175, 176, 187, 188, 189, 190, 192, 195, 196, 197, 205, 207, 210, 212, 213
regulations   11, 16, 17, 20, 21, 32, 48, 61, 70, 74, 80, 89, 93, 95, 102, 138, 142, 150, 153, 156, 157, 159, 160, 163, 164, 165, 170, 173, 180, 187, 188, 193, 203
regulative mechanisms   2, 27, 38, 171
religio-cultural   1, 2, 36, 55, 134
religious values   10, 22, 50, 52, 147, 169, 174, 175, 198, 199, 201, 208

secular   25, 43, 44, 45, 49, 50, 52, 56, 69, 75, 77, 122, 133, 158, 160, 161, 163, 164, 174, 176, 190, 193, 194, 195, 199, 200, 201, 202, 209, 212
security mechanisms   90, 147, 152, 211
self-esteem   3, 25, 27, 41, 46, 67, 90, 96, 106, 117, 187, 189, 191, 194, 195, 196, 199, 202
sex   24, 25, 26, 29, 34, 40, 41, 59, 63, 78, 81, 93, 96, 102, 116, 129, 134, 180, 183, 218
sexuality   27, 33, 37, 95, 217, 220, 222, 230
social harmony   61, 62, 64, 65, 211
social justice   41, 183, 184, 187, 188, 211
sovereign power   90, 145, 156, 157, 171, 172, 173, 174
subject formation   3, 89, 158
subjectivity   1, 8, 9, 13, 22, 35, 42, 55, 74, 96, 97, 111, 126, 155, 158, 168, 175, 183, 192, 198, 200, 202, 206, 209

traditional sensitivities   14, 22, 70, 105, 133
truth regime   3, 4, 12, 23, 25, 206
Turkey   v, vii, ix, 1, 2, 3, 7, 8, 9, 10, 14, 15, 16, 17n.4, 19, 20, 21, 22, 23, 24, 25, 27, 28, 34, 40, 42, 43, 43n.6, 44, 47, 48, 49, 50, 52, 53, 54, 55, 56, 57, 58, 60, 61, 63, 64, 65, 67, 69, 70, 71, 72, 75, 77, 79, 81, 84, 92, 94, 95, 96, 97, 98, 101, 107, 111, 115, 116, 117, 118, 120, 122, 127, 128, 129, 133, 134, 137, 139, 140, 142, 143, 152, 155, 156, 158, 159, 160, 161, 162, 162n.1, 163, 164, 165, 166, 167n.5, 168, 169, 171, 173, 174, 176, 178, 180, 182, 183, 186, 189, 190, 191, 191n.8, 192, 195, 197, 198, 199, 200, 202, 203, 205, 206, 207, 208, 209, 210, 211, 212, 213, 215, 216, 217, 218, 219, 220, 223, 224, 225, 226, 227, 228, 229, 230, 235, 237, 239, 240

values   1, 2, 3, 4, 6, 7, 13, 14, 16, 17n.4, 19, 20, 22, 23, 24, 26, 31, 33, 34, 36, 37, 39, 40, 46, 51, 52, 53, 54, 55, 56, 61, 63, 65, 68, 71, 72, 73, 76n.3, 78, 79, 80, 81, 85, 86, 88, 90, 91, 92, 94, 95, 96, 100, 101, 102, 103, 105, 106, 107, 109, 111, 113, 115, 117, 118, 126, 128, 130, 134, 135, 137, 145, 144, 146, 151, 153, 155, 156, 158, 159, 163, 164, 165, 167, 167n.5, 168, 169, 171, 176, 178, 179, 180, 181, 184, 185, 186, 187, 188, 189, 190, 193, 194, 195, 197, 198, 199, 200, 201, 202, 203, 204, 206, 207, 208, 209, 210, 211
veiling   20, 29, 32, 36, 37, 43, 45, 46, 51, 53, 54, 57, 59, 61, 131, 191, 191n.8, 192, 193, 196, 200, 202, 226
virtues   4, 14, 20, 23, 24, 25, 26, 27, 29, 41, 46, 60, 68, 87, 128, 153, 156, 158, 178, 187, 200

womanhood   1, 2, 3, 5, 7, 8, 9, 10, 11, 15, 16, 17n.4, 20, 21, 22, 23, 25, 26, 27, 31, 32, 33, 35, 36, 37, 38, 39, 40, 41, 43, 44, 45, 46, 47, 48, 52, 53, 54, 55, 58, 60, 64, 66, 68, 69, 70, 75, 76, 77, 78, 79, 86, 87, 88, 91, 92, 95, 99, 102, 109, 111, 112, 113, 114, 115, 116, 117, 118, 120, 125, 128, 132, 133, 135, 137, 138, 139, 144, 145, 148, 152, 153, 155, 156, 157, 173, 174, 177, 179, 185, 186, 189, 192, 195, 197, 198, 201, 202, 203, 205, 206, 207, 208, 209, 211, 212, 213
woman-subjects   2, 8, 202

www.ingramcontent.com/pod-product-compliance
Lightning Source LLC
Chambersburg PA
CBHW052206090526
44583CB00017BA/2175